Lecture Notes in Computer Science

# Lecture Notes in Artificial Intelligence 16785

Founding Editor

Jörg Siekmann

The series Lecture Notes in Artificial Intelligence (LNAI) was established in 1988 as a topical subseries of LNCS devoted to artificial intelligence.

The series publishes state-of-the-art research results at a high level. As with the LNCS mother series, the mission of the series is to serve the international R & D community by providing an invaluable service, mainly focused on the publication of conference and workshop proceedings and postproceedings.

Emily Farran · Angela Schwering ·
Victor R. Schinazi · Jack Parkinson
Editors

# Spatial Cognition XIV

14th International Conference, Spatial Cognition 2026
Glasgow, UK, August 25–28, 2026
Proceedings

Springer

*Editors*
Emily Farran
University of Surrey
Surrey, UK

Angela Schwering
University of Münster
Münster, Nordrhein-Westfalen, Germany

Victor R. Schinazi
Bond University
Robina, QLD, Australia

Jack Parkinson
University of Glasgow
Glasgow, UK

ISSN 0302-9743 ISSN 1611-3349 (electronic)
Lecture Notes in Artificial Intelligence
ISBN 978-3-032-36715-0 ISBN 978-3-032-36716-7 (eBook)
https://doi.org/10.1007/978-3-032-36716-7

LNCS Sublibrary: SL7 – Artificial Intelligence



This Springer imprint is published by the registered company Springer Nature Switzerland AG
The registered company address is: Gewerbestrasse 11, 6330 Cham, Switzerland

# Preface

Welcome to the proceedings of the 14th International Spatial Cognition Conference, held in Glasgow in August 2026. This conference marked a significant gathering of minds dedicated to the exploration of spatial cognition, a field at the intersection of cognitive, developmental, and educational psychology, neuroscience, computer science, geography, and beyond.

The University of Glasgow is one of Scotland's four ancient universities, established in 1451 and celebrating 575 years in 2026. Spatial Cognition 2026 was hosted by the recently launched Turner Kirk Centre for Spatial Reasoning. The Centre has a remit for developing, translating and supporting research in the field of spatial cognition with connections to policy makers, academic researchers, practitioners, and education specialists across the breadth of the sector, and therefore was well suited to host Spatial Cognition 2026.

The scope and purpose of this conference were vast, aiming to delve into the intricate mechanisms behind how humans perceive, reason about, and navigate through space. From understanding the developmental origins of spatial abilities to exploring the applications of spatial cognition in fields such as STEM learning, artificial intelligence, and virtual reality, this conference provided a platform for interdisciplinary exchange and collaboration.

The peer review process was meticulously conducted with a double-blinded approach. Each paper was reviewed by three expert reviewers, and a last expert reviewer resolved any remaining ambiguities via a meta-review, ensuring that only high-quality research contributed to the discourse.

The conference took place over four days in the Glasgow University Union, located on the Gilmorehill Campus of the University of Glasgow, from August 25 to 29. On Day 1, a workshop entitled "Creating Requirements for a Spatial Cognition Grand Challenge", was led by Stephen Gilbert et al.

Each of Days 2, 3, and 4 began with a keynote. The first keynote was delivered by Tom Lowrie of the University of Canberra, who reflected on the journey of his research from initial classroom studies to nation-scale interventions. He discussed the value in continuing to explore, even – or especially – as intervention programmes grow, the underlying mechanisms which make a change, both at the individual level and for a curriculum at scale. This was followed by a paper session: "Navigation Behaviour and Environmental Interaction". On day 2 we also heard lightning talks from 12 Doctoral Colloquium participants, who also took part in a poster session. In addition to the 12 Doctoral Colloquium posters, 12 posters from the poster track were also presented. Two paper sessions took place in the afternoon: "Spatial Perception, Attention and Representation" and "Spatial Thinking and STEM Education".

Lauren Margulieux, Georgia State University, delivered the second keynote. Her talk reflected on the fairly unique capacity for personal achievement provided by spatial skills development. She framed the value of spatial skills as being cross-cutting, with spatial improvements leading to better outcomes in a range of disciplines and practice in those disciplines also leading to spatial gains. She presented this as a tantalising opportunity for the development of training, approaching the possible mechanisms at play from education, cognitive, and neuroscience perspectives. The keynote was followed by two symposia: "Mechanisms Underlying the Spatial–Mathematical Connection", chaired by Ilyse Resnick, and "Spatial Skills Measurement for Cognitive, Developmental and Educational Research: Challenges and Solutions", chaired by Emily Farran. A second poster session with 24 posters was held in the afternoon. Paper sessions on Day 3 covered "Navigation, Cognition and Brain Function" and "Development and Education".

The final keynote was delivered by Sheryl Sorby of the University of Cincinnati, who discussed the crucial role of spatial reasoning skills for engineers. She first explored a broad base of research demonstrating links between spatial skills and various engineering skills and competencies. This led to a discussion of the value of spatial reasoning skills across the engineering discipline and a call to action to consider reforming engineering education to ensure these skills are explicitly developed. This keynote was followed by a final paper session on "Computational Approaches to Spatial Cognition". The final symposium of the conference was "New Perspectives on Individual Differences in Human Navigation", led by Chiara Meneghetti.

In all, the conference accepted 13 full papers, and saw 24 oral presentations, 1 workshop, 3 symposia, 12 Doctoral Colloquium lightning talks, and 48 posters presented.

As editors of these proceedings, we are thrilled to present a compilation of the groundbreaking research and insights shared at the Spatial Cognition 2026 conference. We hope that these proceedings serve as a valuable resource for scholars and practitioners alike, inspiring further exploration and innovation in the dynamic field of spatial cognition. We would also like to thank all who helped to make the conference possible: the Steering Committee for their support and permission to host the conference, the Organizing Committee for their many months of hard work, the staff within the Turner Kirk Centre for Spatial Reasoning at the University of Glasgow, the volunteers who helped during the week, and those who chaired sessions and helped in many other ways.

Emily Farran<br>
Victor R. Schinazi<br>
Angela Schwering<br>
Jack Parkinson

# Organization

## Program Committee Chairs

| | |
|---|---|
| Emily Farran | University of Surrey, UK |
| Victor Schinazi | Bond University, Australia |
| Angela Schwering | University of Münster, Germany |

## Organization Committee

| | |
|---|---|
| Ergi Bufasi | Rīga Stradiņš University, Latvia |
| Estefanía Gamarra Burga | University of Greater Manchester, UK |
| Quintin Cutts | University of Glasgow, UK |
| Anna Doyle | University of Glasgow, UK |
| Zoe Falomir | Umeå University, Sweden |
| Danielle Harris | University of Canberra, Australia |
| Claire Johnson | University of Glasgow, UK |
| Jack Parkinson | University of Glasgow, UK |
| Steve Weisberg | University of Texas at Arlington, USA |
| Caiwei Zhu | University of Twente, Netherlands |

## Steering Committee

| | |
|---|---|
| Liz Chrastil | University of California, Irvine, USA |
| Ruth Dalton | Northumbria University, UK |
| Gavin Duffy | Technological University Dublin, Ireland |
| Alexia Galati | University of North Carolina at Charlotte, USA |
| Christoph Hölscher | ETH Zurich, Switzerland |
| Alexander Klippel | Wageningen University & Research, Netherlands (Chair) |
| Ilyse Resnick | University of Canberra, Australia |
| Jurģis Šķilters | University of Latvia, Latvia |
| David Uttal | Northwestern University, USA |

## Program Committee

| | |
|---|---|
| Kinnari Atit | University of California, Riverside, USA |
| Marios Avraamides | University of Cyprus, Cyprus |
| Oliver Baumann | Bond University, Australia |
| Jeffrey Buckley | Technological University of the Shannon, Ireland |
| Ergi Bufasi | Riga Stradiņš University, Latvia |
| Xiaoli Chen | Zhejiang University, China |
| Liz Chrastil | University of California, Irvine, USA |
| Christophe Claramunt | Naval Academy Research Institute, France |
| Giorgio Colombo | Singapore-ETH Centre, Singapore |
| Sarah Creem-Regehr | University of Utah, USA |
| Zoe Falomir | Umeå University, Sweden |
| Gabriele Filomena | University of Liverpool, UK |
| Estefanía Gamarra Burga | Bangor University, UK |
| Jascha Grübel | Central European University, Austria |
| Danielle Harris | University of Canberra, Australia |
| Mary Hegarty | University of California, Santa Barbara, USA |
| Toru Ishikawa | Toyo University, Japan |
| Kate Jeffery | University of Glasgow, UK |
| Armand Kapaj | University of Zurich, Switzerland |
| Peter Kiefer | ETH Zurich, Switzerland |
| Alexander Klippel | Wageningen University and Research, Netherlands |
| Jakub Krukar | University of Münster, Germany |
| Diarmaid Lane | University of Limerick, Ireland |
| Günter Maresch | University of Salzburg, Austria |
| Maria Rosaria Stufano Melone | Technical University of Bari, Italy |
| Chiara Meneghetti | University of Padua, Italy |
| Debbie Mills | Bangor University, UK |
| Laura Miola | University of Padua, Italy |
| Dan Montello | University of California, Santa Barbara, USA |
| Veronica Muffato | University of Padua, Italy |
| Joanne Mulligan | Macquarie University, Australia |
| Nora Newcombe | Temple University, USA |
| Marianna Pagkratidou | Dublin City University, Ireland |
| Zita Patai | University College London, UK |
| Francesca Pazzaglia | University of Padua, Italy |
| Claudia Quaiser-Pohl | University of Koblenz-Landau, Germany |
| Martin Raubal | ETH Zurich, Switzerland |
| Ilyse Resnick | University of Canberra, Australia |
| Kai-Florian Richter | Umeå University, Sweden |

# Contents

# From Gaze to Choice: Attention, Spatial Cognition, and Seat Choice in Virtual Atrium Spaces

Toshihiro Osaragi[1](✉), Takumi Nishikawa[1], Shokatsu Chen[2], Maki Kishimoto[1], Hiroyuki Kaneko[2], and Junichi Makieda[3]

[1] School of Environment and Society, Institute of Science Tokyo, Meguro, Japan
osaragi.t.20f7@m.isct.ac.jp
[2] Kajima Technical Research Institute, Kajima Corporation, Chofu, Japan
[3] Architectural Design Division, Kajima Corporation, Minato, Japan

**Abstract.** We propose a VR-based evaluation framework to quantify how visual attention to environmental elements influences seat selection in atrium spaces, contributing to the understanding of spatial cognition processes in complex architectural environments. We constructed four large-scale atrium layouts in immersive virtual reality and conducted a seat-choice experiment using a head-mounted display with integrated eye tracking. Participants freely explored each VR environment, shortlisted three candidate seats, and then selected the most preferred seat. To identify what was visually attended to and for how long, we classified environmental elements in omnidirectional images via semantic segmentation and linked the resulting masks with gaze coordinates to compute element-wise fixation durations. We then modeled the observed stepwise decision process—cluster (seat group) selection followed by within-cluster seat choice—using a hierarchical (nested) logit formulation that incorporates both seat/environment attributes and fixation-duration variables. Estimation results indicate a valid hierarchical structure and demonstrate that openness and greenery-related visual attention increase seat utility, whereas stronger visual salience of nearby people decreases it. These findings provide quantitative insight into how visual attention and environmental structure interact in spatial cognition and decision-making during seat selection. The proposed framework enables designers to compare alternative atrium configurations by predicting seat attractiveness and expected selections under controlled modifications of spatial and visual conditions.

**Keywords:** Spatial Cognition · Virtual Reality · Eye Tracking · Spatial Decision-Making · Semantic Segmentation · Nested Logit Model

## 1 Introduction

### 1.1 Background and Related Work

Spatial cognition plays a fundamental role in how people perceive, interpret, and act within built environments. When individuals enter large architectural spaces, they continuously process visual cues, spatial structure, and the presence of other people in order


E. Farran et al. (Eds.): Spatial Cognition 2026, LNAI 16785, pp. 1–17, 2027.
https://doi.org/10.1007/978-3-032-36716-7_1

to understand the environment and make behavioral decisions. Atrium spaces—large vertical voids commonly located at the entrances of mixed-use complexes, hotels, commercial facilities, and office buildings—provide a particularly rich setting for studying such processes because they function as transitional and social environments where people linger, converse, and observe their surroundings. For architects and planners, predicting where users are likely to stay and how spatial configurations influence seat preference is crucial at the design stage. However, quantitatively linking environmental design factors to staying behavior remains challenging, particularly when attempting to identify causal pathways between spatial configuration, spatial cognition, and user behavior.

Research in built-environment studies has long emphasized the difficulty of establishing causal relationships between spatial attributes and human activity patterns. From a spatial cognition perspective, seat selection can be regarded as a form of spatial decision-making in which individuals acquire, interpret, and utilize information about their surroundings to evaluate potential locations. Such decisions involve the integration of visual perception, environmental affordances, and social context. Understanding how attention is allocated to environmental features during this process is therefore important for explaining how spatial representations are translated into behavioral choices. Systematic reviews have noted that correlations are often reported, yet perceptual and cognitive mechanisms mediating these relationships remain insufficiently specified [12]. This methodological gap motivates approaches that directly capture how users visually process architectural environments and how such perceptual processes contribute to spatial cognition and decision-making.

Recent advances in eye-tracking technology have significantly expanded the methodological foundation of architectural research. Reviews focusing on eye-tracking in architecture and built environments [1, 7] document the rapid growth of gaze-based studies in spatial analysis. These works demonstrate that visual attention provides valuable insights into how users perceive spatial structure, openness, enclosure, and social presence, which are central components of spatial cognition in built environments. Similar conclusions have been reported in tourism research [17], where gaze behavior has been shown to reflect cognitive evaluation processes in spatial settings. However, many existing studies remain descriptive, relying primarily on fixation heatmaps or aggregate attention metrics without explicitly integrating gaze measures into predictive behavioral models.

Immersive virtual reality (VR) has further strengthened the potential of gaze-based spatial research. Survey studies on VR-based eye tracking [14] highlight the advantages of immersive environments in systematically manipulating spatial variables while collecting precise gaze data. Empirical studies combining VR and eye tracking have examined user evaluation in urban historical districts [5], residential design [4], and landscape environments [11], demonstrating that gaze patterns correlate strongly with perceived spatial quality and user satisfaction. Nevertheless, these studies typically analyze visual attention and subjective evaluation separately, rather than embedding gaze measures within formal choice models that predict concrete behavioral outcomes such as seat selection.

From a technical standpoint, improvements in gaze estimation and head-mounted display based (HMD-based) tracking have enhanced measurement reliability. Surveys of gaze estimation methods [3] and discussions of gaze interaction in immersive systems [10] have clarified both capabilities and limitations of eye-tracking technologies. Methodological contributions addressing data quality assessment and benchmarking [2, 6] have further strengthened experimental robustness. In parallel, advances in computer vision—particularly convolutional neural network architectures such as U-Net for semantic segmentation [16] and Mask R-CNN for instance detection [8]—enable automated classification of environmental elements within panoramic VR imagery. These developments make it feasible to link gaze coordinates with fine-grained spatial components (e.g., openings, vegetation, columns, and people) at the element level.

Despite these methodological and technological advancements, two gaps remain evident. First, although visual attention is increasingly measured in architectural research, it is rarely incorporated explicitly into discrete behavioral models that predict specific spatial choices. Second, while VR facilitates controlled manipulation of spatial conditions, its potential for modeling multi-stage decision processes in architectural contexts remains underexplored.

To address these gaps, this study proposes an integrated framework that combines immersive VR experimentation, semantic segmentation-based environmental classification, and hierarchical discrete choice modeling. By quantifying element-wise fixation duration and embedding these measures within a nested logit structure, we aim to bridge perceptual processes and spatial choice behavior in atrium environments, thereby contributing to a quantitative understanding of spatial cognition during seat selection in complex architectural spaces.

## 1.2 Objectives and Contributions

This paper investigates how visual attention to environmental elements influences seat selection in atrium spaces under controlled VR conditions, with a particular focus on how these perceptual processes contribute to spatial cognition during seat exploration and evaluation. We hypothesize that seat selection is not a single-stage decision but follows a stepwise structure of spatial decision-making, in which users first narrow down alternatives to clusters of seats with similar characteristics and then select the most preferred seat within that cluster.

Based on this background, the study addresses the following research questions:

RQ1: How does visual attention to environmental elements influence seat-selection behavior in atrium spaces?

RQ2: Can gaze-derived attention measures improve the prediction of seat-choice behavior beyond conventional environmental and seat attributes?

RQ3: Does seat selection follow a hierarchical decision process consisting of seat-cluster screening followed by within-cluster choice?

The main contributions of this study are threefold:

C1 (Integrated VR–attention pipeline): We develop an immersive experimental platform that records navigation trajectories and eye movements during spatial exploration and seat evaluation across multiple atrium layouts.

C2 (Element-level attention quantification): Using semantic segmentation and instance detection techniques [8, 13], we transform panoramic VR images into classified environmental components and compute element-wise fixation durations linked to seat evaluation.

C3 (Attention-informed hierarchical choice modeling): We incorporate visual attention variables into a rigorously specified hierarchical (nested) logit model, enabling quantitative prediction of seat attractiveness and empirical validation of stepwise decision structures.

By explicitly integrating perception-level measurements into a discrete choice framework, this study contributes to evidence-based architectural evaluation and advances methodological approaches for linking built form, visual processing, and spatial behavior, thereby providing a quantitative perspective on spatial cognition in architectural environments.

Figure 1 summarizes the overall analytical framework of the study. The framework consists of four stages: VR-based data collection, visual-attention quantification, seat clustering, and hierarchical choice modeling.

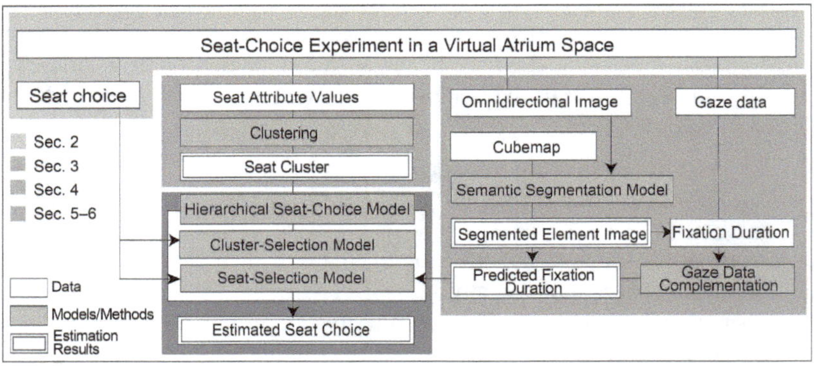


**Fig. 1.** Overview of the analytical framework

## 2 Seat-Choice Experiment in Virtual Atrium Spaces

### 2.1 Construction of the VR Atrium Environments

Four large-scale atrium layouts (Plans A–D) were constructed as immersive virtual environments (Fig. 2). The atrium represents the ground-floor space of a mixed-use complex with a three-story void structure. To ensure systematic exploration, the walkable area was discretized into a grid-based network with a 3 m pitch. At each grid node, a high-resolution (8 K) 360° panoramic image was rendered and linked to adjacent nodes in eight directions using a game engine (Unity). Participants navigated through the VR space by switching between panoramic viewpoints in the direction of gaze.

The base architectural geometry was modeled using a building information modeling (BIM) software (Revit) and imported into a rendering environment (Lumion), where materials, vegetation, furniture, and human figures were added. The number of human figures was fixed at 50 across all plans to maintain comparable social density. When participants selected a seat and pressed the seating switch, the viewpoint height was lowered to simulate the visual perspective of sitting. This allowed consistent reproduction of changes in visual conditions between walking and sitting.

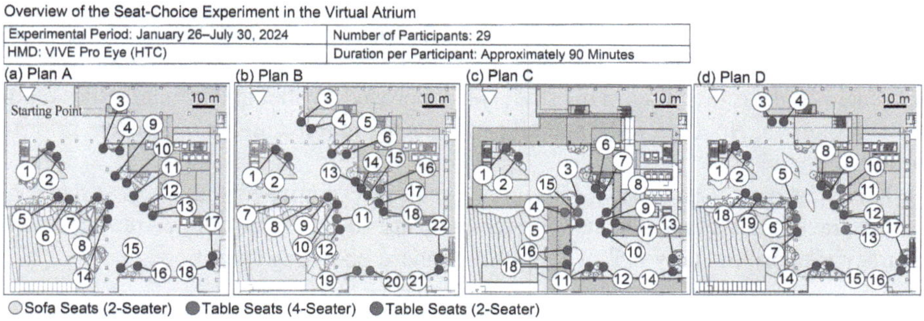


**Fig. 2.** Overview of the seat-choice experiment in the virtual atrium. Experimental setup and participant information. (a–d) Layouts of Plan A–D with seat locations and seating types

The VR system was implemented using an HTC VIVE Pro Eye head-mounted display equipped with integrated binocular eye-tracking functionality operating at 120 Hz. Gaze coordinates, head orientation, and spatial position were recorded continuously with timestamp information throughout the experiment.

A panoramic-image-based VR system was adopted instead of real-time 3D rendering to ensure a consistent visual experience across participants while maintaining high-resolution image quality and stable eye-tracking performance. This approach also facilitated subsequent semantic segmentation and element-level gaze analysis because all participants observed identical visual stimuli.

The four atrium layouts were designed to represent different spatial configurations frequently observed in contemporary mixed-use facilities. Plan A served as a baseline configuration characterized by open circulation and distributed seating. Plan B introduced greater diversity in seating types. Plan C incorporated an elevated corridor structure that created locally enclosed spaces and variations in ceiling height. Plan D combined multiple seating arrangements with a more fragmented circulation pattern. The use of four layouts enabled examination of seat-selection behavior under varying spatial conditions while maintaining a consistent overall building scale.

### 2.2 Experimental Procedure

Twenty-nine university students participated in the experiment (20 males and 9 females; mean age = 22.5 years). Most participants were enrolled in architecture-related programs and were recruited through university mailing lists and classroom announcements. All participants had normal or corrected-to-normal vision.

The experiment was conducted as follows. Participants first underwent calibration of eye tracking. They were then instructed to assume a situation in which they would converse with a friend and to select preferable seats accordingly. Participants freely navigated the VR atrium and selected three candidate seats from 14–21 available seating locations. After sitting at each candidate seat and inspecting the surrounding environment, they chose the most preferred seat among the three.

The procedure was repeated for all four plans (A–D). The presentation order of Plans A–D was randomized across participants to minimize potential order effects. For each participant, navigation trajectories and gaze data were recorded during both walking and seated evaluation phases. This study was approved by the institutional ethics committee (Approval No. 2022174), and all participants provided informed consent prior to participation.

The experiment used an HTC VIVE Pro Eye headset equipped with integrated binocular eye tracking. Eye movements were recorded at 120 Hz. Manufacturer-reported gaze accuracy is approximately 0.5°–1.1° under standard operating conditions.

## 2.3 Overview of Seat-Choice Tendencies

Figure 3 summarizes seat-selection outcomes across the four plans. Although spatial configurations differed considerably, several recurring tendencies were observed.

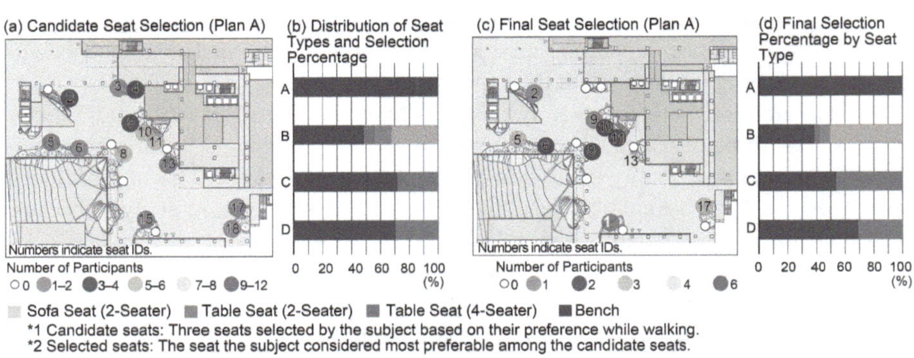


**Fig. 3.** Seat-selection outcomes in Plan A. (a) Candidate seat selection results. (b) Distribution of plan types and corresponding selection percentages. (c) Final seat selection results. (d) Final selection percentage by plan type

In Plan A, seats characterized by visual openness—such as those facing openings or located beneath higher ceilings—were frequently shortlisted. Seats positioned away from main pedestrian circulation also exhibited higher selection frequencies. In Plans B and D, where multiple seating types were introduced (e.g., sofa seats and four-person table seats), seat type strongly influenced choice. Approximately half of participants selected sofa seats as their final choice in Plan B. In Plan C, which included an overhead corridor, seats located beneath the corridor—where ceiling height was reduced—were often selected, suggesting a preference for more enclosed and calm environments. Across plans, selection patterns appeared systematic rather than random, indicating that seat preference can be modeled based on identifiable environmental and visual factors.

# 3 Quantification of Visual Attention

## 3.1 Semantic Segmentation of Environmental Elements

To quantify what participants visually attended to, we classified visual environmental elements in the panoramic images using semantic segmentation (Fig. 4). A U-Net-based neural network architecture was trained on manually annotated samples (219 images) and applied to 871 omnidirectional images. The resulting Dice coefficient was 0.61, indicating acceptable segmentation performance for architectural scene elements.

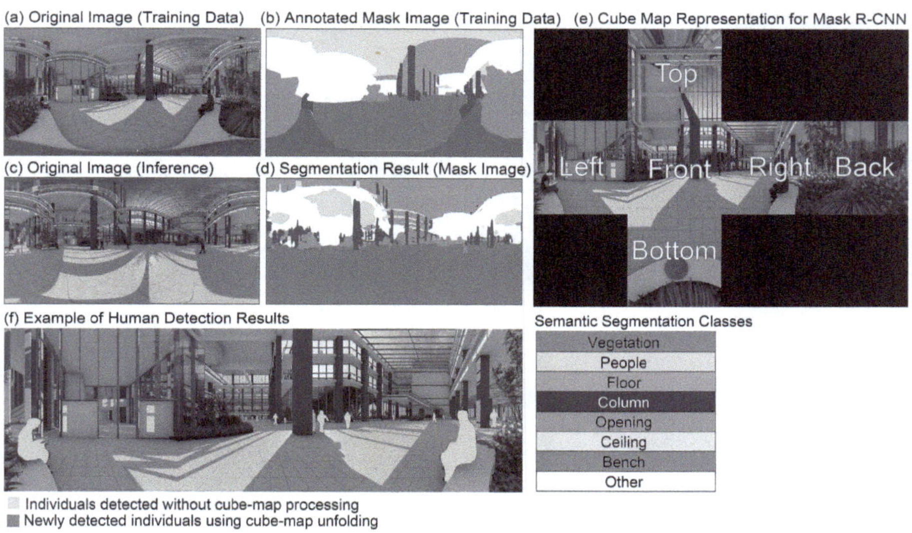


**Fig. 4.** Semantic segmentation and element detection workflow. (a–b) Training data and annotated masks. (c–d) Inference results of environmental element segmentation. (e) Cube-map representation for improved human detection. (f) Example of detected individuals

Because omnidirectional images introduce geometric distortion, each image was unfolded into six planar faces (cube maps) before applying Mask R-CNN for improved human detection. This additional processing significantly improved detection accuracy of distant individuals.

The classified elements included benches, columns, openings, floor, ceiling, vegetation, and people. Pixel counts for each element were computed separately for front, left, and right viewing directions.

## 3.2 Fixation Identification

Fixation detection followed criteria adapted from established eye-tracking studies [2, 6, 9]:

1. gaze remained within the same element for at least 0.2 s,
2. gaze movement velocity was below 100°/s, and
3. angular variance was within 2°.

Prior to fixation classification, raw gaze coordinates were smoothed using a moving-average filter to reduce high-frequency noise associated with micro eye movements and measurement instability (Fig. 5). By linking gaze coordinates to segmented element masks, fixation duration for each environmental element was computed.

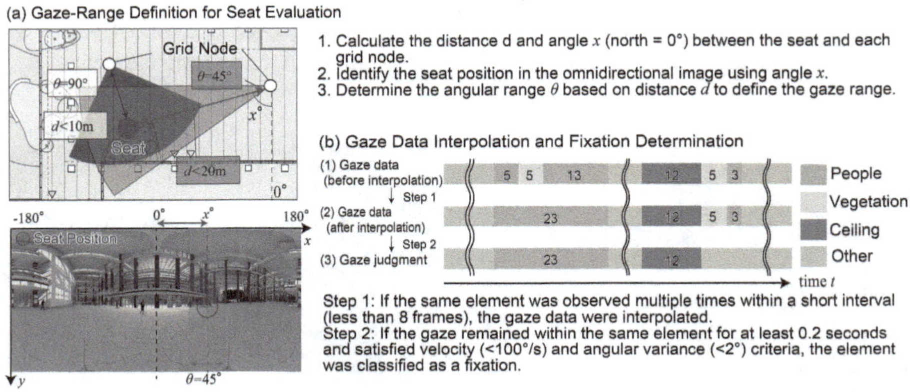


**Fig. 5.** Gaze-range definition and fixation determination procedure. (a) Definition of the angular range used to extract gaze data for seat evaluation. (b) Gaze data interpolation and fixation classification process

### 3.3 Gaze Analysis during Walking and Sitting

Gaze behavior was analyzed separately for walking and sitting phases (Fig. 6). During walking, participants frequently fixated on columns and vegetation while scanning the environment. Columns received relatively frequent fixations during movement. One possible explanation is that they served as visual boundaries between adjacent spaces.

During seated evaluation, fixation concentrated on frontal elements. Vegetation and distant spatial openness received longer fixation durations compared with floor areas. Notably, the fixation duration on people was disproportionately high relative to their pixel area, suggesting heightened sensitivity to social presence.

These findings indicate that visual attention during seat evaluation is structured and element-specific, motivating its inclusion as explanatory variables in seat-choice modeling.

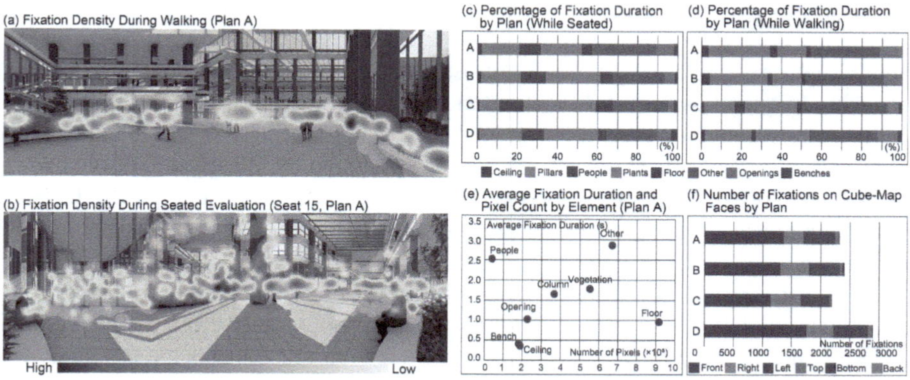


**Fig. 6.** Eye-tracking results. (a) fixation density during walking (Plan A). (b) fixation density during seated evaluation (Seat 15, Plan A). (c–d) percentage of fixation duration by plan during seated and walking phases. (e) relationship between average fixation duration and pixel count by element (Plan A). (f) number of fixations on cube-map faces by plan

# 4 Seat Clustering

## 4.1 Clustering Procedure

To capture the hypothesized stepwise decision process, seats were clustered using $k$-means based on their spatial and environmental attributes (Table 1). Highly correlated features were removed prior to clustering.

**Table 1.** Variables representing seat features

| $k$ | Seat Type | 8 | Number of Columns on Both Sides of the Seat | $k$ | Seating Location |
|---|---|---|---|---|---|
| 1 | Sofa Seat (2-Seater) | 9 | High Ceiling | 16 | Entrance Area |
| 2 | Table Seat (4-Seater) | 10 | Adjacent Seat Present | 17 | Central Area |
| 3 | Table Seat (2-Seater) | 11 | Facing Main Circulation | 18 | Rear Area |
| 4 | Concave Bench | 12 | Proximity to Pedestrians | $k$ | Facing Direction |
| 5 | Convex Bench | 13 | Presence of an Opening | 19 | North-Facing |
| $k$ | Spatial Attributes | 14 | Number of Sightlines | 20 | East-Facing |
| 6 | Presence of Nearby Stairs | 15 | Depth | 21 | West-Facing |
| 7 | Facing an Open Atrium | | | 22 | South-Facing |

For each participant, if at least two of the three shortlisted seats belonged to the same cluster, that cluster was defined as the participant's preferred cluster. Feature selection was conducted prior to model estimation and was based on spatial interpretability rather than model fit or seat-choice outcomes. The clustering process was performed independently of the final seat-choice model estimation.

### 4.2 Clustering Results

Figure 7 presents clustering outcomes. Across plans, features related to openness and seat type were frequently selected. In Plans B and D, clusters were clearly differentiated by seat type and orientation toward openings. In Plan C, clustering was less distinct, likely because corridor-specific features were not fully captured by the selected attributes.

For over 80% of participants, two of the three candidate seats belonged to the same cluster, supporting the hypothesis of preliminary group-based screening prior to final seat choice.

The clustering results suggest that participants tend to evaluate seats in groups sharing similar spatial characteristics. This observation motivates the hierarchical choice structure introduced in the next section, where the identified clusters are interpreted as nests in the seat-selection process.

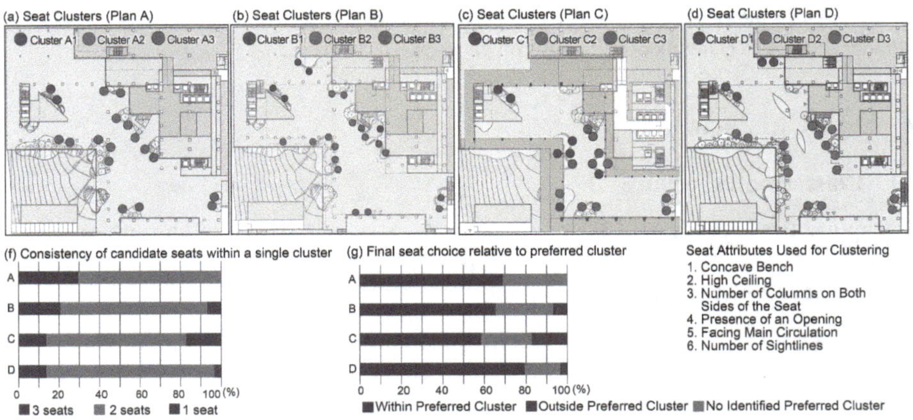


**Fig. 7.** Seat clustering results and validation of the preliminary cluster-selection hypothesis. The high proportion of candidate seats belonging to the same cluster supports the first-stage screening assumption in the hierarchical (nested) logit framework

## 5 Hierarchical Seat-Choice Modeling

### 5.1 Formulation of the Hierarchical Choice Structure

Unlike conventional seat-preference studies that rely solely on physical attributes, the proposed model explicitly incorporates perceptual attention into the utility structure. To quantitatively examine the hypothesized stepwise seat-selection process, we model participants' decisions using a hierarchical (nested) logit framework based on Random Utility Theory (RUT) [13]. Within this framework, individuals are assumed to choose the alternative that maximizes their utility among the available options.

The seat-choice experiment suggests that seat selection is not a single-stage decision. Participants were instructed to first identify three candidate seats and subsequently select the most preferred seat among them. This procedure implies a two-stage decision process consisting of (1) narrowing the available alternatives to a smaller set of preferred seats and (2) making a final selection from that set.

The clustering analysis presented in the previous section further supports this interpretation. The results showed that, for most participants, multiple candidate seats belonged to the same cluster, indicating that seats sharing similar spatial and environmental characteristics were evaluated as a group. Accordingly, the clusters identified in Sect. 4 are interpreted as nests in the subsequent choice model.

A nested-logit formulation is particularly suitable for representing this decision structure. The choice set contains multiple seats with similar characteristics, and the utilities of such seats are therefore likely to be correlated. Under these conditions, the Independence of Irrelevant Alternatives (IIA) assumption underlying the multinomial logit model may not be appropriate. The nested-logit model relaxes this restriction by allowing correlation among alternatives belonging to the same nest while preserving a behaviorally interpretable hierarchical structure.

Let $C$ denote the set of seat clusters and $A_c$ the set of seats belonging to cluster $c$. We assume that participant first selects a cluster $c \in C$ and subsequently chooses a seat $i \in A_c$. Let $V_{(i|c)n}$ denote the deterministic component of the utility obtained by participant from choosing seat $i$ within cluster $c$. The conditional probability that participant selects seat $i$ given cluster $c$, denoted by $P_n(i|c)$, is expressed as

$$P_n(i|c) = \frac{e^{V_{(i|c)n}}}{\sum_{i \in A_c} e^{V_{(i|c)n}}} \tag{1}$$

This expression represents the lower-level seat-choice model.

Let $V_{cn}$ denote the deterministic utility associated with selecting cluster $c$ by participant $n$. The probability of selecting cluster $c$, denoted $P_n(c)$, is defined as:

$$P_n(c) = \frac{e^{V_{cn} + \lambda V^*{}_{cn}}}{\sum_{c \in C} e^{V_{cn} + \lambda V^*{}_{cn}}} \tag{2}$$

where $\lambda$ is a structural parameter representing the degree of independence between alternatives within a cluster.

The composite variable $V^*{}_{cn}$, often referred to as the inclusive value or logsum variable, captures the expected maximum utility from the lower-level seat choices within cluster $c$. It is defined as:

$$V^*{}_{cn} = \ln \sum_{i \in A_c} e^{V_{(i|c)n}} \tag{3}$$

The parameter $\lambda$ must satisfy $0 < \lambda < 1$ for consistency with random utility maximization. If $\lambda = 1$, the model collapses to a standard multinomial logit model without hierarchical structure. If $0 < \lambda < 1$, the nested structure is valid and indicates correlation among alternatives within clusters.

The unconditional probability that participant $n$ selects seat $i$ belonging to cluster $c$, denoted $P_n(i, c)$, is obtained by multiplying the conditional probability and the cluster-selection probability:

$$P_n(i, c) = P_n(i|c) P_n(c) \tag{4}$$

This expression represents the hierarchical seat-choice behavior model.

## 5.2 Specification of Utility Functions

Seat-level utility functions were specified as linear combinations of seat attributes, environmental features, and fixation-duration variables (Table 2).

**Table 2.** Explanatory variables for seat choice behavior model

| $k$ | Seat Attributes | 8 | Facing an Opening | 16 | People |
|---|---|---|---|---|---|
| 1 | Table Seat (4-Seater) | 9 | High Ceiling | 17 | Openings |
| 2 | Table Seat (2-Seater) | 10 | Presence of Nearby Stairs | 18 | Ceiling |
| 3 | Sofa Seat (2-Seater) | 11 | Adjacent Seat Present | 19 | Vegetation |
| 4 | Concave Bench | 12 | Number of Sightlines | 20 | Floor |
| $k$ | Environmental Attributes | 13 | Distance to Main Circulation (*) | 21 | Columns |
| 5 | Presence of Columns on Both Sides of the Seat | 14 | Distance to Stairs (*) | 22 | Benches |
| 6 | Presence of Vegetation Nearby | 15 | Distance to Entrance (*) | 23 | Other |
| 7 | Presence of Nearby Pedestrians | $k$ | Fixation Duration Variables | | |

(*) Distance-related variables are measured using normalized network distance.

The deterministic utility of seat $i$ within cluster $c$ for participant $n$ is specified as a linear function of seat attributes and visual-attention variables:

$$V_{(i|c)n} = \sum_{k=1}^{K_1} \beta_k X_{(i|c)nk} \tag{5}$$

where:

$X_{(i|c)nk}$: the $k$-th explanatory variable describing seat (e.g., seat type, openness indicators, vegetation fixation duration, presence of nearby pedestrians),

$\beta_k$: unknown parameters to be estimated,

$K_1$: number of seat-level explanatory variables.

The inclusion of fixation-duration variables allows direct incorporation of quantified visual attention into the choice model.

Similarly, the cluster-level deterministic utility is defined as:

$$V_{cn} = \sum_{k=1}^{K_2} \theta_k X_{cnk} \tag{6}$$

where:

$X_{cnk}$: the $k$-th attribute of cluster $c$,

$\theta_k$: parameters to be estimated,
$K_2$: number of cluster-level variables.

All parameters $\beta_k$, $\theta_k$, and $\lambda$ were estimated by maximum likelihood estimation. Optimization was performed using the Newton–Raphson method. Statistical significance was evaluated using $t$-statistics derived from the inverse Hessian matrix.

# 6 Estimation Results

## 6.1 Cluster-Level Model

The cluster-selection model achieved an adjusted likelihood ratio of 0.37 (Fig. 8). The estimated $\lambda = 0.26$ satisfies the theoretical condition $0 < \lambda < 1$, supporting the consistency of the nested-logit formulation and suggesting correlation among alternatives within the same cluster.

The hierarchical structure was not imposed solely by the modeling framework but was motivated by the observed decision procedure in the experiment. Participants explicitly narrowed the available alternatives to three candidate seats before making their final selection in a preliminary experiment. This behavior suggests that seat choice is more appropriately represented as a hierarchical process than as a single-stage choice among all available seats. Moreover, because several seats shared similar spatial and environmental characteristics, the Independence of Irrelevant Alternatives (IIA) assumption of the multinomial logit model could be problematic. For these reasons, a nested logit formulation was adopted to represent correlations among similar alternatives while preserving a behaviorally interpretable decision structure.

Clusters characterized by sofa seating and lower social exposure were preferred. Openness-related variables also contributed positively.

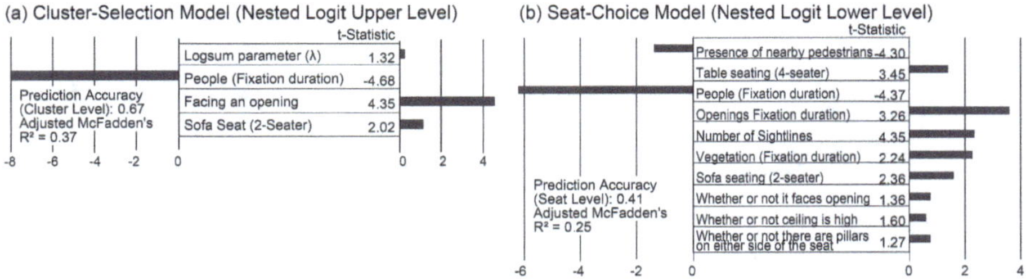


**Fig. 8.** Estimation results of the hierarchical (nested) logit model. (a) Cluster-selection (upper-level) model. (b) Seat-choice (lower-level) model. Bars represent $t$-statistics of estimated parameters. The inclusive value parameter ($\lambda$) confirms the validity of the hierarchical decision structure

## 6.2 Seat-Level Model

Seat-level estimation results (Fig. 9) indicate that seat type, number of visually open directions, vegetation fixation duration, and opening-related attention positively influence utility. In contrast, variables representing strong awareness of nearby people exhibited negative coefficients.

Predicted seat-choice counts closely matched observed counts across plans. Figure 10 shows utility distributions for all seats. Plans incorporating greater spatial diversity (e.g., Plan C) produced more high-utility seats.

The model thus enables quantitative evaluation of alternative atrium configurations by predicting seat attractiveness under modified spatial or visual conditions.

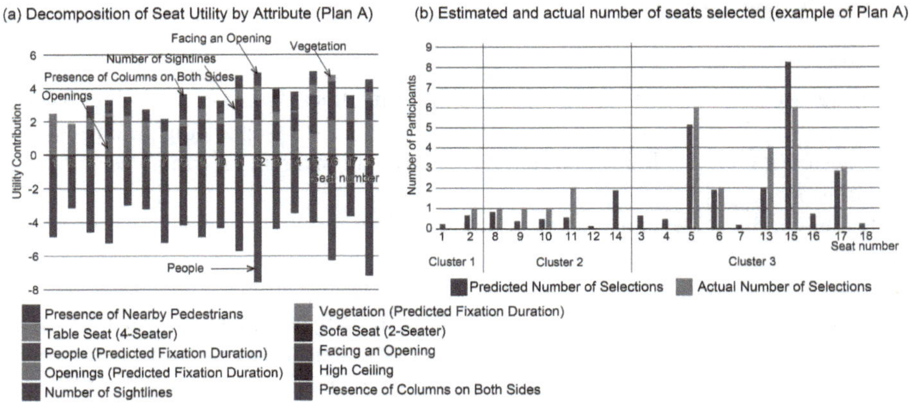


**Fig. 9.** Model validation results (Plan A). (a) Decomposition of deterministic utility into attribute-specific contributions for each seat. (b) Comparison between predicted and observed number of selections

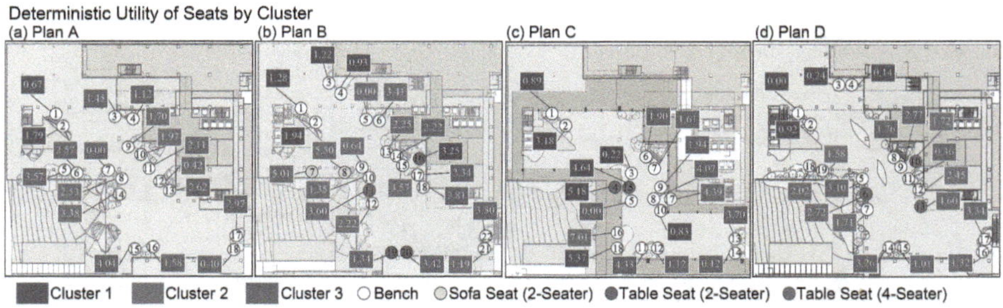


**Fig. 10.** Deterministic utility distribution of seats by cluster across Plans A–D. Colors indicate cluster membership derived from *k*-means clustering. Higher utility values correspond to seats predicted to have greater attractiveness in the nested logit model. Plan C exhibits the largest number of high-utility seats, reflecting the spatial diversity introduced by the corridor configuration

## 7 Conclusion

This study presented an integrated VR-based framework for quantitatively analyzing seat-selection behavior in atrium spaces by explicitly incorporating visual attention into a hierarchical discrete choice model. By combining immersive virtual environments,

HMD-based eye tracking, semantic segmentation of environmental elements, and nested logit modeling, we established a unified pipeline that connects spatial configuration, visual perception, and behavioral outcomes.

The experimental results demonstrate that seat selection is not a single-stage decision but follows a stepwise structure: participants first narrow down alternatives to a cluster of seats with similar characteristics and subsequently select the most preferred seat within that cluster. The estimated nesting parameter confirmed the statistical validity of this hierarchical structure. Importantly, the inclusion of fixation-duration variables revealed that visual attention significantly contributes to seat utility beyond purely geometric or physical descriptors. Seats characterized by greater visual openness and attention to vegetation exhibited higher utility values, whereas increased visual salience of nearby people reduced attractiveness. These findings suggest that perceptual and social-awareness factors jointly shape staying behavior in atrium environments.

From a methodological perspective, the study advances architectural evaluation research in three ways. First, it demonstrates that immersive VR can function as a controllable experimental platform for pre-construction evaluation of spatial alternatives. Second, it provides a practical procedure for translating raw gaze data into element-wise quantitative indicators via semantic segmentation. Third, it integrates these attention measures into a rigorously specified hierarchical choice model, enabling prediction of seat attractiveness and expected selection frequencies under modified design conditions.

The proposed framework is compatible with BIM-based design workflows and can support iterative design processes by enabling scenario comparison at the planning stage. Designers can simulate alternative layouts, seating types, and environmental configurations, and quantitatively assess their behavioral implications before implementation.

Several limitations should be acknowledged. The participant sample consisted primarily of architecture students, whose spatial sensitivity and evaluation criteria may differ from those of general users. Moreover, the experimental scenario was restricted to a conversational setting with a friend, and behavioral responses may vary under different activity contexts (e.g., working, resting alone, waiting). Future research should include participants with more diverse demographic, cultural, and professional backgrounds in order to examine the generalizability of the proposed model and to better capture heterogeneity in spatial cognition and seat-selection behavior. Particular attention should be paid to individual differences in spatial cognition, including variations in environmental preference, social sensitivity, and visual exploration strategies. Modeling such heterogeneity may improve both predictive accuracy and theoretical understanding of spatial decision-making. Additionally, extending the model toward cross-nested formulations may capture heterogeneity in preferences more flexibly. A systematic comparison with alternative formulations such as multinomial logit, mixed logit, or cross-nested logit models would be valuable.

In addition, the semantic segmentation model achieved moderate accuracy. Segmentation errors may introduce noise into estimated fixation-duration variables and consequently affect parameter estimation. Future work should investigate the sensitivity of behavioral predictions to segmentation performance and evaluate the robustness of the proposed framework using more advanced segmentation techniques.

Overall, this study demonstrates that integrating visual attention into hierarchical discrete choice modeling provides a robust and interpretable framework for understanding and predicting staying behavior in complex architectural environments. The approach offers a quantitative bridge between perceptual processes and spatial design decisions, contributing to evidence-based architectural planning in immersive virtual contexts.

**Acknowledgments.** This research was conducted with the approval of the Research Ethics Committee for Human Subjects at Institute of Science Tokyo (Approval Number: 2022174). This paper is an expanded and revised version of [15]. We would like to express our sincere gratitude to the reviewers for their many valuable comments and suggestions.

**Disclosure of Interests.** The authors have no competing interests to declare that are relevant to the content of this article.

## References

1. Aalto, P., Steinert, M.: Emergence of eye-tracking in architectural research: a review of studies 1976–2021. Archit. Sci. Rev. **68**(3), 213–223 (2025)
2. Adhanom, I.B., Lee, S.C., Folmer, E., MacNeilage, P.: Gazemetrics: An open-source tool for measuring the data quality of HMD-based eye trackers. In: Proceedings of the ACM Symposium on Eye Tracking Research and Applications, pp. 1–5. ACM, New York (2020)
3. Akinyelu, A.A., Blignaut, P.: Convolutional neural network-based methods for eye gaze estimation: a survey. IEEE Access. **8**, 142581–142605 (2020)
4. Berni, A., Ruiz-Pastor, L., Borgianni, Y.: User evaluation of a tiny house design through eye-tracking-integrated virtual reality. Int. J. Interact. Des. Manuf. **19**, 4815–4834 (2024)
5. Chen, S., Li, Y., Zhang, H.: An Eye-Tracking Analysis Based on Virtual Reality (VR) Technology: a study on satisfaction with urban historical district renovation. In: 2025 International Conference on Artificial Intelligence and Computational Intelligence (AICI 2025), February 14–16, 2025, Kuala Lumpur, Malaysia. ACM, New York, NY, USA, p. 8 (2025)
6. Chernyak, I., Chernyak, G., Bland, J.K.S., Rahier, P.D.P.: Important considerations of data collection and curation for reliable benchmarking of end-user eye-tracking systems. In: 2021 Symposium on Eye Tracking Research and Applications (ETRA '21 Full Papers), May 25–27, 2021, Virtual Event, Germany, p. 9. ACM, New York, NY, USA 2021
7. Cruz, M.B., Rebelo, F., Pinto, J.C.: eye-tracking advancements in architecture: a review of recent studies. Buildings. **15**(19), 3496 (2025)
8. He, K., Gkioxari, G., Dollár, P., Girshick, R.: Mask R-CNN, In: IEEE International Conference on Computer Vision (ICCV), Venice, Italy, pp. 2980–2988 (2017)
9. Holmqvist, K., Nyström, M., Andersson, R., Dewhurst, R., Jarodzka, H., van de Weijer, J.: Eye Tracking: A Comprehensive Guide to Methods and Measures. Oxford University Press, Oxford (2011)
10. Katsini, C., Abdrabou, Y., Raptis, G.E., Khamis, M., Alt, F.: The role of eye gaze in security and privacy applications: Survey and future HCI research directions. In: Proceedings of the 2020 CHI '20: CHI Conference on Human Factors in Computing Systems, April 25–30, HI, Honolulu, USA (2020)
11. Kim, E.J., Kang, Y.: Analyzing image recognition characteristics in landscape architecture using eye tracking. Front. Archit. Res. **14**(3), 797–811 (2025)
12. McCormack, G.R., Shiell, A.: In search of causality: a systematic review of the relationship between the built environment and physical activity among adults. Int. J. Behav. Nutr. Phys. Act. **8**(125) (2011)

13. McFadden, D.: Conditional logit analysis of qualitative choice behavior. In: Zarembka, P. (ed.) Front. Econ., pp. 105–142. Academic, New York (1974)
14. Moreno-Arjonilla, J., López-Ruiz, A., Jiménez-Pérez, J.R., Callejas-Aguilera, J.E.: Eye-tracking on virtual reality: a survey. Virtual Reality. **28**, 38 (2024)
15. Osaragi, T., Nishikawa, T., Kishimoto, M., Kaneko, H., Chen, S., Makieda, J.: Seat selection behavior analysis based on eye-tracking experiments in VR atrium spaces. J. Archit. Planning (Trans. Archit. Institute Japan). **90**(838), 2692–2700 (2025)
16. Ronneberger, O., Fischer, P., Brox, T.: U-Net: Convolutional Networks for Biomedical Image Segmentation, Medical Image Computing and Computer -Assisted Intervention-MICCAI 2015, Lecture Notes in Computer Science(), vol 9351. Springer (2015)
17. Scott, N., Zhang, R., Le, D., Moyle, B.: A review of eye-tracking research in tourism. Curr. Issue Tour. **22**(10), 1244–1261 (2019)

# An Empirical Study of Pedestrian Comfortable Distances in Real-World Interactions

Mengnan Cai(✉), Ehsan Hamzei, Martin Tomko, and Stephan Winter

University of Melbourne, Parkville 3010, Victoria, Australia
mengnan.cai@student.unimelb.edu.au

**Abstract.** Pedestrian navigation in crowded environments involves a continuous, subtle negotiation of interpersonal space. This research investigates these pedestrian spacing behaviors through the lens of comfortable distance—an invisible yet perceptible psychological boundary that regulates social interactions and collective movement. We examine how pedestrians perceive and manage this spacing as a dynamic response to social and environmental constraints. Using manually labeled pedestrian interactions from 650 pedestrian tracks recorded in two real-world datasets, we provide empirical evidence of how directional context and social configuration systematically structure spatial behavior. We find significant differences in comfortable distances across directional interactions, conditionally influenced by crowd density, pedestrian speed, spatial freedom, and relative positions. Group membership systematically modifies these associations, although its effect on encountered non-group pedestrians remains limited. By quantifying these spacing patterns, we establish a reproducible baseline for spatial organization, informing socially-aware navigation.

**Keywords:** Comfortable Distance · Directional Interactions · Pedestrian Interaction · Walking behavior

## 1 Introduction

Pedestrians navigate freely, using perception and judgment to coordinate movement and avoid collisions. These interactions are governed by social norms and the drive to preserve personal space, which are long studied in sociology and anthropology [11], and form invisible psychological boundaries similar to territorial behavior [2], typically expressed through distances to others, obstacles, or spatial boundaries. Pedestrian interaction is a process of perceiving, organizing, and regulating interpersonal space in real-world environments.

Where possible, pedestrians maintain a minimum distance with which they feel comfortable [12], acting as a dynamic spatial representation depending on personal habits, environmental constraints, crowdedness, and interaction types


E. Farran et al. (Eds.): Spatial Cognition 2026, LNAI 16785, pp. 18–33, 2027.
https://doi.org/10.1007/978-3-032-36716-7_2

[5]. This distancing is anisotropic: physiological responses are stronger in face-to-face than in face-to-back encounters, affecting spatial decision-making [9]. Although interpersonal distancing is sometimes treated as intuitive or self-evident, real-world evidence on how directional context, environmental, and social configuration systematically and conditionally shape this organization of space remains limited. Whether assumed influences persist or invert under specific conditions is a critical question that lacks systematic quantification.

This gap extends to pedestrian models, such as the social force model [13] regulates interpersonal spacing, but does not explicitly account for interaction direction. Furthermore, movement often occurs in groups where cohesion supports collective travel [7], while individual adaptations within groups affect nearby pedestrians and overall dynamics [10]. Yet it remains unclear how comfortable distance differs between group and non-group pedestrians, whether single pedestrians maintain different distances when, or how group membership interacts with density, speed, spatial freedom, and relative positioning. This study provides empirical constraints for future pedestrian modelling.

This research investigates *comfortable distance*, defined as the minimum distance pedestrians maintain to preserve private space without requiring evasive maneuvers. This concept is especially relevant in the low- to medium-density environments, where pedestrians have the flexibility to adjust movement. We examine how density, speed, spatial freedom, and relative positioning—key factors in crowd dynamics [7]—influence comfortable distance across various directional interactions and social configurations (group vs. single). Specifically, we ask:

- How do comfortable distances differ between aligned directional interactions and opposing directional interactions?
- How are comfortable distances associated with speed, density, spatial freedom, and relative position to obstacles in low- to medium-density crowds?
- How do these relationships change in the presence of group members?

By systematically analyzing two real-world datasets, we:

- demonstrate robust direction-dependent differences in comfortable distances, confirming direction as a fundamental and systematic determinant and quantifying when the effect is amplified or attenuated;
- identify a consistent association structure among density, speed, spatial freedom, and relative positioning with comfortable distances, revealing when observations hold, when they fail, and when they reverse.
- reveal systematic contrasts between group and non-group pedestrians in comfortable distance patterns and responsiveness to contextual factors, refining intuitive expectations about group presence and social-spatial dynamics.

These contributions advance empirical understanding of pedestrian spacing in low- to medium-density urban environments and provide a reproducible behavioral baseline for spatial planning, crowd management, and refinement of socially-aware pedestrian dynamics models [24].

## 2 Background

Interpersonal interactions stem from the human need to preserve personal space, a concept rooted in psychological and social behavior [6]. We refer to this as the *comfortable distance* - an invisible dynamic boundary that protects physical safety and supports psychological well-being [11]. Consequently, crowding can trigger endocrine-related physiological and psychological responses [3], reflecting the strain of boundary intrusion. Comfortable distance regulation is thus a multifaceted behavioral, physiological, and psychological process that may vary with interaction direction [9].

Group dynamics introduce further complexity as members maintain spatial cohesion for communication and collective movement [14], influencing trajectories, route choices, and spacing [7]. Groups adapt dynamically; a single member's shift in speed or position can propagate spatially and affect nearby pedestrians [10], which yield collective behaviors. Furthermore, density, speed, spatial freedom, and relative positioning shape trajectories and crowd flow [23].

Despite these foundations, the association of structural influence of contextual factors on directional interactions remains insufficiently quantified. We address this by operationalizing personal space as *comfortable distance*, treating it as a reproducible proxy for personal space with empirical practice [25] and for comparison across contexts.This framework bridges behavioral observation with proxemics theory [25] to analyze how directional, social, and environmental constraints structure interpersonal spacing, with the expectation that these factors systematically modulate pedestrian spacing behavior.

## 3 Method

Rather than proposing new algorithms, this study advances behavior understanding through rigorous empirical stratification and validation of widely used measures under distinct social configurations, ensuring methodological choices are justified for real-world pedestrian interactions. Our goal is methodological sufficiency, transparency, and principled validation.

### 3.1 Assumptions

The following are our assumptions in this study:

- Observed pedestrian behaviors are assumed to be statistically homogeneous within same interaction type and environmental context. This enables scenario-level analysis of average tendencies but omits inter-individual variability.
- Conflicting interactions occur when other pedestrians break the limits of one's own comfortable distance, prompting dynamic adjustment in moving direction or speed, or alternatively, to tolerate the intrusion.

- Comfortable distance is defined as the minimum Euclidean distance between pedestrians at the moment of closest approach. This provides a consistent, rotation-invariant proxy for interpersonal spacing, though not capturing the full anisotropy of personal space.
- Group-level behavior is represented by the behavior and characteristics of group members, assuming statistical homogeneity within each group, while acknowledging the potential for within-group heterogeneity.

While comfortable distances, given their rationalization in the individual psyche, are probably individual, we take these assumptions to study their average patterns under defined contexts. Our inferences therefore concern scenario-level tendencies, not individual-level variability.

### 3.2 Data

We study pedestrian interactions in the Main Building and Hotel scenes from the *BIWI Walking Pedestrians* dataset [20], recorded at 25 fps and annotated at 2.5 fps ($\Delta t = 0.4$ s). This benchmark dataset is widely used in pedestrian dynamics research [1,26]. It provides manually annotated pedestrian positions and speeds in two ETH Zurich scenes under low- to medium-density conditions [15]. We selected these two scenes because they represent two distinct real-world social settings. In total, 650 pedestrian tracks were recorded over 25 minutes. Pedestrian speeds are relatively stable, with minimal rapid acceleration or deceleration events. Positions and velocities are given in meters through a homography transformation from image to real-world coordinates. We exclude pedestrians at scene borders to reduce effects from objects outside the camera view. The dataset also records pedestrian groups, enabling analysis of both individual and group dynamics, while demographic attributes such as gender, age, and residency status fall outside the scope of this research.

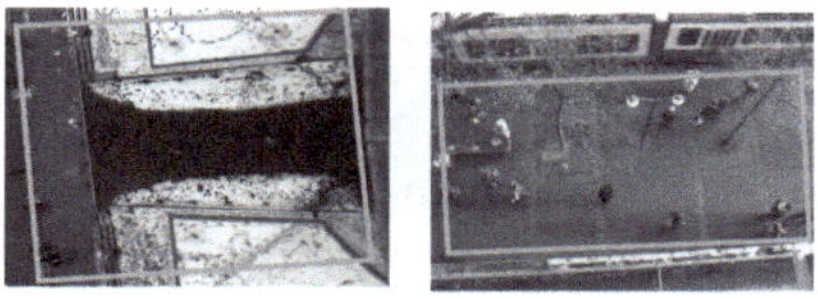

**Fig. 1.** Snapshots of the Main Building dataset and the Hotel dataset [20].

Our processing focuses on trajectories within the green boundaries in Fig. 1. We manually annotated frame-by-frame interactions within 3 meters based on changes in relative position, speed, or path. Only unanimous labels were retained. Exact-match agreement was 73%, 92% (81%, 93% with a one-frame tolerance). This produced two datasets: (1) the **Main Building** and (2) the **Hotel** interaction dataset, with the structure *frame_number, pedestrian_id, pos_x, pos_y, speed_x, speed_y, interaction status*. Interaction duration averages 0.82 s (SD

= 0.50, 75% under 1.2 s) in the Main Building interaction dataset and 1.18 seconds (SD = 1.01, median = 0.8 s) in the Hotel interaction dataset. Preliminary kernel density and spatial occupancy analyses confirmed low- to medium-density conditions and sufficient space for voluntary spacing adjustments.

To examine directional interactions, we classify interactions as aligned ($< 75°$) or opposing ($> 105°$), excluding the 75°–105° transition zone (1/440 cases). The angle distribution is bimodal, with nearly all interactions in 0°–45° or 135°–180° and only 2.5% in 45°–135°. These cutoffs follow the observed bimodality and are consistent with a perceptual transition near 75° [19]. The identified interactions are listed in Table 1.

**Table 1.** Trajectory information and manually labeled data for conflicting pedestrian-pedestrian interactions from the two datasets.

| | Main Building | Hotel |
|---|---|---|
| Speed Mean Value (m/s) | 1.39 | 1.04 |
| Speed Standard Deviation (m/s) | 0.47 | 0.70 |
| Interaction pairs during aligned directional interaction (pairs) | 94 | 156 |
| Interaction pairs during opposing directional interactions (pairs) | 74 | 116 |

### 3.3 Feature Extraction

To ensure methodological validity, we conducted preliminary checks before finalizing analysis parameters, ensuring parameters were adopted based on contextual adequacy and empirical stability.This research captures the following parameters (features) for each pedestrian in each time frame:

- The pedestrian *speed* is calculated as follows:

$$\text{speed} = \sqrt{v_x^2 + v_y^2}$$

  where $v_x$ and $v_y$ are the velocity components (in meters per second) derived from positional data between consecutive time frames, and the frame rate.
- Pedestrian *density* is calculated as the number of pedestrians within a 2-meter radius circle centered on each individual, divided by the area of that circle ($\pi \cdot r^2$ m$^2$), yielding a measure in persons per square meter (p/m$^2$). We adopt a fixed radius ($r = 2$ m), near the personal–social boundary in proxemics theory [8] and commonly used in empirical precedent [22]. It captures a behaviorally relevant zone while avoiding dilution from distant pedestrians;
- *Comfortable distance*: The shortest Euclidean distance (in meters) between two interacting pedestrians is used to represent comfortable distance as a robust baseline measure and an operational proxy, capturing the empirically observed point of maximum spatial constraint during an interaction. This measure is independent of directional classification, which is determined from

relative movement angles. As an operational proxy, it is rotation-invariant and appropriate for the low-to-medium density settings studied here, capturing voluntary spacing rather than enforced minima. This operationalization follows proxemics theory and is consistent with empirical work that quantify interpersonal spacing using Euclidean distance [25], however, it does not directly measure comfort, cognition, or psychological boundaries. Its limitations regarding anisotropy are discussed in Sect. 6.

- *Relative position*: We quantify pedestrians' spatial freedom using distances from the navigable space boundary (or obstacles) ahead (*head freedom*) and on both sides of the body (*side freedom*). We define $freedomshort$ and $freedomlong$ as the shorter and longer distances from the sides of a pedestrian's body to the boundaries of the navigable space. *Head freedom* is the distance from a pedestrian's position to the nearest boundary ahead in the direction of movement. *Side freedom* is the nearest lateral distance, measured horizontally from both sides of the pedestrian's body to the closest boundaries, perpendicular to the movement direction in the same plane. We introduce *ratio* $freedomshort/freedomlong$ to capture the pedestrian's relative lateral position in pedestrian flow within the navigable space. Ratios close to 1 indicate a central position, whereas ratios near 0 indicate proximity to boundaries. In the Hotel dataset, fixed obstacles such as benches and trees are also included in these calculations. Figure 2 illustrates head freedom, side freedom, and how $freedomshort$ and $freedomlong$ relate to obstacles or boundaries at a specific moment in a pedestrian's trajectory.

  To reflect the real-world conditions represented in the datasets, particularly concerning the head freedom and side freedom experienced by pedestrians, we assume that the sidewalks in the up-down direction in Fig. 1(a) and the left-right direction in Fig. 1(b) are sidewalks expanding straight beyond the visible area (confirmed on maps). For these calculations we set the spatial boundaries at (−100 m, 100 m), consistently with [18].

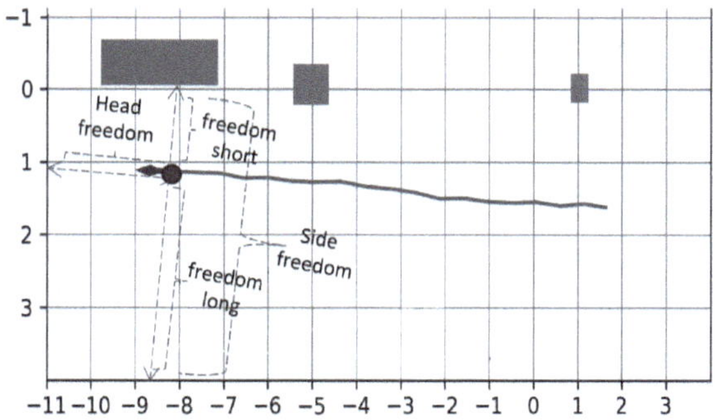


**Fig. 2.** Illustration of how head freedom, side freedom, freedomshort, and freedomlong work, here for Frame: 18061.

### 3.4 Statistical Analysis

For each interaction unanimously agreed upon by all annotators, we classify it as aligned (angles $< 75°$) or opposing (angles $> 105°$). For every interaction, we compute speed, local density, comfortable distance, and relative position. We use the Mann–Whitney U test [16] and Pearson [4] and Spearman correlation coefficients [17] to compare aligned and opposing directional interactions between individuals as well as group members. The Mann–Whitney U test is appropriate because comfortable distance distributions are positively skewed with long tails and slightly unequal sample sizes (Table 1). Spearman's $\rho$ captures monotonic associations and is more robust to skewness, tied values, and bounded variables such as ratio, while Pearson's $r$ is used to assess linear covariation. Using both coefficients [21] helps distinguish linear from monotonic relationships and provides a robustness check. This study intentionally prioritizes empirical regularity and cross-dataset reproducibility over model novelty, providing behavioral constraints essential for future mechanistic and simulation work. Given the exploratory nature of this research, the Bonferroni correction or similar adjustments are not applied, as the focus is on identifying potential patterns and relationships for future investigation rather than testing specific hypotheses. Applying stringent correction methods in this context could obscure valuable preliminary insights.

## 4 Results

### 4.1 Comfortable Distances

Comfortable distances vary over time. In the Main Building interaction dataset, the median distance is 0.94 m (range: 0.49–2.25 m; SD: 0.36 m), while the Hotel interaction dataset shows a smaller median of 0.89 m but a wider range (0.27–2.87 m; SD: 0.43 m). Maximum individual ranges reach 1.46 m and 1.59 m, respectively, highlighting significant individual differences in spatial adjustment during interactions.

The violin plots (Figure 3) show *opposing interactions* maintain larger comfortable distances than *aligned* ones. In both datasets, *aligned directional interactions* show an earlier truncation at larger values, indicating fewer interactions with large comfortable distances, whereas *opposing directional interactions* exhibit a broader distribution with a wider spread at larger values. This may be purely due to the problem of *identifying* the interactions. The range of $mean \pm 1$ std further confirms higher variability in *opposing directional interactions*, while *aligned directional interactions* remain more tightly concentrated. This suggests that pedestrians maintain a more consistent and tighter comfortable distance in *aligned directional interactions*, possibly due to greater predictability of surrounding movement, whereas *opposing directional interactions* require lower density under more rapidly changing pedestrian proximity.

To ensure that these findings are not caused by observational variance, we examined the video resolution. Each pixel represents approximately 4.6 cm,

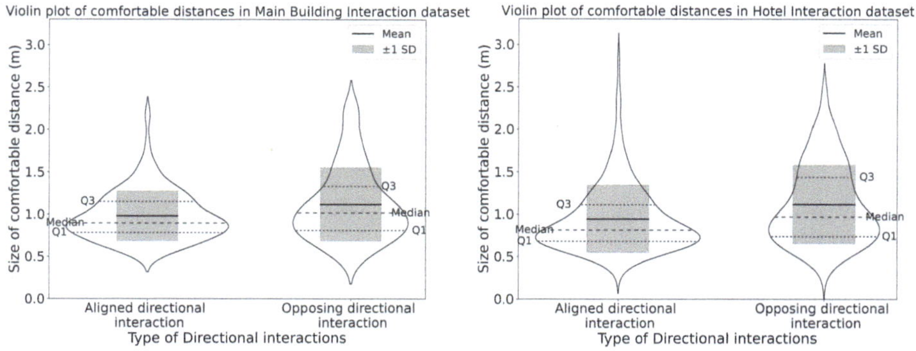


**Fig. 3.** Distribution of the comfortable distances during aligned and opposing directional interactions. Violin widths reflect kernel density estimation.

introducing only minor measurement error relative to the analyzed distances. Since all calculations involve distances exceeding a single pixel, this error is negligible.

We perform a Mann–Whitney U test to verify the significance of the differences, with the null hypothesis assuming no significant difference between the medians of *aligned directional interaction* and *opposing directional interaction*, and the alternative hypothesis $Ha : M1 < M2$.

For the Main Building Interaction dataset, the mean comfortable distance is 0.98 m in aligned directional interaction ($M1 = 0.98$, standard deviation = 0.29) and 1.12 m in opposing directional interaction ($M2 = 1.12$ m, SD = 0.43 m), an increase of approximately 14.3%. The U statistic is 9438.00 with $p = 0.02$, indicating a statistically significant difference at $\alpha = 0.05$. For the Hotel Interaction dataset, the mean comfortable distance is 0.94 m in aligned directional interaction ($M1 = 0.94$ m, SD = 0.40 m) and 1.12 m in opposing directional interaction ($M2 = 1.12$ m, SD = 0.46 m), an increase of approximately 19.1%. The U statistic is 25012.50 with $p = 5.13e^{-6}$, also indicating a statistically significant difference. In both datasets, opposing directional interaction shows a significantly higher median comfortable distance than aligned directional interaction. These results reflect significant differences in average comfortable distances rather than individual variations, and we do not control for surrounding traffic effects, as the aim here is only to identify whether average comfortable distances differ significantly between aligned and opposing directional interactions.

### 4.2 Features' Correlation with the Comfortable Distances

We evaluate both linear and nonlinear relations between comfortable distances during interactions and pedestrian density, speed, heading freedom, and lateral (side) body freedom, as shown in Table 2. Pearson and Spearman correlations indicate that, in both aligned and opposing directional interactions, density shows the strongest negative correlation with comfortable distance, followed by speed (positive). These effects are consistent in both Pearson and Spearman correlations, and are stronger in opposing interactions. Lower density generally corresponds to greater and more predictable comfortable distances, whereas higher density forces space reduction or faster movement to clear others. By contrast, pedestrian mobility freedom and lateral position in pedestrian flow show weak and inconsistent relationships across datasets. The ratio of body side freedom (lateral position in the flow) has a small, negative, and variable correlation with comfortable distance.

**Table 2.** Correlation of different variables with comfortable distance in the Main Building and Hotel interaction dataset.

| Datasets | Case | Correlation | density | speed | heading freedom | body side freedom | ratio |
|---|---|---|---|---|---|---|---|
| Main Building interaction dataset | aligned directional interaction | Pearson | -0.34 | 0.10 | -0.05 | -0.08 | -0.07 |
| | | Spearman | -0.31 | 0.09 | -0.09 | -0.03 | -0.10 |
| | opposing directional interaction | Pearson | -0.54 | 0.12 | -0.01 | -0.04 | -0.07 |
| | | Spearman | -0.47 | 0.15 | -0.05 | -0.00 | -0.03 |
| Hotel interaction dataset | aligned directional interaction | Pearson | -0.23 | 0.17 | -0.13 | 0.05 | -0.06 |
| | | Spearman | -0.09 | 0.11 | -0.16 | 0.14 | -0.01 |
| | opposing directional interaction | Pearson | -0.63 | 0.26 | 0.02 | 0.00 | -0.09 |
| | | Spearman | -0.62 | 0.26 | -0.02 | -0.00 | -0.13 |

Spearman evaluates whether the ordering of observations is preserved, whereas Pearson captures linear covariation. Divergences between Pearson's $r$ and Spearman's $\rho$ provide additional insights:

- *Density*: In all cases, $r > \rho$, indicating that the robust negative association is captured well linearly. The attenuation after ranking, most pronounced in the Hotel–aligned case ($r = -0.23$, $\rho = -0.09$), suggests that influential observations or departures from strict monotonicity are downweighted in $\rho$. Still, the consistently negative $\rho$ confirms that higher density almost always corresponds to shorter comfortable distances.
- *Speed*: In aligned interactions $r > \rho$, consistent with a weak but approximately linear positive relation. In opposing interactions $\rho \geq r$, suggesting a modest monotonic effect that remains at least as strong after ranking, consistent with mild nonlinearity or improved robustness to skew or outliers.
- *Ratio*: Correlations are uniformly small and unstable across contexts. Signs are negative but magnitudes are near zero, indicating a weak, context-dependent association rather than a robust linear or monotonic trend. This pattern is compatible with the ratio's bounded nature in $[0, 1]$, which compresses variation near boundaries and makes correlations sensitive to spatial layout. Fixed obstacle distributions may further shift ratio values across environments, limiting cross-context consistency.

Pearson's $r$ and Spearman's $\rho$ are generally close for density and for speed in opposing flows, indicating predominantly linear and monotonic associations.

For speed in aligned flows, the difference suggests mild departures from monotonicity, possibly due to leverage points or tied ranks. The consistently weak and sign-unstable coefficients for ratio and freedom reflect context-dependent effects, consistent with their bounded nature and sensitivity to spatial constraints.

As a robustness check, we additionally fitted a Random Forest regression model to examine whether non-linear effects or higher-order interactions would overturn the correlation-based ranking of predictors. Variable importance scores were qualitatively consistent with the correlation analysis.

We interpret the possible reasons for these observations across the two datasets:

- *Density*: Negative association: higher density reduces comfortable distance, with a stronger effect in opposing interactions, likely because denser environments force pedestrians to reduce space to avoid collisions and face-to-face encounters may increase discomfort.
- *Speed*: Positive association: higher speed increases comfortable distance. The effect is smaller in aligned interactions, where minor adjustments may suffice, but larger in opposing interactions, where high relative speed shortens reaction time and requires more space for course adjustment.
- *Lateral body side freedom*: Negligible and unstable association. Lateral body side freedom may have little regular effect on comfortable distance because lateral movement is irregular during collision avoidance and may depend on environmental factors, personal habits, or other external conditions.
- *Heading freedom*: Larger effect in aligned interactions, possibly because pedestrians can adjust behavior based on available space ahead, whereas in opposing interactions they focus more on avoiding immediate collisions than on longer-term path planning.
- *Ratio*: The weak and inconsistent negative correlation suggests that pedestrians closer to one lateral boundary may maintain slightly larger distances as a compensatory measure. However, the lack of consistent patterns across datasets and correlation methods indicates that this effect is unstable, context-dependent, or sensitive to outliers.

### 4.3 Group Dynamics

Using the original dataset group-membership annotations [20], which identify pedestrians as belonging to groups of 2–6 members, we examine group effects on comfortable distances; because observations for larger groups are sparse, the analysis focuses on comparisons between grouped and non-grouped pedestrians across three perspectives and five scenarios Fig. 4.

- Aligned: within group members vs. whole population (**S1**). Opposing: involving group members vs. the whole population (**S2**).
- Aligned: within group members vs. without group members (**S3**).
- Opposing: group member in involving pair vs. single pedestrian in involving pair(**S4**). without group members vs. single pedestrian in involving pair (**S5**) (Table 3).

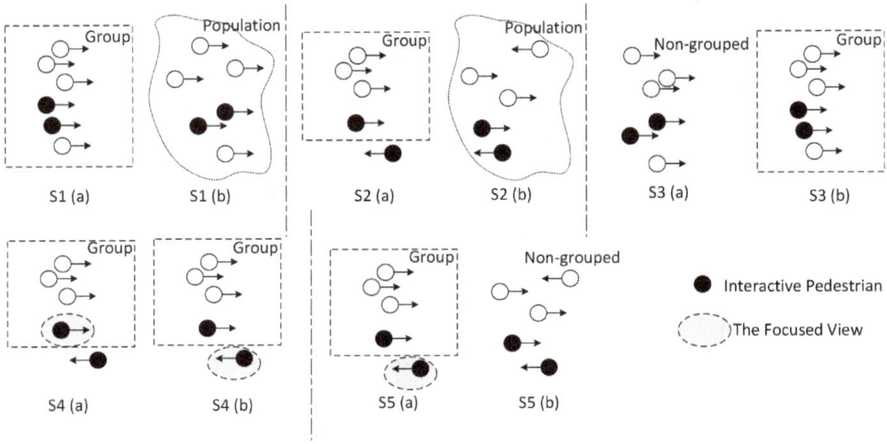


**Fig. 4.** Illustration of the five interaction scenarios that consider the presence of group dynamics.

In aligned interactions ($S1$), group members maintain smaller comfortable distances than the average. This effect is more pronounced in the Hotel interaction dataset than in the Main Building interaction dataset, where campus constraints may naturally limit distances. Group dynamics weaken the influence of density and speed on comfortable distances. While correlations with heading and lateral freedom vary, heading freedom remains negative but nears zero within groups. Notably, the speed-comfortable distances correlation in the Main Building interaction dataset shifts from positive to negative within groups, though the overall impact remains minimal as group integrity overrides individual speed adjustments.

In opposing interactions ($S2$), differences in comfortable distances between interactive pairs involving one group member and the general population are subtle. Group-involved pairs show slightly more constrained distances, particularly in the Main Building interaction dataset, suggesting environmental factors may limit group effects. While density and speed correlations weaken for group members, spatial freedom correlations remain inconsistent. Notably, in the Hotel interaction dataset, Pearson correlations for speed persist while Spearman correlations decline, suggesting maintained linearity despite rank-order consistency diminished.

Direct comparison ($S3$) shows group members exhibit wider comfortable distance ranges than non-grouped pedestrians, reflecting greater spatial preference variation when as part of a group. Conversely, in aligned interactions, groups maintain narrower ranges, indicating stronger cohesion. Group dynamics weaken most feature correlations, though density remains consistently negative. While speed correlates positively and monotonically with comfortable distances for non-grouped individuals, this effect weakens for groups. Similarly, non-grouped pedestrians prioritize forward space (heading freedom), whereas

**Table 3.** Correlation coefficient between the pedestrian comfortable distances and potential features (Label $a$ versus Label $b$ in $S1$ - $S5$) in the two datasets.

| Datasets | Cases | Correlation | Density | Speed | Heading Freedom | Body Side Freedom | Ratio |
|---|---|---|---|---|---|---|---|
| Main Building Interaction dataset | The whole population ( S1 (b) ) | Pearson | -0.34 | 0.10 | -0.05 | -0.08 | -0.07 |
| | | Spearman | -0.31 | 0.09 | -0.09 | -0.03 | -0.10 |
| | Within group members ( S1 (a) ) | Pearson | -0.17 | -0.02 | -0.16 | -0.03 | -0.12 |
| | | Spearman | -0.20 | -0.03 | -0.13 | -0.02 | -0.14 |
| Hotel Interaction dataset | The whole population ( S1 (b) ) | Pearson | -0.23 | 0.17 | -0.13 | 0.05 | -0.06 |
| | | Spearman | -0.09 | 0.11 | -0.16 | 0.14 | -0.01 |
| | Within group members ( S1 (a) ) | Pearson | -0.15 | 0.06 | -0.01 | -0.11 | 0.02 |
| | | Spearman | -0.10 | 0.02 | -0.00 | 0.01 | 0.03 |
| Main Building Interaction dataset | The whole population ( S2 (b) ) | Pearson | -0.54 | 0.12 | -0.01 | -0.04 | -0.07 |
| | | Spearman | -0.47 | 0.15 | -0.05 | -0.00 | -0.03 |
| | Involving group member ( S2 (a) ) | Pearson | -0.45 | 0.08 | -0.02 | 0.00 | -0.06 |
| | | Spearman | -0.37 | 0.04 | -0.05 | -0.05 | 0.02 |
| Hotel Interaction dataset | The whole population ( S2 (b) ) | Pearson | -0.63 | 0.26 | 0.02 | 0.00 | -0.09 |
| | | Spearman | -0.62 | 0.26 | -0.02 | -0.00 | -0.13 |
| | Involving group member ( S2 (a) ) | Pearson | -0.42 | 0.28 | -0.01 | -0.01 | -0.24 |
| | | Spearman | -0.33 | 0.17 | -0.04 | 0.02 | -0.21 |
| Main Building Interaction dataset | Without group members ( S3 (a) ) | Pearson | -0.45 | 0.13 | 0.12 | -0.27 | 0.15 |
| | | Spearman | -0.39 | 0.26 | 0.06 | -0.28 | 0.24 |
| | Within group members ( S3 (b) ) | Pearson | -0.17 | -0.02 | -0.16 | -0.03 | -0.12 |
| | | Spearman | -0.20 | -0.03 | -0.13 | -0.02 | -0.14 |
| Hotel Interaction dataset | Without group members ( S3 (a) ) | Pearson | -0.47 | 0.21 | 0.03 | 0.08 | -0.27 |
| | | Spearman | -0.42 | 0.19 | 0.00 | 0.00 | -0.25 |
| | Within group members ( S3 (b) ) | Pearson | -0.15 | 0.06 | -0.01 | -0.11 | 0.02 |
| | | Spearman | -0.10 | 0.02 | -0.00 | 0.01 | 0.03 |
| Main Building Interaction dataset | Group member in involving pair ( S4 (a) ) | Pearson | -0.29 | -0.02 | -0.24 | 0.10 | -0.17 |
| | | Spearman | -0.14 | -0.05 | -0.18 | 0.02 | -0.04 |
| | Single pedestrian in involving pair ( S4 (b) ) | Pearson | -0.48 | 0.06 | 0.36 | 0.44 | -0.06 |
| | | Spearman | -0.39 | 0.07 | 0.31 | 0.06 | 0.03 |
| Hotel Interaction dataset | Group member in involving pair ( S4 (a) ) | Pearson | -0.11 | 0.06 | -0.08 | 0.11 | -0.15 |
| | | Spearman | -0.19 | 0.00 | -0.00 | 0.03 | -0.13 |
| | Single pedestrian in involving pair ( S4 (b) ) | Pearson | -0.58 | 0.39 | 0.05 | -0.19 | -0.20 |
| | | Spearman | -0.48 | 0.33 | 0.05 | -0.00 | -0.15 |
| Main Building Interaction dataset | Without group members ( S5 (b) ) | Pearson | -0.53 | -0.05 | -0.00 | -0.12 | -0.06 |
| | | Spearman | -0.48 | 0.09 | -0.02 | -0.03 | -0.09 |
| | Single pedestrian in involving pair ( S5 (a) ) | Pearson | -0.48 | 0.06 | 0.36 | 0.44 | -0.06 |
| | | Spearman | -0.39 | 0.07 | 0.31 | 0.06 | 0.03 |
| Hotel Interaction dataset | Without group members ( S5 (b) ) | Pearson | -0.62 | 0.22 | 0.08 | -0.07 | -0.04 |
| | | Spearman | -0.61 | 0.26 | 0.08 | -0.16 | -0.02 |
| | Single pedestrian in involving pair ( S5 (a) ) | Pearson | -0.58 | 0.39 | 0.05 | -0.19 | -0.20 |
| | | Spearman | -0.48 | 0.33 | 0.05 | -0.00 | -0.15 |

group members exhibit opposite trend. Lateral and relative positioning remaining unstable.

In $S4$ interactions, the group member in interactive pairs maintains narrower comfortable distance ranges and weaker density correlations, reflecting more constrained spatial negotiation strategies shaped by group cohesion. Conversely, non-grouped pedestrians in pairs exhibit greater spatial flexibility and stronger responses to density and speed. Notably, heading freedom correlation is negative for group members but positive for non-grouped individuals. For both, relationships involving lateral freedom and relative positioning remain unstable.

$S5$ reveals that non-grouped single pedestrians in interactive pairs maintain stable comfortable distances indicating they maintain similar spatial preferences whether interacting with group members or with other non-grouped pedestrians. While density remains the primary driver, its correlation is slightly lower for non-grouped single pedestrians interacting with group members. Speed effects are context-dependent: in the Main Building interaction dataset, the correlation shifts from weakly negative to positive, whereas in the Hotel interaction dataset, positive associations strengthen. Spatial freedom features show no clear pattern. Overall, non-grouped single pedestrians exhibit resilient spatial preferences, primarily density-driven with minor, context-specific speed adjustments.

These scenarios demonstrate that while group dynamics may not drastically shift absolute comfortable distances, they consistently alter their regulation. Grouping typically weakens associations between comfortable distances and features, though density remains the most stable factor. In contrast, non-grouped pedestrians and non-grouped single pedestrians exhibit more consistent, density-driven spatial adaptation that remains stable across diverse interaction contexts.

## 5 Discussion on Datasets

Synthesizing the key findings, while both datasets show consistent trends, notable variations exist. For instance, in opposing interactions, correlation coefficient for density is nearly twice as high in the Main Building interaction dataset and three times higher in the Hotel interaction dataset compared to aligned interactions (Table 2).

Despite higher density, the Main Building dataset exhibits orderly movement, while the Hotel dataset's variable flow and correlation discrepancy suggests a more chaotic environment. In the Main Building dataset, diverse group sizes and synchronized campus travel lead to consistent density effects but cause sign reversals in weaker predictors like speed. Conversely, the Hotel dataset's predominant two-person groups amplify density and speed associations. These contrasts indicate that while pedestrians in the Main Building likely adjust trajectories proactively. Environmental and social contexts fundamentally shape group spatial behavior. In the Main Building dataset, complex multi-person groups foster predictability but weaken the rank-order consistency of secondary predictors (e.g., Spearman results). Conversely, the Hotel dataset's homogeneous small-group structure yields stronger, more consistent group effects, requiring continual adaptation to variable flow. While density remains the dominant driver, group dynamics reshape the stability and direction of other predictors, underscoring the need to incorporate group structure when interpreting pedestrian behavior.

## 6 Conclusion

This research advances empirical understanding of comfortable distances during directional interactions and social configuration in low- to medium-density urban settings through explicit and reproducible statistical estimates. Across datasets, comfortable distances are significantly larger in opposing than in aligned interactions, confirming a robust direction-dependent spatial preference. Density is the primary driver (negatively correlated), followed by speed, which shows stronger positive associations in opposing flows. Conversely, heading, lateral freedom, and relative positioning show unstable, context-dependent effects. Group involvement weakens density and speed associations and reduces rank-order consistency, particularly in the Main Building interaction dataset's heterogeneous groups. While group members maintain smaller, more stable comfortable distances due to cohesion, non-grouped pedestrians remain consistently density-driven spatial strategies whether they encounter single pedestrians or group members. Ultimately, social composition reorganizes the regulation of spacing determinants rather than merely shifting absolute levels. The findings therefore reveal a conditional association structure and non-monotonicity in spatial organization, showing where assumed influences weaken, disappear, or reverse.

Several methodological boundaries define the scope of results. First, aggregating behavior within same interaction type and context enables scenario-level pattern identification but overlooks inter-individual and within-group heterogeneity. Second, using minimum Euclidean distance approach ensures objective reproducibility and rotation invariance but omits the anisotropic geometry of personal space directional weighting could refine it in the future. Third, while a 2 m density radius is theoretically grounded and consistent with proxemics theory, future work could explore multi-radius robustness and higher frame (resolution) rates to capture sub-second micro-adjustments in spatial perception. Furthermore, this analysis prioritizes interpretability by focusing on the nearest interactant, excluding factors like demographics or gaze cues. Future work could incorporate these findings in high-density and utilize longitudinal across culturally diverse settings; the Zurich scenes are not globally representative, and cities with larger family-like groups may be closer to Main Building than Hotel.

These findings provide an empirical characterization of pedestrian spacing in low- to medium-density urban settings, revealing distinct spatial management strategies. By establishing a reproducible behavioral baseline and a direction-sensitive structure of spacing determinants, this study informs spatial cognition on how human perceive, organize, and regulate interpersonal space in real environments and supports future theory and crowd management. These insights can refine pedestrian dynamics models, such as the social force model, by incorporating directional configuration, group structure, and the stability of interpersonal spacing rank-order.

## References

1. Alahi, A., Goel, K., Ramanathan, V., Robicquet, A., Fei-Fei, L., Savarese, S.: Social LSTM: human trajectory prediction in crowded spaces. In: Proceedings of the IEEE Conference on Computer Vision and Pattern Recognition, pp. 961–971 (2016)

2. Altman, I.: The environment and social behavior: privacy, personal space, territory, and crowding, ERIC (1975)
3. Baum, A., Paulus, P.: Crowding. Handbook of Environmental Psychology, pp. 293–335 (1983)
4. Cohen, I., et al.: Pearson correlation coefficient. In: Noise Reduction in Speech Processing, pp. 1–4 (2009)
5. Colombi, A., Scianna, M.: Modelling human perception processes in pedestrian dynamics: a hybrid approach. Royal Soc. Open Sci. **4**(3), 1–23 (2017)
6. Demerath, L., Levinger, D.: The social qualities of being on foot: a theoretical analysis of pedestrian activity, community, and culture. City Commun. **2**(3), 217–237 (2003)
7. Do, T., Haghani, M., Sarvi, M.: Group and single pedestrian behavior in crowd dynamics. Transp. Res. Rec. **2540**(1), 13–19 (2016)
8. Federici, M.L., Gorrini, A., Manenti, L., Vizzari, G.: Data collection for modeling and simulation: case study at the university of Milan-Bicocca. In: Cellular Automata: 10th International Conference on Cellular Automata for Research and Industry, pp. 699–708. Springer (2012)
9. Feese, S.F.: Observing Teams with Wearable Sensors, ETH Zurich (2014). Ph.D. Thesis
10. Gorrini, A., Bandini, S., Sarvi, M., Dias, C., Shiwakoti, N.: An empirical study of crowd and pedestrian dynamics: the impact of different angle paths and grouping. Transp. Res. Rec. **41**, 1–12 (2013)
11. Hall, E.T.: The Silent Language. Anchor (1973)
12. Hedeker, D., Gibbons, R.D.: Mixor: a computer program for mixed-effects ordinal regression analysis. Comput. Meth. Prog. Biomed. **49**(2), 157–176 (1996)
13. Helbing, D., Molnar, P.: Social force model for pedestrian dynamics. Phys. Rev. E **51**(5), 1–5 (1995)
14. Knowles, E.S.: Boundaries around group interaction: the effect of group size and member status on boundary permeability. J. Pers. Soc. Psychol. **26**(3), 327–331 (1973)
15. Luan, Q.Y., Liu, S.B., Fu, Z.J., Lyu, J.Y.: Experimental and modelling studies of collision avoidance strategy choices and behavioural characteristics in interweaving pedestrian flow. Royal Soc. Open Sci. **9**(7), 1–25 (2022)
16. MacFarland, T.W., Yates, J.M.: Mann-Whitney U test. Introd. Nonparam. Statist. Biolog. Sci. Using R **1**(1), 103–132 (2016)
17. Myers, L., Sirois, M.J.: Spearman correlation coefficients, differences between. Encyclop. Statist. Sci. **12**, 1–2 (2004)
18. Park, H.C., Park, C.H., Kim, D.K., Chon, K.S.: Minimum pedestrian flow estimation for installing a moving sidewalk. In: Proceedings of the Eastern Asia Society for Transportation Studies, vol. 8. pp. 241–251. Eastern Asia Society for Transportation Studies (2011)
19. Peli, E., Apfelbaum, H., Berson, E.L., Goldstein, R.B.: The risk of pedestrian collisions with peripheral visual field loss. J. Vis. **16**(15), 5–5 (2016)
20. Pellegrini, S., Ess, A., Schindler, K., Van Gool, L.: You'll never walk alone: modeling social behavior for multi-target tracking. In: IEEE 12th International Conference on Computer Vision, pp. 261–268 (2009)
21. Rovetta, A.: Raiders of the lost correlation: a guide on using Pearson and spearman coefficients to detect hidden correlations in medical sciences. Cureus **12**(11), 1–7 (2020)
22. Steffen, B., Seyfried, A.: Methods for measuring pedestrian density, flow, speed and direction with minimal scatter. XXPhys. A **389**(9), 1902–1910 (2010)

23. Vanumu, L.D., Ramachandra Rao, K., Tiwari, G.: Fundamental diagrams of pedestrian flow characteristics: a review. Eur. Transp. Res. Rev. **9**, 1–13 (2017)
24. Von Krüchten, C., Schadschneider, A.: Empirical study on social groups in pedestrian evacuation dynamics. XXPhys. A **475**(1), 129–141 (2017)
25. Wąs, J., Gudowski, B., Matuszyk, P.J.: Social distances model of pedestrian dynamics. In: International Conference on Cellular Automata, pp. 492–501 (2006)
26. Zhang, P., Xue, J., Zhang, P., Zheng, N., Ouyang, W.: Social-aware pedestrian trajectory prediction via states refinement LSTM. IEEE Trans. Pattern Anal. Mach. Intell. **44**(5), 2742–2759 (2022)

# Computational Spatial Fluency: A Framework for Interactive 3D Making From the Design of Flock XR

Tracy Gardner[1(✉)] and Yasemin Allsop[2]

[1] Flip Computing, London, UK
tracy@flipcomputing.com
[2] University College London, London, UK
y.allsop@ucl.ac.uk

**Abstract.** This paper introduces Computational Spatial Fluency (CSF), a theoretical construct that emerged from the development of Flock XR and pedagogical experiences with other three-dimensional creative making spaces. CSF articulates how spatial and computational reasoning are integrated in practice within interactive 3D making environments, where spatial systems are constructed, tested, and refined through executable processes over time. The construct reframes spatial reasoning as an expressive, multimodal fluency enacted through the coordination of representations, embodied interaction, and iterative design, rather than as a set of isolated cognitive skills. It responds to a gap in existing accounts, which have given limited attention to how spatial reasoning develops in dynamic, computational contexts. The paper presents a framework and associated design principles grounded in this work, and outlines a research agenda for investigating implications for pedagogy, creativity, and equitable participation in K12 education.

**Keywords:** Spatial cognition · Computational thinking · Digital making · Constructionism · Three-dimensional environments · Computational spatial fluency · K-12

## 1 Introduction

Spatial thinking is a foundational form of cognition that supports learning across mathematics, science, geography, engineering, and computing [25,26,44]. It enables learners to interpret and construct spatial representations, from maps and models to digital environments [17,32]. In interactive three-dimensional digital environments, this reasoning is increasingly intertwined with computational processes, as learners design, manipulate, and test spatial structures that change over time. Digital making environments such as Minecraft show how spatial reasoning can develop through construction, navigation, and debugging rather than passive interaction with three-dimensional visuals [18].


E. Farran et al. (Eds.): Spatial Cognition 2026, LNAI 16785, pp. 34–48, 2027.
https://doi.org/10.1007/978-3-032-36716-7_3

This paper introduces Computational Spatial Fluency (CSF), a theoretical construct for understanding how learners develop spatial reasoning through computationally organised design activity in interactive three-dimensional environments. CSF foregrounds how spatial relations are constructed, tested, and refined through rule-governed action, and conceptualises spatial reasoning as emerging through cycles of creation, interaction, and revision within executable spatial systems.

We argue that three-dimensional digital making environments can be designed as constructionist microworlds in which learners develop CSF through meaningful creative activity [36]. In these environments, spatial reasoning is enacted through embodied interaction, coordinated representations, perspective switching, and iterative problem solving, while computational processes make spatial relations testable and revisable over time.

This paper responds to calls for more authentic and contextually grounded accounts of spatial learning [32,43]. It contributes by (1) introducing CSF as a theoretical construct, (2) describing how it is operationalised within a three-dimensional creative tool, and (3) proposing a research agenda to investigate its development and implications for pedagogy and equitable access. The paper addresses the following research questions:

1. How can three-dimensional creative digital spaces be theorised as environments for the development and application of spatial thinking during digital making?
2. What design affordances support embodied cognition and perspective taking in such environments?
3. In what ways does Computational Spatial Fluency extend traditional conceptions of spatial thinking and computational thinking?

## 2 Literature Review

Spatial thinking is a multidimensional construct involving spatial concepts (e.g. location, distance, orientation), spatial representations (internal and external), and spatial reasoning processes such as transformation and perspective taking [26,44]. While early work focused on internal mental representations, more recent research emphasises the embodied nature of spatial cognition, grounded in perception and action [4,46]. Children's spatial reasoning develops through activities such as manipulating objects, navigating environments, and coordinating multiple representations [14,33]. These embodied processes extend into digital contexts, where learners build, navigate, and transform structures across physical and virtual environments [11,47]. Spatial thinking is increasingly understood as situated and distributed, shaped by the representational and material environments in which learners act. Studies of physical and digital making contexts show that spatial reasoning becomes visible through actions such as manipulating objects, reorganising structures, and coordinating representations [11,13]. These findings position spatial thinking as a competence that develops through interaction with tools and environments, rather than as a fixed internal ability. At a cognitive level, spatial thinking relies on working memory, attention control and visuospatial processing systems [3]. This capacity is not fixed, and digital environments can support the transfer of these skills. Research on digital making environments suggests that experience with three-dimensional representations can support broader spatial reasoning, including transfer to tasks such as interpreting two-dimensional nets [1]. Digital making environments extend constructivist and constructionist approaches by enabling learners to externalise and test spatial ideas through interaction with artefacts [36]. Such environments support iterative cycles of planning, acting, testing, and revising, in which errors function as opportunities for learning [28]. Research on platforms such as Minecraft demonstrates that spatial reasoning develops through sustained engagement in construction and debugging tasks, particularly when activities involve meaningful constraints that prompt planning and revision [18]. Hughes et al. [18] found preliminary evidence suggesting that spatial reasoning does not emerge automatically from unstructured exploration; it requires intentional challenges, such as dimensional limits, to prompt systematic planning, hypothesis testing, and iterative debugging. Similarly, modelling environments such as TinkerCAD support spatial reasoning through the manipulation of three-dimensional forms and the development of mental models [7,42]. These environments also highlight the role of representation in shaping spatial reasoning. Learners coordinate multiple perspectives, including egocentric and allocentric frames of reference, as they navigate and design within three-dimensional spaces. This coordination is central to embodied cognition and supports the development of concepts such as orientation, scale, and transformation [47]. Studies of hybrid and computational environments further show how programming can act as a representational tool, making spatial relations explicit, testable, and revisable [13,40]. Spatial thinking also plays a central role in creativity and problem solving. It supports the generation and transformation of representations, enabling learners to explore alternatives, restructure problems, and iteratively refine solutions [35]. In design-oriented activities, spatial reasoning is enacted through cycles of exploration, evaluation, and revision, positioning it as a generative resource rather than a supporting skill. Despite growing recognition of its importance, spatial thinking is often addressed in isolation from the contexts in which it is enacted, with a focus on discrete abilities such as mental rotation or visualisation rather than on how spatial reasoning develops through interaction with dynamic, computational environments [34]. This gap is particularly evident in contexts where learners design and manipulate spatial systems whose behaviour unfolds over time. In such settings, spatial relations are not only represented but constructed, tested, and revised through computational processes, yet this form of reasoning remains under-theorised.

# 3 Computational Spatial Fluency: A Constructionist Framework for Three-Dimensional Creative Learning Spaces

This paper introduces Computational Spatial Fluency (CSF) as a theoretical construct describing how learners develop the capacity to create and reason about spatial systems through computational processes during digital making. CSF extends the constructionist tradition of computational fluency [6,38], understood as the expressive and purposeful use of computation for creation, debugging, and participation, into domains where the primary object of reasoning and creation is spatial structure and behaviour within three-dimensional digital environments. It builds on Papert's notion of technological fluency [36], emphasising expressive and creative use of computational tools, and applies this perspective to contexts in which spatial systems themselves become the medium of computational expression.

Educational research has often treated spatial thinking and computational thinking as complementary but distinct domains [37]. Comparatively little attention has been given to contexts in which learners design spatial systems whose behaviour emerges from computational processes. CSF names a productive intersection that warrants study in its own right: one with emergent properties that are not fully captured when spatial thinking and computational thinking are considered separately, and framed as expressive fluency rather than cognitive skill—with significant implications for how capability develops, how it is assessed, and who is able to participate.

CSF emerges when learners must simultaneously coordinate spatial relationships, embodied experience, and computational behaviour in a 3D digital learning space. For example, a learner creating a scripted camera path through a virtual environment must reason about geometry, perspective, movement, timing, and program execution as an integrated system. Similarly, constructing a procedurally generated structure requires anticipating both spatial form and the consequences of algorithmic rules. These activities require forms of prediction, debugging, and revision that are not fully explained by either spatial thinking or computational thinking in isolation.

## 3.1 Defining Computational Spatial Fluency

Computational Spatial Fluency is the ability to encode spatial intent into executable behaviour within interactive three-dimensional making environments. It focuses on the design of spatial systems whose behaviour emerges through computational processes, where spatial relations are constructed, tested, and refined over time. Executable behaviour includes imperative programming, but also physics behaviours resolved by the runtime from authored objects and applied forces. This integration positions CSF as a construct that connects spatial thinking with creativity, problem solving, and computational thinking.

CSF conceptualises spatial reasoning as emerging through cycles of creation, interaction, and revision. Learners externalise spatial ideas into manipulable artefacts, explore their behaviour through interaction, and iteratively refine designs in response to feedback. Computational processes make spatial relations explicit, persistent, and revisable over time, supporting forms of reasoning that extend beyond internal mental transformation. CSF requires learners to bridge the gap between allocentric logic (the global coordinate system) and egocentric experience (the first-person perspective of the avatar or camera).

CSF can be understood through four interrelated characteristics: (a) externalisation of spatial ideas into manipulable artefacts (b) coordination of embodied and symbolic representations (c) iterative tinkering and debugging (d) progressive application of computational structures to spatial objects, behaviours and reference frames. For example, a learner constructing a virtual maze may first arrange walls through direct manipulation, then introduce procedural rules that generate additional pathways or respond to user interaction. Success depends not only on understanding the geometry of the space or the syntax of the program, but on coordinating both while anticipating how the environment will behave when executed. This coupling of spatial structure and computational behaviour illustrates the distinctive focus of CSF.

### 3.2 Implications for Three-Dimensional Creative Learning Environments

Three-dimensional creative environments provide contexts in which spatial reasoning and computational processes are closely integrated. Learners construct and manipulate spatial artefacts within systems governed by computational rules, requiring them to reason about both spatial form and system behaviour. In such environments, perspective-taking, transformation, and interaction become integral to design activity rather than isolated cognitive skills.

From a constructionist perspective, learning occurs through iterative cycles of building, testing, and refining artefacts [36]. Tinkering and debugging play a central role, as learners encounter mismatches between intended and realised configurations and revise their designs accordingly. Through these cycles, spatial reasoning becomes increasingly organised through computational strategies, such as applying constraints, repeating transformations, and decomposing complex structures. In this sense, Papert's objects-to-think-with become programmable three-dimensional **objects-to-create-with**, where transformations are executable, relationships testable, and behaviours inspectable through the act of making itself.

CSF also reframes assumptions about individual spatial ability by emphasising the role of interaction and representation in supporting spatial reasoning. Learners with differing levels of internal visualisation skill may engage with spatial problems through alternative strategies, including the use of external representations, computational structures, and iterative manipulation of artefacts. Accessibility is integral to this process. Reported spatial skill differences across gender [5,45] are increasingly understood as shaped by stereotype threat and differential access to spatial experience rather than fixed ability [30,39], and similar patterns emerge across socio-economic and cultural backgrounds [16,24].

Furthermore, spatial cognition is not strictly visual or neurotypical; learners construct functional representations through diverse profiles, including deaf individuals [27], blind and visually impaired learners [12,21], those with physical disabilities [9], and neurodivergent learners with conditions such as autism, dyslexia, ADHD, or aphantasia [22,23,29,31]. Following the principles of Universal Design for Learning (UDL) for Computer Science [8,20], environments must be proactively designed for this variability. For example, Angeli and Valanides [2] found a significant interaction between gender and scaffolding strategy in early childhood robot programming: boys benefited more from individual, kinesthetic card-based activity while girls benefited more from collaborative writing, reinforcing why inclusive tools must offer multiple, equivalent entry points.

Together, these characteristics position CSF as a framework for understanding spatial reasoning as a dynamic, interactive, and computationally mediated process. It provides a basis for analysing how learners engage with spatial systems in digital making environments and for designing tools that support diverse pathways into spatial reasoning.

Learners may engage in spatial-computational reasoning through multiple modalities, including visual, auditory, embodied, textual, and collaborative approaches. This perspective challenges assumptions that spatial reasoning depends primarily on mental visualisation and instead recognises that computationally mediated environments can provide alternative routes into spatial understanding. Consequently, the design of accessible tools is not merely supportive of CSF development; it is fundamental to enabling participation in the forms of spatial-computational practice that CSF seeks to describe.

## 4 Design Principles of Flock XR

Flock XR [10] is a block-based 3D creative coding environment designed to provide equitable access to spatial computing in formal and informal education. The tool is implemented as an open source, browser-based environment built on Blockly and Babylon.js. Users construct interactive scenes through visual programming blocks and direct manipulation of scene objects. The environment supports object creation, transformation, camera control, events, animation, hierarchy, and constructive solid geometry within a real-time runtime, allowing spatial structures and computational processes to remain tightly coupled during design and debugging. As a free, open source, browser-based platform, [tool name] provides an ecologically valid and transparent foundation for further research [19].

The Computational Spatial Fluency (CSF) construct is informed by a broader ecosystem of 3D creative tools—including Blender, Autodesk, and Unreal Engine—which increasingly require the coordination of spatial and algorithmic thinking. Flock XR differs in its pedagogical and research orientation: it lowers barriers to entry through block-based interaction while preserving the relationship between spatial structure and executable behaviour. From a CSF perspective, these platforms may all support computational spatial fluency, but with different accessibility, abstraction, and scaffolding characteristics.

CSF emerged from sustained engagement with this wider landscape, but was crystallised through the co-design of Flock XR with educators and learners, making it constructionist in origin. It is proposed as a theoretical lens for understanding the forms of spatialcomputational reasoning that become visible across immersive creative environments.

The design principles presented below operate at two levels. At the theoretical level, they describe characteristics that may support the development of CSF across a range of spatial-computational environments, including game engines, CAD systems, virtual world editors, GIS platforms, and educational making tools. At the implementation level, Flock XR provides one concrete tool that integrates these principles. The examples presented are therefore tool-specific, while the underlying principles are intended to generalise beyond this platform.

### Design Principle 1: Executable 3D Worlds Enable Spatial Authorship Through Embodied Objects-to-Create-With

Extending Papert's objects-to-think-with [36], spatial authorship involves creating executable worlds that support identity, aesthetic expression, and meaningful participation. Learners are positioned as embodied participants rather than detached manipulators of geometric form.

Customisable avatars, characters, and environments can be modified visually or programmatically at runtime as in Fig. 1. Diverse skin tones, materials, and textures support identity and representation. Learners inhabit and refine the worlds they construct, coordinating egocentric and allocentric perspectives within executable space. These objects-to-create-with enable interactive narratives, simulated systems, and expressive digital spaces analogous to game design, data visualisation, and digital twin modelling.

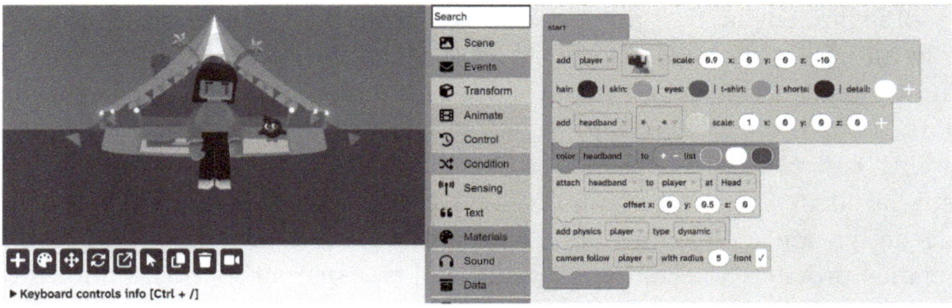


**Fig. 1.** Scene with colourful customisable character avatar.

## Design Principle 2: Coordinated Embodied and Symbolic Representations Offer Multiple Cognitive Frames for Constructing and Interpreting Spatial Transforms and Properties

Spatial transforms and properties can be specified through direct manipulation in the 3D scene or through block-based code as in Fig. 2. These representations are synchronised: spatial manipulation updates symbolic parameters, and programmatic specification is enacted perceptually in the environment.

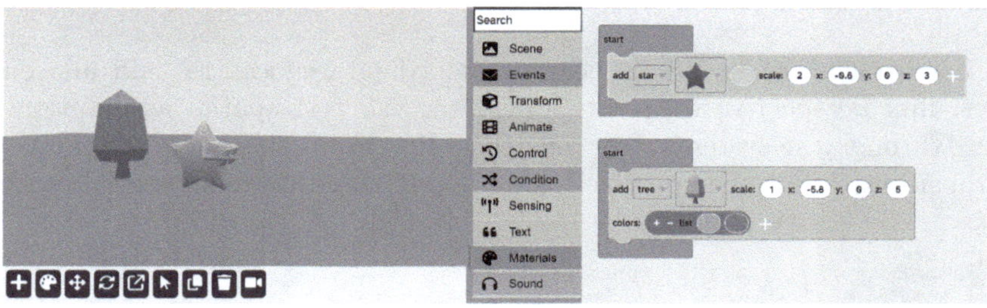


**Fig. 2.** Scene with gizmo shown transforming object and corresponding code.

This bidirectional coordination makes spatial computation inspectable across modalities. Learners move between embodied and symbolic frames, translating and integrating representations of the same transforms and properties. Consistent with UDL principles, neither manipulation nor abstraction is privileged—both are equivalent entry points to the same computational spatial concepts.

## Design Principle 3: Executable Spatial Systems Extend Spatial Reasoning From Static Configuration to Dynamic Processes

Within a real-time event-driven runtime, spatial reasoning extends beyond generating geometry to coordinating state, causality, and temporal change. Learners must anticipate not only what structures are, but how they behave over time. Objects respond to events, physics, hierarchy, and programmed transformations. Programmable constructive solid geometry enables primitive forms to be combined or modified at runtime, situating spatial form within executable systems.

When a project runs, spatial relationships are enacted over time as in Fig. 3. This supports iterative development through debugging, refinement, and the progressive application of computational structures to spatial forms and relations.

## Design Principle 4: Perspective is a Computationally Authored Element of Spatial Design

Cameras can be positioned, moved, and scripted within the scene as in Fig. 4, making viewpoint an explicit element of spatial authorship rather than a

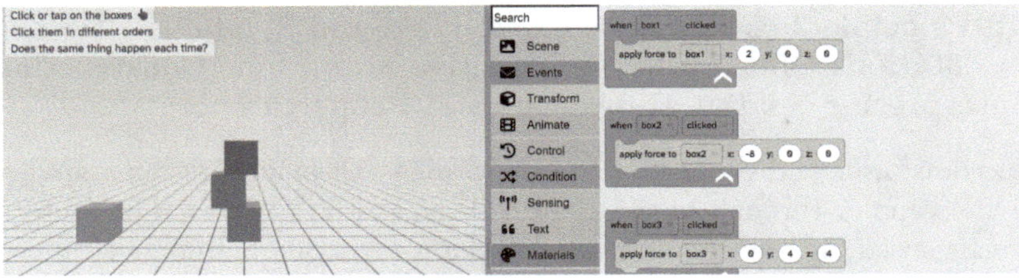


**Fig. 3.** Screenshot showing transformation.

fixed condition of observation. Learners coordinate egocentric and allocentric frames, link perspective to events and data, and test spatial assumptions by moving through the systems they construct. Programmable cut scenes and camera transitions situate perspective-taking within computational spatial practice.

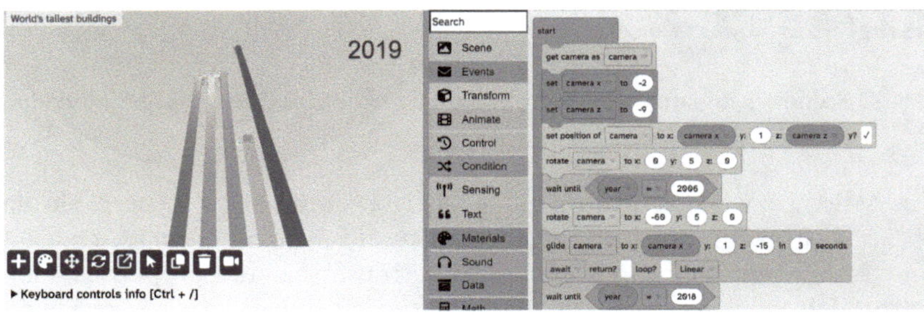


**Fig. 4.** Programmable camera moving to capture different perspectives over time.

## Design Principle 5: Spatial Computational Fluency Extends Across Physical and Digital Contexts

Augmented reality situates digital objects within physical environments as in Fig. 5. Sensor-driven inputs connect physical context to computational spatial systems, and fabrication workflows extend executable designs into material form. These affordances align educational practice with the hybrid physicaldigital ecology of contemporary spatial computing.

## Design Principle 6: Spatial Computational Fluency Requires Multiple Modalities of Access Across Diverse Cognitive, Sensory, and Situational Profiles

Accessibility is treated as a foundational condition for equitable participation. Spatial cognition is multimodal, and computational spatial fluency must be achievable across diverse cognitive, sensory, and physical profiles—including

**Fig. 5.** Augmented reality scene combining digital assets with a camera view.

blind and visually impaired learners, wheelchair users, deaf individuals, and those with specific cognitive differences. Current support includes a clean interface with clear language, adaptive game controller compatibility, spatial audio for non-visual outputs, and support for low-cost devices.

Block-based drag-and-drop coding tools have historically been inaccessible to some learners [41], though this is changing with improvements in the Blockly library that underpins many of these tools. Building on this work, keyboard navigation in Flock XR is under development to support users with fine motor challenges and enable adaptive switch access. Future support will build on Blockly screen reader capabilities to improve access for blind and visually impaired learners.

These capabilities reflect a design philosophy in which accessibility is built into the architecture of the tool. Interaction pathways determine how learners engage with spatial systems and therefore shape the development of spatial reasoning itself.

## 5 Research Agenda

We plan to pursue this agenda through empirical work in primary schools. This research will focus on the following areas:

*Understanding CSF Development.* Little is currently known about how computational spatial fluency develops in practice. How do learners progress from initial spatial manipulation to confident authorship of executable 3D systems? How do we assess CSF across diverse learner artefacts, processes, and discourse?

*Equity and Access.* CSF must develop across diverse learners, not only those with prior spatial or computational experience. What spatial and creative knowledge do learners bring from existing engagement with 3D digital worlds, and how can this be built on equitably? How do we ensure that the construct does not reproduce the exclusions it seeks to address?

*Spatial Computing and Transfer.* Does computational spatial creation develop transferable capabilities such as perspective-taking, spatial orientation, and the coordination of reference frames? What is the relationship between CSF and meaningful participation in the emerging spatial computing landscape?

*Improving Pedagogy and Tool Design.* What pedagogical approaches best support fluency across diverse learners and contexts? How can tool design, scaffolding, and learning sequences be iteratively refined in response to evidence?

*Assessing CSF.* Although CSF is introduced here as a conceptual framework, its components suggest several dimensions for future assessment. Potential indicators include: (1) spatial-computational artefact complexity, such as the use of hierarchical structures, transformations, procedural generation, or multiple coordinate frames; (2) process measures derived from learner interactions, including debugging cycles, revision patterns, and transitions between symbolic and embodied representations; (3) perspective-coordination measures that assess learners' ability to move between egocentric and allocentric viewpoints; and (4) transfer measures that evaluate whether learners apply spatial-computational strategies in novel design contexts.

Learning analytics collected from the environment may provide additional evidence of development over time. Examples include frequency and diversity of spatial transformations, use of abstraction mechanisms, creation of dynamic behaviours, and the complexity of executable spatial relationships. These measures can be triangulated with artefact analysis, think-aloud protocols, and established spatial reasoning instruments.

Consistent with work on navigation and virtual environments [15], future studies must distinguish between operational proficiency with interfaces and the underlying development of CSF. Dynamic assessment approaches may be particularly valuable because spatial-computational reasoning and interaction competence often co-develop during design activity.

## 6 Conclusion

This paper has introduced Computational Spatial Fluency as a construct for understanding spatial reasoning as a dynamic, designable, and computationally mediated process in 3D digital making environments. Grounded in constructionist theory, and emerging from the iterative development of Flock XR, CSF positions spatial–computational capability as something that develops through making.

In response to the three research questions posed, the paper has argued: first, that three-dimensional creative digital spaces can be theorised as constructionist microworlds in which spatial relations become executable, persistent, and revisable, affording cycles of creation, interaction, and revision; second, that coordinated embodied and symbolic representations, programmable perspective, and iterative debugging constitute design affordances that directly support embodied cognition and perspective taking; and third, that CSF extends traditional conceptions by framing spatial–computational capability as expressive fluency rather than cognitive skill, with emergent properties that neither spatial thinking nor computational thinking alone captures—and with significant implications for equitable participation.

The construct integrates authentic contemporary spatial computing practice, learners' lived experience of 3D environments, equity of access and participation, and fluency as expressive creative capability. Flock XR illustrates how CSF can be operationalised through design principles that support its development in a creative digital making space.

Spatial skills are linked to success across STEM, and spatial computing is emerging as a major frontier in industry, human–computer interaction, and artificial intelligence. These capabilities are developable, but only if the conditions for learning are deliberately and inclusively designed. CSF provides both a theoretical framework and a practical agenda for doing so. We invite researchers, educators, and the spatial computing community to participate, to ensure that all young people, regardless of background, identity, prior experience, disability, or neurodivergence, have the opportunity not only to develop computational spatial fluency as a future-facing literacy, but to shape the spatial systems and environments of the future.

**Acknowledgements.** The development of Flock XR has been supported by the UK Games Fund and by NLnet through the NGI Zero Commons Fund, part of the European Commission's Next Generation Internet initiative under Horizon Europe grant agreement No. 101135429. The views expressed in this paper are those of the authors and do not necessarily reflect those of the funders.

## References

1. Allsop, Y.: An Examination of Children's Thinking, Learning and Metacognition When Making Computer Games, Manchester Metropolitan University (2019). Ph.D. Thesis
2. Angeli, C., Valanides, N.: Developing young children's computational thinking with educational robotics: an interaction effect between gender and scaffolding strategy. Comput. Hum. Behav. **105** (2020). https://doi.org/10.1016/j.chb.2019.03.018
3. Baddeley, A.: Working memory: looking back and looking forward. Nat. Rev. Neurosci. **4**(10), 829–839 (2003). https://doi.org/10.1038/nrn1201
4. Barsalou, L.W.: Grounded cognition. Annu. Rev. Psychol. **59**, 617–645 (2008). https://doi.org/10.1146/annurev.psych.59.103006.093639
5. Bartlett, K.A., Camba, J.D.: Gender differences in spatial ability: a critical review. Educ. Psychol. Rev. **35**(1), 8 (2023). https://doi.org/10.1007/s10648-023-09728-2
6. Bers, M.U.: Coding as a playground: programming and computational thinking in the early childhood classroom. Routledge (2020). https://doi.org/10.4324/9781003022602
7. Bhaduri, S., Biddy, Q.L., Bush, J., Suresh, A., Sumner, T.: 3DnST: a framework towards understanding children's interaction with Tinkercad and enhancing spatial thinking skills. In: Proceedings of the 20th Annual ACM Interaction Design and Children Conference (IDC '21), pp. 257–267. ACM (2021). https://doi.org/10.1145/3459990.3460717
8. Creative Technology Research Lab, University of Florida College of Education: UDL+CS guidelines for K–12 CS education. Universal Design for Learning for Computer Science (UDL4CS). https://udl4cs.education.ufl.edu/

9. Farran, E.K., Critten, V., Courbois, Y., Campbell, E., Messer, D.: Spatial cognition in children with physical disability: what is the impact of restricted independent exploration? Front. Hum. Neurosci. **15**, 669034 (2021). https://doi.org/10.3389/fnhum.2021.669034
10. Flip Computing: Flock XR: Creative coding in 3D (2026). https://github.com/flipcomputing/flock
11. George, R., Howitt, C., Oakley, G.: Young children's use of an augmented reality sandbox to enhance spatial thinking. Children's Geograph. **18**(2), 209–221 (2020). https://doi.org/10.1080/14733285.2019.1614533
12. Giudice, N.A.: Navigating without vision: principles of blind spatial cognition. In: Montello, D.R. (ed.) Handbook of Behavioral and Cognitive Geography, pp. 260–288. Edward Elgar Publishing (2018). https://doi.org/10.4337/9781784717544.00024
13. Gkreka, C., Kynigos, C.: Spatial thinking with dynamically linked digital and embodied representations. Int. Res. Geograph. Environ. Educat. (2025). https://doi.org/10.1080/10382046.2025.2473706
14. Glenberg, A.M.: Embodiment as a unifying perspective for psychology. Wiley Interdiscip. Rev.: Cognit. Sci. **1**(4), 586–596 (2010). https://doi.org/10.1002/wcs.55
15. Grübel, J., Thrash, T., Hölscher, C., Schinazi, V.R.: Evaluation of a conceptual framework for predicting navigation performance in virtual reality. PLOS ONE **12**(9) (2017). https://doi.org/10.1371/journal.pone.0184682
16. Haun, D.B.M., Rapold, C.J., Janzen, G., Levinson, S.C.: Plasticity of human spatial cognition: spatial language and cognition covary across cultures. Cognition **119**(1), 70–80 (2011). https://doi.org/10.1016/j.cognition.2010.12.009
17. Hegarty, M., Waller, D.: Individual differences in spatial abilities. In: Shah, P., Miyake, A. (eds.) The Cambridge Handbook of Visuospatial Thinking, pp. 121–169. Cambridge University Press (2005). https://doi.org/10.1017/CBO9780511610448.005
18. Hughes, B.E., Lux, N., Frank, B., Willoughby, S.D., LaMeres, B.J., Weyerbacher, R.C.: Minecraft learning system for spatial reasoning in middle grades learners. In: Proceedings of the ASEE Annual Conference (2020). https://doi.org/10.18260/1-2-34974
19. Hundhausen, C.D., Olivares, D.M., Carter, A.S.: IDE-based learning analytics for computing education: a process model, critical review, and research agenda. ACM Trans. Comput. Educat. **17**(3) (2017). https://doi.org/10.1145/3105759
20. Israel, M., Ribuffo, C., Smith, S.: Universal design for learning: recommendations for teacher preparation and professional development. Tech. Rep. IC-7, Collaboration for Effective Educator Development, Accountability, and Reform Center, University of Florida (2014). http://ceedar.education.ufl.edu/tools/innovation-configurations/
21. Kane, S.K., Bigham, J.P.: Tracking @stemxcomet: teaching programming to blind students via 3D printing, crisis management, and Twitter. In: Proceedings of the 45th ACM Technical Symposium on Computer Science Education, pp. 247–252. ACM (2014). https://doi.org/10.1145/2538862.2538975
22. von Károlyi, C., Winner, E., Gray, W., Sherman, G.F.: Dyslexia linked to talent: global visual-spatial ability. Brain Lang. **85**(3), 427–431 (2003). https://doi.org/10.1016/S0093-934X(03)00052-X
23. Keogh, R., Pearson, J.: The blind mind: no sensory visual imagery in Aphantasia. Cortex **105**, 53–60 (2018). https://doi.org/10.1016/j.cortex.2017.10.012

24. Levine, S.C., Vasilyeva, M., Lourenco, S.F., Newcombe, N.S., Huttenlocher, J.: Socioeconomic status modifies the sex difference in spatial skill. Psychol. Sci. **16**(11), 841–845 (2005). https://doi.org/10.1111/j.1467-9280.2005.01623.x
25. Liu, D., Yi, L., Kang, R.: The impact of a digital game on spatial reasoning for elementary school students. J. Comput. Assist. Learn. **41**(6), e70138 (2025). https://doi.org/10.1111/jcal.70138
26. Lowrie, T., Logan, T., Hegarty, M.: The influence of spatial visualization training on students' spatial reasoning and mathematics performance. J. Cogn. Dev. **20**(5), 729–751 (2019). https://doi.org/10.1080/15248372.2019.1653298
27. Marschark, M., et al.: Understanding language, hearing status, and visual-spatial skills. J. Deaf Stud. Deaf Educat. **20**(4), 310–330 (2015). https://doi.org/10.1093/deafed/env025
28. Marshman, M., Woolcott, G., Dole, S.: Engaging pre-service mathematics teachers in creating spatially-based problems in a 3D virtual environment: a CAVE2 experience. In: Proceedings of the 40th Annual Conference of the Mathematics Education Research Group of Australasia, pp. 365–372. MERGA (2017)
29. Martinussen, R., Hayden, J., Hogg-Johnson, S., Tannock, R.: A meta-analysis of working memory impairments in children with attention-deficit/hyperactivity disorder. J. Am. Acad. Child Adolescent Psych. **44**(4), 377–384 (2005). https://doi.org/10.1097/01.chi.0000153228.72591.73
30. McGlone, M.S., Aronson, J.: Stereotype threat, identity salience, and spatial reasoning. J. Appl. Dev. Psychol. **27**(5), 486–493 (2006). https://doi.org/10.1016/j.appdev.2006.06.003
31. Nejati, V., Khoshroo, S., Mirikaram, F.: Review of spatial disability in individuals with attention deficit-hyperactivity disorder: toward spatial cognition theory. Clin. Child Psychol. Psych. **29**(1), 312–337 (2024). https://doi.org/10.1177/13591045231176707
32. Newcombe, N.S.: Thinking spatially in the science classroom. Current Opinion Behav. Sci. **10** (2016). https://doi.org/10.1016/j.cobeha.2016.04.010
33. Newcombe, N.S., Frick, A.: Early education for spatial intelligence: why, what, and how. Mind Brain Educ. **4**(3), 102–111 (2010). https://doi.org/10.1111/j.1751-228X.2010.01089.x
34. Newcombe, N.S., Shipley, T.F.: Thinking about spatial thinking: new typology, new assessments. In: Studying Visual and Spatial Reasoning for Design Creativity, pp. 179–192 (2015). https://doi.org/10.1007/978-94-017-9297-4_10
35. Palmiero, M., Srinivasan, N.: Creativity and spatial ability: a critical evaluation. In: Manjaly, J.A., Indurkhya, B. (eds.) Cognition, Experience and Creativity, pp. 189–214. Orient Blackswan (2015)
36. Papert, S.: Mindstorms: Children, Computers, and Powerful Ideas, Basic Books (1980)
37. Parkinson, J., Cutts, Q.: Improving primary school pupils' spatial skills leads to computational thinking gains. In: Proceedings of the 30th ACM Conference on Innovation and Technology in Computer Science Education, vol. 1. pp. 646–652. ITiCSE 2025 (2025). https://doi.org/10.1145/3724363.3729075
38. Resnick, M.: Lifelong Kindergarten: cultivating creativity through projects, passion, peers, and play. MIT Press (2017). https://doi.org/10.7551/mitpress/11017.001.0001
39. Shenouda, C.K., Danovitch, J.H.: Effects of gender stereotypes and stereotype threat on children's performance on a spatial task. Rev.Int. Psychol. Soc. **27**(3–4), 53–77 (2014)

40. Soleimani, A., Green, K.E., Herro, D., Walker, I.D.: A tangible, story-construction process employing spatial, computational-thinking. In: Proceedings of the Interaction Design and Children Conference, pp. 157–166 (2016). https://doi.org/10.1145/2930674.2930703
41. Stefik, A., Allee, W., Contreras, G., Kluthe, T., Hoffman, A., Blaser, B., Ladner, R.: Accessible to whom? Bringing accessibility to blocks. In: Proceedings of the 55th ACM Technical Symposium on Computer Science Education, vol. 1 (SIGCSE 2024), pp. 1286–1292. ACM (2024). https://doi.org/10.1145/3626252.3630770
42. Sun, Y.: Action-based embodied design: spatial-mathematical learning experiences with Tinkercad 3D modeling for elementary students. Digit. Exper. Math. Educ. **9**, 492–507 (2023). https://doi.org/10.1007/s40751-023-00129-2
43. Uttal, D.H., Cohen, C.A.: Spatial thinking and STEM education: when, why, and how? Psychol. Learn. Motiv. **57**, 147–181 (2012). https://doi.org/10.1016/B978-0-12-394293-7.00004-2
44. Uttal, D.H., et al.: The malleability of spatial skills: a meta-analysis of training studies. Psychol. Bull. **139**(2), 352–402 (2013). https://doi.org/10.1037/a0028446
45. Voyer, D., Postma, A., Brake, B., Imperato-McGinley, J.: Gender differences in object location memory: a meta-analysis. Psych. Bulletin Rev. **14**(1), 23–38 (2007). https://doi.org/10.3758/BF03194024
46. Wilson, M.: Six views of embodied cognition. Psych. Bulletin Rev. **9**(4), 625–636 (2002). https://doi.org/10.3758/BF03196322
47. Ying, S., Zhuang, Y., Huang, L., Wang, H., Yin, Z.: Analysis of the correlation between spatial cognitive abilities and wayfinding decisions in 3D digital environments. Behav. Info. Technol. **40**(8), 809–820 (2021). https://doi.org/10.1080/0144929X.2020.1726468

# Clarification of Developmental Topographical Disorientation (DTD): Identification of a Distinct Navigation Profile

Midas M. Stöfsel[1], Martine J. E. van Zandvoort[2,3], and Ineke J. M. van der Ham[1,4](✉)

[1] Department of Health, Medical, and Neuropsychology, Leiden University, Leiden, the Netherlands
c.j.m.van.der.ham@fsw.leidenuniv.nl
[2] Department of Neurology, UMC Utrecht Brain Center, University Medical Center Utrecht, Utrecht, the Netherlands
[3] Department of Experimental Psychology, Utrecht University, Utrecht, The Netherlands
[4] Faculty of Architecture and the Built Environment, Delft University of Technology, Delft, the Netherlands

**Abstract.** Developmental Topographical Disorientation (DTD) is the recently uncovered lifelong inability to orient in even extremely familiar surroundings despite the absence of any acquired brain damage or neurological disorder. Descriptive criteria have been proposed, but clear objective criteria would be helpful to create a better conceptual definition of DTD. We examined navigation ability in a group of people with DTD in more detail with objective and subjective measures. Navigation ability was assessed with the Leiden Navigation Test (LNT), which includes scores for landmark knowledge, location knowledge (allocentric and egocentric) and path knowledge (route and survey). The results showed that people with DTD showed varied levels of navigational performance. At group level they showed a distinct pattern of navigation inability in comparison to people without DTD. People with DTD showed better landmark memory and impaired path knowledge and allocentric location knowledge compared to the general population. In addition, people with DTD scored lower on navigation self-assessments compared to the general population but reported a comparable level of spatial anxiety to the general population, a sharp contrast with the high levels of anxiety found when navigation impairment occurs after acquired brain injury. In conclusion, we uncovered a distinct navigation profile for individuals with DTD, characterized by specific impairment in path knowledge and allocentric location knowledge, while landmark knowledge is particularly well developed. The current study reveals a distinct strategic navigation profile for people with DTD, which can be detected with the LNT, a brief online assessment. This distinct profile is a pivotal step towards a clear conceptual definition of DTD, which supports the acknowledgement and accommodation of DTD.

**Keywords:** Developmental Topographical Disorientation · Navigation · Spatial strategy · Landmark knowledge · Behavioral Assessment


E. Farran et al. (Eds.): Spatial Cognition 2026, LNAI 16785, pp. 49–62, 2027.
https://doi.org/10.1007/978-3-032-36716-7_4

# 1 Introduction

The ability to navigate is an essential aspect of our daily lives. Clinical research shows that navigation ability is positively correlated with quality of life [1]; limited navigational ability directly impacts a person's well-being. Such topographical disorientation [2] commonly occurs because of acquired brain injury (e.g [3–5].). Topographical disorientation is not restricted to clinical populations, however. Substantial variation in navigation ability is typically found within healthy individuals (see e.g [6].), but there is a condition within the healthy population that shows remarkable levels of topographical disorientation. In 2009, Iaria and his colleagues [7] first described a case of Developmental Topographical Disorientation (DTD). DTD is defined as a lifelong inability to orient in even extremely familiar surroundings despite the absence of any acquired brain damage or neurological disorder [8]. Individuals with DTD lose their way in both new and familiar environments [9], experience difficulties in various tasks related to spatial orientation and cannot use cognitive maps [9, 10]. However, a comprehensive cognitive description for DTD is currently lacking, as existing studies show significant variability in the navigational aspects of individuals with DTD and the neurological mechanisms behind DTD are still unknown [11, 12]. With the current research, we aim to create a more detailed understanding of the general cognitive characteristics of DTD to lay a foundation for effective support and treatment.

The currently leading DTD criteria are derived from the initial work by Iaria and Barton [13]: (1) getting lost daily or often (1 to 5 times per week) in the most familiar environment, (2) since childhood, (3) no memory complaints or other cognitive problems affecting daily activities and (4) no known brain injury [9, 11, 13]. In the early work concerning DTD, there seemed to be a core characteristic of impaired mental map formation and use, whereas later additions to the literature also included topographical disorientation linked to other cognitive processes such as landmark recognition and route knowledge (see [12] for a review). The criterion of 'frequently getting lost' is unable to differentiate between these different forms of topographical disorientation, while they are distinctly different. Clinical work has shown that requirements for effective detection and intervention strategies are very different for the different forms of disorientation (e.g [5].). Additionally, the recent normalization of using GPS support for navigation has obscured how people provide the subjective indication of getting lost frequently. It should be noted that in DTD, GPS support is frequently perceived as confusing rather than supportive. Given the developments in literature and technological advances, there is a clear need for more discrete and objective criteria to define DTD. Ideally, these criteria could support the development of diagnostic and intervention tools.

Recently, van der Ham and Claessen [12] attempted to clarify the cognitive correlates of the topographic impairment reported in literature. Previous work designed to grasp navigation impairment in a clinical context provided a useful framework [14]: Landmark knowledge, location knowledge (allocentric and egocentric), and path knowledge (route and survey) are the key components of navigation ability and in case of impairment, these components are typically selectively impaired. Landmark knowledge refers to the ability to memorize and recognize distinct landmarks. Location knowledge refers to the spatial positions of these landmarks and can be assessed from both an egocentric and allocentric perspective [15, 16]. Egocentric perspective taking involves encoding spatial information from the observer's perspective [17]. An allocentric perspective, in contrast, involves encoding spatial locations based on external cues [18]. Path route knowledge refers to the knowledge of the order and elements of a route, such as turns and sequences, which is essential for effective navigation [19]. In contrast, path survey knowledge refers to knowledge about the spatial relationships between landmarks, which helps in making distance comparisons and creating an overview of the environment [20]. The literature review showed that both allocentric location knowledge and path survey knowledge are consistently impaired across studies with DTD participants. Path route knowledge is affected in a significant number of reports but appears intact in some cases. Additionally, landmark knowledge generally remains intact. Furthermore, egocentric location knowledge is rarely included in DTD studies, whereas it may provide additional refinement to the cognitive features of DTD. Therefore, we have suggested that future research should include a comprehensive assessment of navigational abilities, including egocentric location knowledge, to contribute to an objective diagnosis of DTD [12].

Until recently, standardized testing materials for large-scale spatial functioning were lacking [21–24]. Several tests have been developed, such as Sea Hero Quest [25] and the Leiden Navigation Test [26]. The Leiden Navigation Test (LNT) was specifically developed for clinical use and measures the clinically meaningful domains of navigation separately in a comprehensive test format, including egocentric location knowledge. This makes the LNT suitable to assess the cognitive features of DTD. Thus far, Burles and Iaria (e.g [11].) studied a range of cognitive skills in DTD through self-reported performance, which shows that individuals with DTD rated themselves lower on a range of navigation aspects, compared to a control group. The clinically validated Wayfinding Questionnaire (WQ) was therefore included as a potential initial screening tool to assess subjective navigation performance, as well as spatial anxiety in DTD (see [26]).

In the current study we therefore administered both the WQ and LNT in person, in a group of individuals with suspected DTD. This group was composed after publishing case I.S. in a national newspaper in the Netherlands, the first reported Dutch case of DTD [27]. Case I.S. met the existing DTD criteria of [13]. After an indepth interview with case I.S. and one of the authors (I.H.) in de Volkskrant [28], 22 individuals with similar symptoms have spontaneously contacted the principal investigator. This created the opportunity to investigate whether a DTD navigation profile exists in a larger group of Dutch DTD participants.

The qualitative findings of the case study I.S. added an additional interest, mental imagery ability. In addition to our primary navigation measures LNT and WQ, the VVIQ (Visual Vividness of Imagery Questionnaire; [29]) was also included, to gain a better understanding of the general ability to mentally generate visuospatial information. The VVIQ is typically used to determine aphantasia, the phenomenon of inability to generate mental images of objects (e.g [30].). The interview with case I.S. suggested there may be a problem with mental image generation, as she clearly described 'when I think of spatial structures like my kitchen, or what can be seen after that turn in our street, I just see black'. This is further substantiated by the assumption that individuals with DTD specifically have difficulty acquiring mental representations of their environment [11], while individuals with aphantasia have difficulty acquiring mental representations in general [30, 31]. Burles and Iaria [11] found that people with DTD rated themselves lower, compared with a control group, on the ability to imagine familiar faces, objects and places. This may indicate that individuals with DTD also generally have more difficulty making voluntary visual mental representations. Clarifying a potential connection between DTD and aphantasia would thus be an additional step in understanding the cognitive architecture of DTD.

## 2 Methods

### 2.1 Participants

The final sample involved 12 participants (1 male and 11 females) aged 26 to 78 years old (M = 51.5, SD = 15.8) who voluntarily contacted the researchers after recognizing themselves in the detailed case description of a person with DTD in de Volkskrant. From the original 22 volunteers, 10 were not included after screening during the initial contact by email or phone conversation, reasons included suspicion or medical record of neurological events, very young (<18 years) or old age (>80 years), and logistic limitations in traveling to the lab location.

We used the following inclusion criteria in the recruitment; participants had to meet the DTD criteria as described by [13], including: (1) getting lost in the most familiar environment daily or frequently (1 to 5 times per week), (2) since childhood, (3) no memory complaints or other cognitive problems affecting daily activities, and (4) no known brain injury. When there was comorbidity with other disorders, the participant was excluded to avoid biasing symptoms by these additional conditions. Participants had normal or corrected to normal vision. Also, participants were not allowed to be under the influence of medication that affects responsiveness. Lastly, if a participant failed both performance validity tasks (PVTs), that person was also excluded. None of the participants were excluded based on this rule. Informed consent was signed prior to participation. Monetary compensation consisted of reimbursement of travel expenses. The experiment was approved by the Leiden University Psychology Research Ethics Committee (application #5100).

### 2.2 Measures

The presence of DTD was assessed by examining whether the participant met the DTD criteria as described by [13]. The data of the participants was compared with control groups from the general population through single case study statistics [32], matched in age, gender and education level. In addition, the Cognitive Failure Questionnaire (CFQ) was used as a control, to check that participants did not have cognitive problems. The CFQ is a questionnaire for measuring subjective cognitive functioning [33, 34]. The questionnaire consists of 25 questions divided into four subscales: scatteredness (7 items), scatteredness in social situations (4 items), names and words (3 items) and orientation (3 items). The participants must indicate how often they make mistakes on a five-point scale, ranking from 1: 'very often' to 5: 'never'. To determine the total score, the scores were transformed as follows: a score of 1 becomes 4, 2 be-comes

3, 3 becomes 2, 4 becomes 1 and 5 becomes 0. A high score on the CFQ indicates more cognitive mistakes. One of the subtasks of the CFQ is 'orientation', which has a significant impact on the total score of the CFQ. As a result, the validity of this task for the current purpose was not optimal. For this reason, achieving a passing score on the CFQ was not a strict requirement and a qualitative evaluation was conducted to check for any abnormalities. Further, the Rey 15-item recognition test (FIT), and in the case of failing on the FIT, the Structured Inventory of Malingered Symptomatology (SIMS) were also used to evaluate whether the tests provide a reliable indication of participants' actual performance. The FIT is a task consisting of two parts. In the first part, participants had to memorize 15 figures within 10 s. Then, they must directly reproduce these figures via free reproduction. In the second part, participants were faced with 30 figures, where they had to circle the correct 15 figures. The total number of correctly figures in both parts was calculated together, subtracting false positives from task 2. A cut-off point of $<20$ was used [35]. The SIMS questionnaire is used to determine whether a person intentionally simulates psychological symptoms [36]. The SIMS is a self-report instrument consisting of 75 questions about bizarre and non-existent symptoms. The SIMS include subscales addressing memory complaints, low intelligence and psychotic, affective and neurological symptoms. Answer options are "yes" or "no". A cut-off point of $>16$ is used. Thereby, the sensitivity is 0.95 and the specificity is 0.51 [37].

Navigation performance was assessed using two different navigation tasks: the Leiden Navigation Task (LNT) and the Virtual Tübingen Task (VTT). The LNT [24] consisted of two parts: memorizing a short video route (69 s) through a fictional environment and asking questions about various aspects of navigation ability. Participants first memorized a route and then their performance was assessed on five subtasks: land-mark knowledge, egocentric and allocentric location knowledge, path route knowledge and path survey knowledge. For each subtask, the proportion of correct answers is calculated. The LNT measures five functionally distinct domains of navigation ability. A higher score on a subtask of the LNT indicates better ability or accuracy in understanding, remembering and interpreting specific aspects of navigational ability. The VTT is the predecessor of the LNT, also developed for clinical assessment of navigation impairment. It entails a more elaborate set of behavioral measurements and uses a highly realistic digital environment. First, the participants watched 2 times a 5-min video of a real-life route through the city of Tübingen. After the video, participants performed a series of 8 subtasks. These subtasks consisted of recognizing landmarks, arranging arrows to turn off the route, indicating turns at landmarks, arranging landmarks in order of appearance, referring back to the starting point from different landmarks, estimating relative distances between two points on the route, judging the accuracy of a trio of locations presented as dots with screenshots, identifying the correct map of the route between distractors and indicating landmarks on a map. For each subtask, the number of correct answers is calculated. A higher score on a subtask of the VTT indicates better navigation abilities for a specific navigation aspect.

Self-reported navigational experience is measured with the Wayfinding Questionnaire (WQ). The WQ consists of 22 items divided into three subscales: navigation and orientation (NO), distance estimation (DE) and spatial anxiety (SA). Scores ranged from

1 ('Not applicable to me at all') to 7 ('Completely applicable to me'), where a lower score indicates more navigation complaints (all 8 SA items were reversed) [21].

Mental imagery was measured with the Vividness of Visual Imagery Questionnaire (VVIQ). The VVIQ consists of 16 items. The participant was asked to form a visual image and consider their experience carefully. Then, for each image, the partic-ipant had to indicate how vivid it is on a five-point scale, ranking from 1: "No image at all, you only "know" that you are thinking of the object" to 5: "Perfecting clear and lively as real seeing". A higher final score indicates a higher rating for the vividness of the mental images [38, 39]. In this study, the commonly used threshold of ≤16 is applied for aphantasia, to indicate who cannot form visual images at all, and a threshold of 17 ≤ VVIQ ≤32 for those who can form weak or vague images [40].

### 2.3 Procedure

First, we contacted potential participants via e-mail with an information letter. After reviewing the information letter, an on-site appointment was scheduled by phone. In the appointment confirmation e-mail, a demographic questionnaire and the CFQ, through Qualtrics software. On location, after completing the informed consent, the study began with a semi-structured interview of approximately 1 h. Through a narrative interview, participants were given the opportunity to share their personal experience regarding DTD. Next, the LNT, VTT and the FIT were presented. In case of failure on the FIT, the SIMS was also conducted. This was followed by the VVIQ and WQ.

### 2.4 Statistical Analyses

Participants' individual performances on each navigation sub-task of the LNT and the VTT was examined. For the LNT, each participant was compared to a matched control group taken from the general population based on age, gender and education level, derived from a large norm group from the study by van der Ham and Claessen (2022). In the absence of a comprehensive norm group for the VTT, an existing control group from the study by [22] was used. In addition, the VTT subtasks were grouped into four functional clusters: landmark knowledge, location knowledge, path route knowledge, and path survey knowledge. Z-scores were calculated for the individual scores using the control groups, then the mean z-scores for each subtask were determined. A one-sample t-test was performed on the mean z-scores of all LNT and VTT subtasks, with a significance level (α) of .05 and a test value of 0. Based on available literature, one-tailed tests were applied for allocentric location knowledge and path survey knowledge, while two-tailed tests were applied for all other subtasks and clusters due to inconsistent or limited empirical evidence.

For the WQ, each participant was compared to a matched control group based on age and gender, derived from a large norm group from the study by van der Ham and Claessen [26]. Z-scores were calculated for the individual scores using the matched control groups. A one-sample t-test was performed on the mean z-scores of the WQ subtasks, with a significance level (α) of .05 and a test value of 0. Two-tailed testing was used due to the subjective nature of the assessment. To examine the extent to which objective neuropsychological navigation tasks correlate with self-reported navigation experiences in individuals with DTD, correlation analyses were conducted between the subtasks of the WQ and LNT.

To investigate the quality of visual imaging in individuals with DTD, we used the thresholds of the VVIQ. Previous research by [40] has shown that the VVIQ can divide individuals into three groups: individuals who cannot form visual images at all (aphantasia), individuals who can form weak or vague images and individuals who have no problems forming images. The analyses were performed in SPSS 29.

## 3 Results

Fig. 1 shows the mean z-scores for each subtask of the LNT. No significant effect was found for egocentric location knowledge and path survey knowledge, t(11), $p > .05$. For landmark knowledge a significant effect was found, t(11) = 4.190, p = .002 (two-tailed), d = 1.21, indicating performance was significantly higher than performance of the controls. For allocentric location knowledge a significant effect was found, t(11) = −2.842, p = .008 (one-tailed), d = −.82, reflecting performance significantly lower than the controls. A similar pattern was found for path route knowledge, t(11) = −2.895, p = .015 (two-tailed), d = −.84, also reflecting performance significantly lower than the controls.

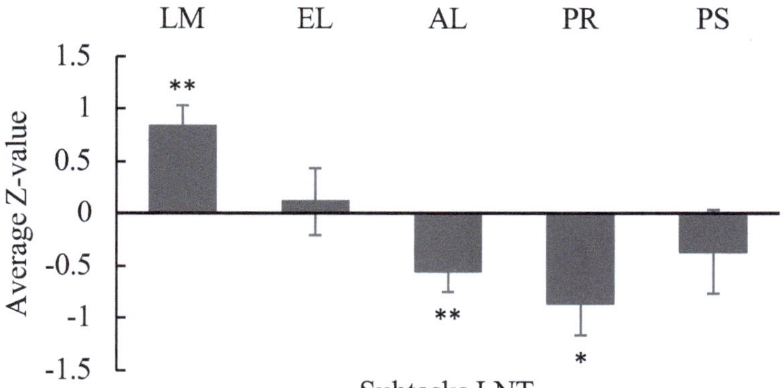


**Fig. 1.** Mean z-scores per subtask for the LNT. Leiden Navigation Task (LNT), landmark knowledge (LM), egocentric location knowledge (EL), allocentric location knowledge (AL), path route knowledge (PR) and path survey knowledge (PS). Statistical significance from *t*-tests is indicated as $p < .05$ (*), $p < .01$ (**). For the error bars, the standard error of the mean was used. Lower scores indicate lower mean performance of DTD participants relative to controls.

A similar approach was used for the WQ. Fig. 2 shows average z-scores for each subtask of the WQ. No significant effect was found for spatial anxiety, t(11), $p > .05$. A significant difference was found for the subscale navigation and orientation, t(11) = −8.873, p = <.001 (two-tailed), d = −2.56, with DTD individuals scoring notably lower than the matched control sample. Similarly, a significant effect was found for the subscale distance estimation, t(11) = −5.698, p = <.001 (two-tailed), d = −1.65, indicating a significantly lower score for the DTD sample compared to the matched controls.

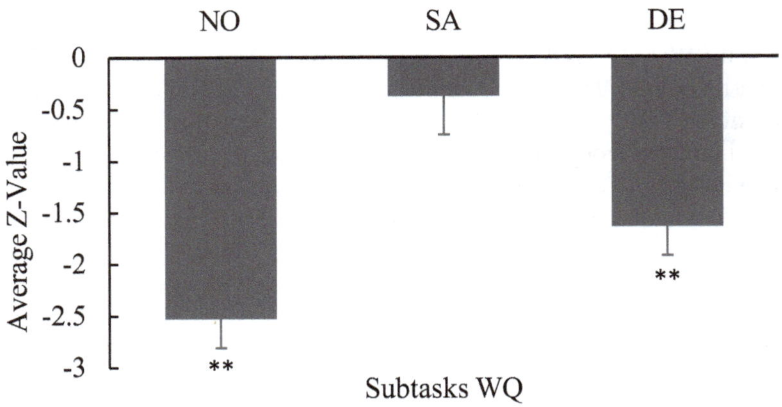


**Fig. 2.** Mean z-scores per subtask for the Wayfinding Questionnaire (WQ). Navigation and orientation (NO), distance estimation (DE) and spatial anxiety (SA). Statistical significance from *t*-tests is indicated as $p < .05$ (*), $p < .01$ (**). For the error bars, the standard error of the mean was used. Lower scores indicate lower mean performance of DTD participants relative to con-trols.

The VTT was examined as an additional measure of spatial navigation. The various subtasks were divided into functionally meaningful clusters. The first cluster was Landmark knowledge and includes only the subtask recognizing landmarks. The second cluster was path route knowledge and includes the subtasks arranging arrows to turn off the route, indicating turns at landmarks and arranging landmarks in order of appearance. The third cluster was Location knowledge and includes the subtasks refer-ring back to the starting point from different landmarks, estimating relative distances between two points on the route and judging the accuracy of a trio of locations presented as dots with screenshots. The fourth cluster was path survey knowledge and includes the subtasks identifying the correct map of the route between distractors and indicating landmarks on a map.

Fig. 3 showed the mean z-scores for each cluster of the VTT. No significant effect was found for landmark knowledge and location knowledge, t(11), p > .05. For path route knowledge a significant effect was found, t(11) = −4.879, p = <.001 (two-tailed), d = −1.41, with DTD individuals scoring notably lower than the control sample. Lastly, for path survey knowledge a significant effect was found, t(11) = −2.171, p = .026 (one-tailed), d = −.63, indicating a lower score for the DTD sample compared to the control group.

Table 1 shows results of correlation analyses between the subtasks of the LNT and WQ. The table showed that only one significantly strong negative correlation was found, between the subtask navigation and orientation of the WQ and the subtask allo-centric location knowledge of the LNT, r = −.613, p = .034.

The VVIQ scores among participants ranged from 32 to 77, with an average score of 53.50 (SD = 11.98) and a median also of 53.50. One participant reported a notably weak or vague imagination with a score of 32, while another had a boundary score of 33. The remaining 10 participants did not report any issues with their visual imagination, as their scores were consistently higher and closer to the maximum of 80.

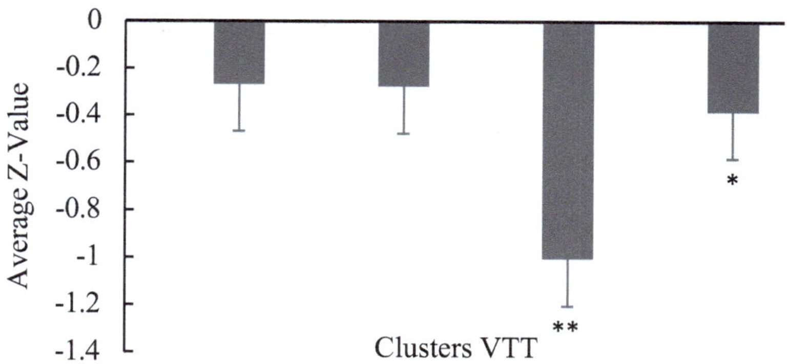


**Fig. 3.** Mean z-scores per cluster for the Virtual Tübingen Task (VTT). Landmark knowledge (LM), location knowledge (LK), path route knowledge (PR), path survey knowledge (PS). Statistical significance from *t*-tests is indicated as $p < .05$ (*), $p < .01$ (**). For the error bars, the standard error of the mean was used. Lower scores indicate lower mean performance of DTD participants relative to controls

**Table 1.** Correlations between Leiden Navigation Task and Wayfinding Questionnaire. Landmark knowledge (LM), egocentric location knowledge (EL), allocentric location knowledge (AL), path route knowledge (PR), path survey knowledge (PS), navigation and orientation (NO), distance estimation (DE) and spatial anxiety (SA). The table shows the correlation coefficients between the different subtasks of LNT and WQ. * Correlation is significant at the 0.05 level (two-tailed)

| | 1. | 2. | 3. | 4. | 5. | 6. | 7. |
|---|---|---|---|---|---|---|---|
| 1. LM (LNT) | 1 | | | | | | |
| 2. EL (LNT) | −0.162 | 1 | | | | | |
| 3. AL (LNT) | 0.019 | −0.010 | 1 | | | | |
| 4. PR (LNT) | 0.137 | −0.355 | 0.386 | 1 | | | |
| 5. PS (LNT) | 0.316 | −0.037 | 0.192 | 0.179 | 1 | | |
| 6. NO (WQ) | 0.322 | 0.228 | −0.613* | −0.299 | −0.481 | 1 | |
| 7. SA (WQ) | −0.114 | −0.148 | 0.382 | −0.174 | 0.062 | −0.244 | 1 |
| 8. DE (WQ) | 0.217 | −0.145 | 0.107 | −0.127 | 0.410 | −0.237 | 0.127 |

## 4 Discussion

The current research aimed to better understand the characteristics of DTD. To redefine DTD with more concrete and objective criteria, it is important to identify measurable characteristics that distinguish individuals with DTD from those without this phenomenon. Our goal was to identify common characteristics that contribute to a better understanding of DTD. Additionally, we investigated a possible link between DTD and lower visual imagery.

The study shows that the DTD group shows a distinct navigation profile, with weaknesses in path knowledge and allocentric location knowledge. In contrast, landmark knowledge is found to be a well-developed strength. From literature, especially the earlier reports concerning DTD, it was expected that DTD participants would have difficulty acquiring and using a cognitive map specifically [11, 41] Path survey knowledge and location knowledge require the use of a cognitive map. A cognitive map is a mental representation of an individual's spatial environment, including information about locations, objects and the spatial relationships between them [42]. Forming a cognitive map enables the individual to be able to navigate and understand spatial relationships [43]. Therefore, the expectation from the literature was that people with DTD have more difficulty with path survey knowledge and allocentric location knowledge [11, 13, 41]. The current study clearly shows that DTD participants perform worse compared to the general population on path route knowledge. This supports the statement from the literature that individuals with DTD have difficulty with mental map acquisition and use. In contrast, the study shows that DTD participants performed significantly better on landmark knowledge compared to the general population. This can be explained through the use of strategies to remember landmarks, indicating that DTD participants developed this strategy. The use of landmarks can be an efficient strategy for route memorization (e.g [44].). During interviews, DTD participants often emphasized their specific focus on remembering landmarks to maintain route awareness. The strengths and weaknesses profile of navigation ability among DTD participants identified in our study is found in both navigation tasks included. This is the first time that such a distinct navigation profile has been observed in DTD research.

A detailed analysis of navigation aspects showed that the DTD group had significantly more difficulty with path route knowledge compared to the general population. This suggests that people with DTD have more difficulty remembering which direction they went in when seeing a familiar landmark. Contrarily, the study shows that DTD participants performed significantly better on landmark knowledge compared to the general population. Regarding path survey knowledge, no significant differences at the group level were found. Overall, the DTD group performed lower compared to the general population. This could be the result of substantial variations between DTD individuals. The review by [12] confirms that such variation at group level is also apparent in previous studies. The final navigation aspect, location knowledge, was divided into allocentric and egocentric location knowledge. As a group, DTD participants performed at the same level as the general population on the composite domain of location knowledge in general. In contrast, further examination on the LNT showed that DTD participants performed significantly worse on the allocentric aspect of location knowledge, which is in line with the existing literature [11, 45, 46]. In contrast, no difference was found for the egocentric aspect. However, there is currently limited empirical research on egocentric location knowledge in individuals with DTD. Therefore, additional work focusing on egocentric performance in DTD is recommended for future research.

In addition, the study shows that participants with DTD rated themselves significantly lower on their navigational ability compared to the general population, both in distance estimation (DE) and navigation and orientation (NO). This is in line with expectations from previous research [11]. In contrast, no difference was found in the assessment on spatial anxiety (SA) compared to the general population. This is markedly different for acquired brain injury patients with navigational complaints, where increased SA is especially expected [21]. Despite difficulties in estimating distances and navigation, DTD participants report relatively low spatial anxiety. The most likely cause of this difference is the lifelong exposure to navigation impairment versus a sudden onset of the impairment.

Only one negative relationship between the subjectively reported navigation and orientation ability and the objective allocentric location knowledge was found. Individuals with DTD who rated themselves lower on navigation and orientation ability, compared to other DTD participants, had better allocentric location knowledge. Allocentric location knowledge is the task that relies strongly on mental map quality and may also been considered most exemplary of spatial navigation for the general public, and people with DTD specifically. It is important to note that DTD participants perform significantly lower on both subjective and objective measures involved than the general population. No other significant relationships were found, which suggests that individuals with DTD are less accurate in estimating their navigation abilities, compared to people without DTD (see [24]), resulting in no meaningful relationship between their estimated ability to actual performance. The relatively small sample size in the current study might also play a role in this observation and this effect should therefore be interpreted with caution.

Finally, the relationship between DTD and visual imagery was examined. The study shows that the majority of DTD participants have no difficulty creating voluntary mental images. Furthermore, exploratory research was conducted on the relationship between the ability of creating voluntary mental images and objective navigation ability. As the prevalence of aphantasia is estimated at 2.5%, the frequency of VVIQ scores indicative of limited mental imagery ability is rather high at 16.7%. Yet, a larger sample size would be appropriate to create a reliable estimation of the frequency of aphantasia in the DTD sample.

The current study used a self-identified target group. As a result, sampling bias may have potentially occurred [47]. In addition, the typical pattern a female majority in volunteering was found. However, due to possible sampling bias, no conclusion can be made about the gender ratio. The pattern of self-overestimation among men and self-underestimation among women regarding navigation abilities [48] might also have influenced the gender ratio. Taking this into account, there are no clear cues that DTD amy occure more in females compared to males. We have used the FIT and SIMS to control for undesirable sampling bias and to restrict the impact of this potential limitation.

In addition to the LNT, the VTT offers ecological validity by closely resembling reality through a virtual environment mimicking the city of Tübingen in Germany. However, this results in longer testing time, so only a limited number of control participants were available for the current study. In contrast, the LNT is quick to administer and has a very large, general population-based control group, but includes fewer items in total. In follow-up research, it is important to consider various options. These could involve expanding the existing navigation tests or developing an adjusted task specifically for DTD.

## 5 Conclusion

In conclusion, a clear and consistent navigational profile is observed in people with DTD that most likely reflects their strategic approach to navigation, characterized by weaknesses in path knowledge and allocentric location knowledge, while landmark knowledge is a strength. This suggests a compensatory approach where landmark recognition in used to counteract the low quality of mental map knowledge. The consistency found in the DTD profile contributes to the development of objectively measurable criteria in the future. Future research should focus on identifying measurable thresholds for diagnosing DTD and increasing awareness about the phenomenon. The LNT has proven effective in detecting the DTD profile and can be used as a screening tool in future research. Current research takes us one step further in the cognitive understanding of DTD.

**Acknowledgments.** The authors wish to thank the DTD participants for sharing their personal stories and joining in the experiments.

**Disclosure of Interests.** The authors have no competing interests to declare that are relevant to the content of this article.

## References

1. Van der Ham, I.J., Kant, N., Postma, A., Visser-Meily, J.M.: Is navigation ability a problem in mild stroke patients? Insights from self-reported navigation measures. J. Rehabil. Med. **45**(5), 429–433 (2013)
2. Iaria, G., Incoccia, C., Piccardi, L., Nico, D., Sabatini, U., Guariglia, C.: Lack of orientation due to a congenital brain malformation: a case study. Neurocase. **11**(6), 463–474 (2005)
3. Barrash, J.: A historical review of topographical disorientation and its neuroanatomical correlates. J. Clin. Exp. Neuropsychol. **20**(6), 807–827 (1998)
4. Van der Ham, I.J., van Zandvoort, M.J., Meilinger, T., Bosch, S.E., Kant, N., Postma, A.: Spatial and temporal aspects of navigation in two neurological patients. Neuroreport. **21**(10), 685–689 (2010)
5. Van der Kuil, M.N.A., Visser-Meily, J.M.A., Evers, A.W.M., van der Ham, I.J.M.: Navigation ability in patients with acquired brain injury: a population-wide online study. Neuropsychol. Rehabil. **32**(7), 1405–1428 (2022)
6. Hegarty, M., Montello, D.R., Richardson, A.E., Ishikawa, T., Lovelace, K.: Spatial abilities at different scales: individual differences in aptitude-test performance and spatial-lay-out learning. Intelligence. **34**(2), 151–176 (2006)
7. Iaria, G., Bogod, N., Fox, C.J., Barton, J.J.: Developmental topographical disorientation: case one. Neuropsychologia. **47**(1), 30–40 (2009)
8. Iaria, G., Burles, F.: Developmental topographical disorientation. Trends Cogn. Sci. **20**(10), 720–722 (2016)
9. Iaria, G., et al.: Developmental topographical disorientation and decreased hippocampal functional connectivity. Hippocampus. **24**(11), 1364–1374 (2014)
10. Bianchini, F., et al.: Developmental topographical disorientation in a healthy subject. Neuropsychologia. **48**(6), 1563–1573 (2010)
11. Burles, F., Iaria, G.: Behavioural and cognitive mechanisms of developmental topographical disorientation. Sci. Rep. **10**(1) (2020)

12. Van der Ham, I.J., Claessen, M.H.: Always getting lost: defining developmental topographical disorientation – a systematic literature review. Neuropsychol. Rev.. in press
13. Iaria, G., Barton, J.J.: Developmental topographical disorientation: a newly discovered cognitive disorder. Exp. Brain Res. **206**, 189–196 (2010)
14. Claessen, M.H., Visser-Meily, J.M., Meilinger, T., Postma, A., de Rooij, N.K., van der Ham, I.J.: A systematic investigation of navigation impairment in chronic stroke patients: evidence for three distinct types. Neuropsychologia. **103**, 154–161 (2017)
15. Klatzky, R. L.: Allocentric and egocentric spatial representations: definitions, distinctions, and interconnections. In: Spatial Cognition: An Interdisciplinary Approach to Representing and Processing Spatial Knowledge (pp. 1–17). Springer, Berlin, Heidelberg (1998)
16. Burgess, N.: Spatial memory: how egocentric and allocentric combine. Trends Cogn. Sci. **10**(12), 551–557 (2006)
17. Wang, R.F., Spelke, E.S.: Updating egocentric representations in human navigation. Cognition. **77**(3), 215–250 (2000)
18. Thornberry, C., Cimadevilla, J.M., Commins, S.: Virtual Morris water maze: opportunities and challenges. Rev. Neurosci. **32**(8), 887–903 (2021)
19. Wolbers, T., Weiller, C., Büchel, C.: Neural foundations of emerging route knowledge in complex spatial environments. Cogn. Brain Res. **21**(3), 401–411 (2004)
20. Chrastil, E.R., Warren, W.H.: Active and passive spatial learning in human navigation: acquisition of survey knowledge. J. Exp. Psychol. Learn. Mem. Cogn. **39**(5), 1520 (2013)
21. De Rooij, N.K., Claessen, M.H.G., van der Ham, I.J., Post, M.W.M., Visser-Meily, J.M.A.: The wayfinding questionnaire: a clinically useful self-report instrument to identify navigation complaints in stroke patients. Neuropsychol. Rehabil. **29**(7), 1042–1061 (2019)
22. Van der Kuil, M.N., Evers, A.W., Visser-Meily, J.M., van der Ham, I.J.: The effectiveness of home-based training software designed to influence strategic navigation preferences in healthy subjects. Front. Hum. Neurosci. **14**, 76 (2020)
23. Poos, J.M., van der Ham, I.J., Leeuwis, A.E., Pijnenburg, Y.A., van der Flier, W.M., Postma, A.: Short digital spatial memory test detects impairment in alzheimer's disease and mild cognitive impairment. Brain Sci. **11**(10), 1350 (2021)
24. Van der Ham, I.J., Claessen, M.H., Evers, A.W., van der Kuil, M.N.: Large-scale assessment of human navigation ability across the lifespan. Sci. Rep. **10**(1), 3299 (2020)
25. Spiers, H.J., Coutrot, A., Hornberger, M.: Explaining world-wide variation in navigation ability from millions of people: citizen science project sea hero quest. Top. Cogn. Sci. **15**(1), 120–138 (2023)
26. Van der Ham, I.J., Claessen, M.H.: A clinical guide to assessment of navigation impairment: standardized subjective and objective instruments and normative data. J. Clin. Exp. Neuropsychol. **44**(7), 487–498 (2022)
27. Van der Ham, I.J., Claessen, M.H.: A case of developmental topographical disorientation: impact on diagnostic trajectory and everyday life. Neurocase. **31**(2), 53–61 (2025)
28. Veldhuizen, R.: Anna raakt altijd de weg kwijt. De volkskrant boeken & wetenschap. **22-23** (2021)
29. Marks, D.F.: Visual imagery differences in the recall of pictures. Br. J. Psychol. **64**(1), 17–24 (1973)
30. Pearson, J.: The human imagination: the cognitive neuroscience of visual mental imagery. Nat. Rev. Neurosci. **20**(10), 624–634 (2019)
31. Jacobs, C., Schwarzkopf, D.S., Silvanto, J.: Visual working memory performance in aphantasia. Cortex. **105**, 61–73 (2018)
32. Crawford, J.R., Garthwaite, P.H.: Comparison of a single case to a control or normative sample in neuropsychology: development of a Bayesian approach. Cogn. Neuropsychol. **24**(4), 343–372 (2007)

33. Broadbent, D.E., Cooper, P.F., FitzGerald, P., Parkes, K.R.: The cognitive failures questionnaire (CFQ) and its correlates. Br. J. Clin. Psychol. **21**(1), 1–16 (1982)
34. Ponds, R.W.H.M., van Boxtel, M., Jolles, J.: De cognitive failure questionnaire als maat voor subjectief cognitief functioneren. Tijdschrift voor neuropsychologie. **2**, 37–45 (2006)
35. Boone, K.B., Salazar, X., Lu, P., Warner-Chacon, K., Razani, J.: The Rey 15-item recognition trial: a technique to enhance sensitivity of the Rey 15-item memorization test. J. Clin. Exp. Neuropsychol. **24**(5), 561–573 (2002)
36. Merckelbach, H., Smith, G.P.: Diagnostic accuracy of the structured inventory of malingered symptomatology (SIMS) in detecting instructed malingering. Arch. Clin. Neuropsychol. **18**(2), 145–152 (2003)
37. Clegg, C., Fremouw, W., Mogge, N.: Utility of the structured inventory of malingered symptomatology (SIMS) and the assessment of depression inventory (ADI) in screening for malingering among outpatients seeking to claim disability. J. Forensic Psychiatry Psychol. **20**(2), 239–254 (2009)
38. Campos, A., Pérez-Fabello, M.J.: Psychometric quality of a revised version vividness of visual imagery questionnaire. Percept. Mot. Skills. **108**(3), 798–802 (2009)
39. Zeman, A., Dewar, M., Della Sala, S.: Lives without imagery–congenital aphantasia. Cortex. **73**, 378–380 (2015)
40. Takahashi, J., et al.: Diversity of aphantasia revealed by multiple assessments of visual imagery, multisensory imagery, and cognitive style. Front. Psychol. **14**, 1174873 (2023)
41. Barclay, S.F., et al.: Familial aggregation in developmental topographical disorientation (DTD). Cogn. Neuropsychol. **33**(7–8), 388–397 (2016)
42. O'keefe, J., Nadel, L.: The Hippocampus as a Cognitive Map. Oxford University Press (1978)
43. Tolman, E.C.: Cognitive maps in rats and men. Psychol. Rev. **55**(4), 189–208 (1948)
44. Waller, D., Lippa, Y.: Landmarks as beacons and associative cues: their role in route learning. Mem. Cogn. **35**(5), 910–924 (2007)
45. Bianchini, F., et al.: Where am I? A new case of developmental topographical disorientation. J. Neuropsychol. **8**(1), 107–124 (2014)
46. Rusconi, M.L., et al.: Developmental topographical disorientation with concurrent face recognition deficit: a case report. Frontiers. Psychiatry. **12**, 654071 (2021)
47. Panzeri, S., Magri, C., Carraro, L.: Sampling bias. Scholarpedia. **3**(9), 4258 (2008)
48. Van der Ham, I.J., van der Kuil, M.N., Claessen, M.H.: Quality of self-reported cognition: effects of age and gender on spatial navigation self-reports. Aging Ment. Health. **25**(5), 873–878 (2021)

# Performance Convergence as a Driver of Visual Strategy

## A Study Focusing on Scanpath Similarities in Mental-Rotation Tasks

Mirko Saunders(✉) and Claudia Quaiser-Poh

University of Koblenz, Universitätsstaße 1, 56070 Koblenz, Germany
mirkosaunders@uni-koblenz.de

**Abstract.** Eye-tracking research in spatial cognition has aimed to describe the visual strategies individuals employ during spatial problem solving and to identify sources of inter-individual differences in these strategies. It remains unclear, however, whether similarities in visual exploration patterns reflect shared cognitive processes or merely superficial statistical properties of gaze. The present study introduces a dyadic framework to examine inter-individual scanpath similarity in a mental rotation task. Seventy-three participants completed 28 mental rotation items. Scanpaths were encoded as sequences of area-of-interest (AOI) labels and compared using normalized Levenshtein distance (N = 68,357 dyadic observations). Linear mixed-effects models with crossed random effects were used to examine the influence of stimulus characteristics (rotational axis: picture plane vs. in-depth, stimulus type: concrete vs. abstract) and performance-related factors (Balanced Integration Score, BIS). Stimulus properties did not significantly predict scanpath similarity, whereas performance-related variables, particularly item-specific performance differences, emerged as consistent predictors of scanpath divergence (β_std = 0.26). At the individual level, mean scanpath distance negatively predicted overall performance ($\beta\_std = -0.31, R^2 = .094$). These findings suggest that scanpath similarity is more closely linked to shared task-related visual strategies associated with similar performance than to stimulus-driven processes. By conceptualizing scanpaths as relational structures, the dyadic approach provides a useful framework for investigating how visual strategies align across individuals during spatial problem solving.

**Keywords:** Spatial Cognition · Mental Rotation · Eye Tracking · Scanpath Similarity · Dyadic Analysis · Levenshtein Distance · Performance Convergence

## 1 Introduction

Understanding how individuals solve spatial problems is a central question in spatial cognition research, and a key goal of eye-tracking studies in this field has been to describe and compare the visual strategies people employ. Eye movements are tightly coupled with cognitive operations and reflect processes that are otherwise not directly observable [9], enabling fine-grained analysis of problem-solving strategies beyond what behavioral measures alone can reveal.


E. Farran et al. (Eds.): Spatial Cognition 2026, LNAI 16785, pp. 63–76, 2027.
https://doi.org/10.1007/978-3-032-36716-7_5

Mental-rotation tasks have been widely used to investigate the cognitive processes underlying spatial reasoning. Classic work demonstrated that response times increase linearly with angular disparity [20], and early eye-tracking studies by Just and Carpenter [7] showed that fixation patterns reflect the incremental transformation of mental representations. Mental rotation places substantial demands on visuospatial working memory [1], which may constrain strategy selection and shape visual exploration patterns. Individuals differ systematically in their approaches: some rely on holistic mental simulation, while others use analytical, feature-based comparison strategies [3, 4]. More recent eye-tracking work has shown how individuals select and flexibly adapt strategies depending on task demands [14].

Scanpaths, defined as sequences of fixations across areas of interest (AOIs), provide a structured representation of visual exploration and have been widely used to study visual cognition [5]. Early theoretical work by Noton and Stark [15] proposed that scanpaths reflect meaningful cognitive structures underlying visual processing. When scanpaths are encoded as AOI sequences and compared using the Levenshtein distance, a low distance between two observers means they inspected the same regions in a similar order with a similar transition structure. Scanpath similarity computed in this way therefore captures structural convergence in visual exploration: not merely whether two people looked at the same areas, but whether they traversed them in a comparable sequential manner. A central unresolved question is what drives such structural similarity or divergence. Increasing evidence suggests that in goal-directed tasks, eye movements are predominantly guided by top-down processes rather than bottom-up stimulus saliency [21], suggesting that structural scanpath similarity may serve as a behavioral marker of shared cognitive strategies rather than of stimulus-driven attention.

Research on scanpath similarity across expertise levels supports this view. Studies in professional domains have consistently found that scanpaths are more similar within than between expertise groups, reflecting convergence on shared cognitive models for effective task performance [13, 24]. This pattern suggests that observers who approach a task successfully tend to converge on similar visual exploration sequences, while less successful observers show more idiosyncratic gaze behavior.

### 1.1 Research Question and Hypothesis

The present study is guided by three hypotheses derived from the theoretical framework outlined above. First, given that eye movements in goal-directed tasks are primarily driven by top-down processes rather than bottom-up stimulus saliency [21], we expect stimulus characteristics (rotational axis, stimulus type) to have only minor effects on scanpath similarity. Second, if scanpath similarity reflects shared visual strategies [2, 6] and similar performance levels are associated with similar strategy use [4], then higher performance similarity should be associated with more convergent scanpaths. Third, conversely, larger performance differences should be associated with greater scanpath divergence, reflecting differences in underlying visual problem-solving strategies. Accordingly, we hypothesize:

a) Stimulus properties (rotational axis, stimulus type) will have only minor effects on scanpath similarity, operationalized as normalized Levenshtein distance between dyadic AOI sequences.

b) Higher similarity in performance between individuals will be associated with more convergent scanpaths (lower normalized Levenshtein distance), reflecting shared visual strategies.
c) Larger BIS differences in performance between individuals (BIS_item_diff) will be associated with greater scanpath divergence (higher normalized Levenshtein distance), indicating differences in underlying visual problem-solving strategies.

## 2 Method

### 2.1 Participants

Seventy-three participants (59 female, 14 male; age $M = 21.64$, $SD = 2.85$) were recruited from a two-subject Bachelor program with psychology as a major. Participation was compensated with one course credit. All participants had normal or corrected-to-normal vision.

### 2.2 Material and Procedure

**Mental-Rotation Task.** Participants completed a computerized mental-rotation task based on established paradigms [23], programmed in PsychoPy and adapted to allow for eye-tracking analysis, following the design described in [10]. The task consisted of two test parts differing in rotational axis. Test part 1 (picture-plane rotation, z-axis) included 16 items in which objects were rotated around the z-axis within the two-dimensional picture plane. Test part 2 (in-depth rotation, x/y-axis) consisted of 12 items requiring rotation around the x- or y-axis in three-dimensional space. Both test parts contained a mixture of concrete and abstract stimuli. Test part 1 additionally included four items depicting animals and letters that consisted of purely two-dimensional figures without depth information and had no equivalent items in the second test part. Each item presented one standard stimulus and four comparison stimuli, two of which were correctly rotated versions of the standard stimulus and two of which were mirror-reversed distractors. Participants were instructed to select the two correctly rotated comparison stimuli. Accuracy was coded as correct only when both correct alternatives were selected. Because the present study focused on inter-individual scanpath similarity across the full task, all 28 items were retained in the analysis. Item order within each test part was randomized per participant. Test part 1 had a time limit of 5 min; test part 2 had a time limit of 8 min, reflecting the greater difficulty of in-depth rotations [10]. Accuracy and response times were recorded for all items.

### 2.3 Eye Tracking and Scanpath Encoding

Eye movements were recorded using a Tobii Pro Spectrum eye tracker (sampling rate: 60 Hz). The experimental paradigm was implemented in PsychoPy. Fixations were identified using the I-DT (dispersion-threshold) algorithm with a dispersion threshold of $1^\circ$ of visual angle and a minimum duration of 60 ms [17]. These parameters were chosen to provide a balance between sensitivity to short fixations and robustness against noise in structured visual comparison tasks.

Areas of interest (AOIs) were defined using **PeriTag (Version 1.0.0) [19]**, a custom software tool for automatic AOI boundary detection. AOIs were generated with a single click per stimulus, ensuring consistent, observer-independent definition across all items. This procedure minimized observer-dependent variability in AOI definition and increased reproducibility across stimuli.

Each fixation was mapped to the corresponding AOI based on its spatial location, yielding a discrete AOI label for each fixation. AOIs were encoded using alphabetical symbols (e.g., A, B, C); fixations falling outside any AOI were assigned a separate symbol ("N").

Based on this labeling, scanpaths were represented as sequences of AOI labels. Two representations were derived:

1. Full Scanpath Representation

A fixation-based sequence preserving all temporal information, including repeated AOI visits and fixations outside defined AOIs.

2. Compact Scanpath Representation
   A reduced representation in which (a) fixations outside any AOI ("N") were removed prior to further processing and (b) consecutive repetitions of the same AOI were collapsed (run-length compression). For example, a sequence such as AAABNNCC was transformed into ABC.

This compression procedure is commonly recommended in scanpath research to reduce noise introduced by fixation duration and sampling rate, while preserving the structural order of visual exploration [5, 6]. The compact representation was used for all between-subject similarity analyses, as it emphasizes the sequential structure of visual exploration while minimizing the influence of dwell time. All scanpath processing, including run-length compression, Levenshtein distance calculation, and dyadic similarity analysis, was implemented in Iriscope (Version 1.0.0) [18], a custom software environment for sequence-based scanpath analysis. The use of a custom pipeline ensured full control over preprocessing steps and consistency across all dyadic comparisons.

## 2.4 Scanpath Similarity and Dyadic Analysis

Similarity between scanpaths was quantified using the Levenshtein distance (edit distance), a sequence-based measure that captures the minimal number of insertions, deletions, and substitutions required to transform one sequence into another [11]. The application of edit-distance approaches to scanpath comparison is well established in eye-tracking research, as it allows for the direct comparison of sequential visual behavior [2]. Importantly, this measure captures differences in the order and structure of visual exploration rather than purely spatial proximity, making it particularly suitable for assessing strategy similarity in sequential gaze behavior.

To ensure comparability across scanpaths of different lengths, distances were normalized by the maximum sequence length:

$$d_{norm}(s_1, s_2) = \frac{d_{lev}(s_1, s_2)}{\max(|s_1|, |s_2|)}$$

where $d_{lev}$ denotes the Levenshtein distance and $|s|$ the length of sequence $s$. The resulting values range from 0 (identical scanpaths) to 1 (maximally dissimilar scanpaths).

For each stimulus, scanpath similarity was computed pairwise between all participants, resulting in a dyadic dataset of scanpath comparisons. Each observation represents the similarity between two participants' scanpaths for a given item. Because not all participants provided valid responses for all items, the number of available participants varied across items; consequently, the number of dyadic comparisons differs between items, and the total number of observations reflects all valid pairwise comparisons after preprocessing. This results in a dyadic dataset in which all participants providing valid data for a given item are compared pairwise. This approach allows scanpath similarity to be treated as a relational measure, capturing how visual exploration strategies converge or diverge across individuals. Only trials with valid eye-tracking data and behavioral responses were included in the analysis; trials were excluded if fixation data could not be reliably assigned to AOIs or if response data were missing. This ensured that all dyadic comparisons were based on complete and interpretable scanpath sequences.

For each participant and stimulus, summary metrics were derived from the dyadic similarity structure, including the mean, median, and minimum normalized Levenshtein distance to all other participants. These measures quantify the extent to which an individual's scanpath resembles or differs from those of others within the same task context. Mean and median distances reflect overall convergence, whereas the minimum distance indicates the closest match to another participant's scanpath within the sample. In the present study, the mean normalized Levenshtein distance was used for the individual-level analysis. All analyses were implemented in Iriscope, which provides a modular pipeline for AOI-based scanpath extraction and similarity computation.

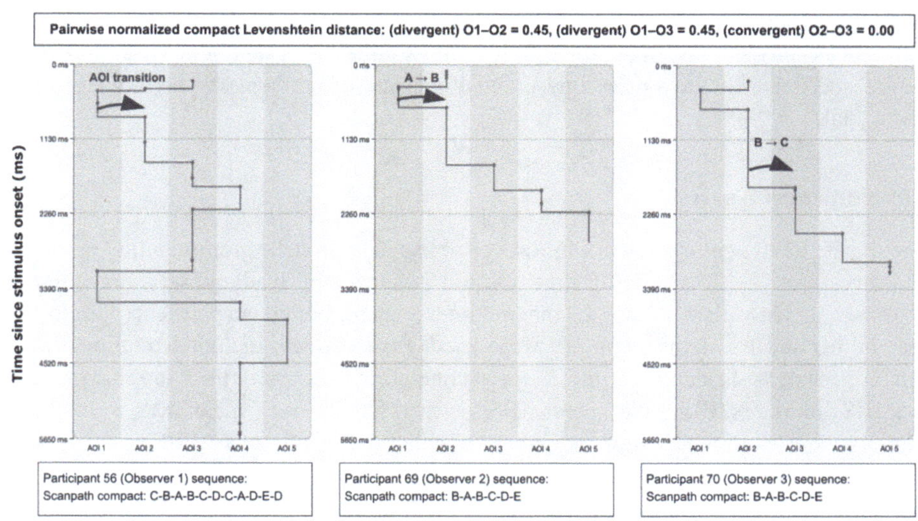


**Fig. 1.** illustrates this measure for three participants viewing the same stimulus, contrasting a convergent pair with identical compact AOI sequences (distance 0.00) against a divergent sequence (distance 0.45).

Figure 1 Compact scanpath similarity for three participants, labelled Observers 1–3, viewing the same stimulus (Item 1). The y-axis represents time (in ms); the stepped paths trace each participant's fixated AOIs at their real viewing times, and shaded bands denote AOI columns. The compact Levenshtein distance is computed on the AOI sequence alone and does not take this timing into account. Observers 2 and 3 share the identical compact AOI sequence (B–A–B–C–D–E) and therefore have a normalized compact Levenshtein distance of 0.00, whereas Observer 1 follows a divergent sequence (C–B–A–B–C–D–C–A–D–E–D), with a distance of 0.45 to each of the others. The visible differences between the paths of Observers 2 and 3 reflect dwell-time and fixation-count differences only; on the raw, non-compressed sequences these two observers differ (normalized raw distance 0.56). The compact representation thus captures the order of AOI transitions rather than their timing

## 2.5 Performance Measure: Balanced Integration Score

To quantify cognitive performance, the Balanced Integration Score [BIS; 12] was used. This measure integrates response time and accuracy with equal weighting and effectively controls for speed-accuracy trade-offs, providing a more robust index of information processing efficiency than either measure alone. BIS was computed at three levels: overall (BIS_total), per rotation layer (picture-plane vs. in-depth; BIS_layer_mean), and per item (BIS_item_mean). Corresponding difference scores (BIS_layer_diff, BIS_item_diff) represent the absolute difference between two participants' BIS values and quantify the degree of performance convergence within a dyad. Larger values indicate greater divergence in performance, whereas smaller values reflect more similar performance levels and, potentially, more similar cognitive processing demands. BIS_layer variables capture performance aggregated within a given rotation layer, reflecting layer-level performance differences across items. In contrast, BIS_item variables represent item-specific performance and thus provide a more fine-grained measure of momentary performance on a given trial.

## 2.6 Statistical Analysis

The dyadic analytical framework follows established approaches for modeling pairwise data structures [8]. To account for the non-independence of dyadic observations, linear mixed-effects models with crossed random intercepts for both dyad partners (vpn_lo_id, vpn_hi_id) and for items (item_id) were used. Fixed effects included rotational axis (picture-plane vs. in-depth), stimulus type (concrete vs. abstract), their interaction, and four BIS predictors (BIS_layer_mean, BIS_layer_diff, BIS_item_mean, BIS_item_diff). Models were estimated using maximum likelihood (REML = FALSE), and model comparisons were conducted via likelihood-ratio tests. To assess whether the results depended on the scanpath representation, the full model was additionally re-estimated on the full, non-compressed scanpaths (retaining repeated AOI visits and out-of-AOI fixations). This robustness analysis is reported in Sect. 3.5.

# 3 Results

## 3.1 Variance Components

A null model including only random effects (crossed intercepts for both dyad partners and items) revealed that the largest proportion of variance was attributable to residual variance (*Var* = 0.0215, *SD* = 0.147), followed by variance between participants (vpn_lo_id: *Var* = 0.0030; vpn_hi_id: *Var* = 0.0029) and between items (*Var* = 0.0002). The intraclass correlation coefficient (*ICC* = .205) indicated that approximately 20.5% of the variance in scanpath similarity was attributable to systematic differences between participants and items, justifying the use of mixed-effects modeling.

## 3.2 Effects of Stimulus Features

In line with Hypothesis (a), stimulus-related predictors did not significantly influence scanpath similarity. Model comparisons confirmed that adding rotational axis ($\chi^2$ = 0.51, p = .474), stimulus type ($\chi^2$ = 0.001, p = .971), or their interaction ($\chi^2$ = 0.40, p = .527) did not improve model fit. Distributions of normalized Levenshtein distances were highly similar across all stimulus conditions, with substantial overlap between groups, indicating that stimulus characteristics had negligible impact on the structural organization of visual exploration.

## 3.3 Performance-Related Effects

In contrast, performance-related variables showed robust and consistent effects on scanpath similarity, supporting Hypotheses (b) and (c). The full model including BIS predictors (m4) significantly improved model fit compared to the stimulus-only model ($\chi^2$ = 6676.9, $p < .001$). Standardized coefficients and partial $\eta^2$ values are reported in Table 1.

**Table 1.** Standardized coefficients (β_std) and partial $\eta^2$ for the full mixed model (m4)

| Predictor | β_std | 95% CI | partial $\eta^2$ |
|---|---|---|---|
| Rotation axis (3D) | −0.02 | [−0.09, 0.06] | – |
| Stimulus type (abstract) | −0.02 | [−0.09, 0.06] | – |
| Rotation × Stimulus type | 0.01 | [−0.10, 0.12] | – |
| BIS_layer_mean | −0.03 | [−0.05, −0.01] | < .001 |
| BIS_layer_diff | 0.03 | [0.02, 0.03] | < .001 |
| BIS_item_mean | −0.04 | [−0.04, −0.03] | < .001 |
| BIS_item_diff | 0.26 | [0.25, 0.27] | .057 |

***Note.*** Stimulus predictors were non-significant (p > .05) and are included for completeness. CI = confidence interval. Partial $\eta^2$ (derived from term-wise F-tests via drop1) reported only for statistically significant predictors (p < .001).

The strongest effect was observed for item-specific performance differences (BIS_item_diff: *beta_std* = 0.26, 95% CI [0.25, 0.27], partial $\eta^2 = .057$), indicating that greater differences in performance between two participants on a given item were associated with substantially more divergent scanpaths. Higher mean performance (BIS_item_mean) was associated with slightly more similar scanpaths (*beta_std* = −0.04), suggesting that better-performing individuals tended to converge on similar visual exploration strategies. Effects for BIS_layer_mean and BIS_layer_diff were also significant but small in magnitude (|beta_std| < = 0.03). This pattern is illustrated in Fig. 2, where higher-performing dyads show lower scanpath distances and reduced variability, consistent with the model-based results.

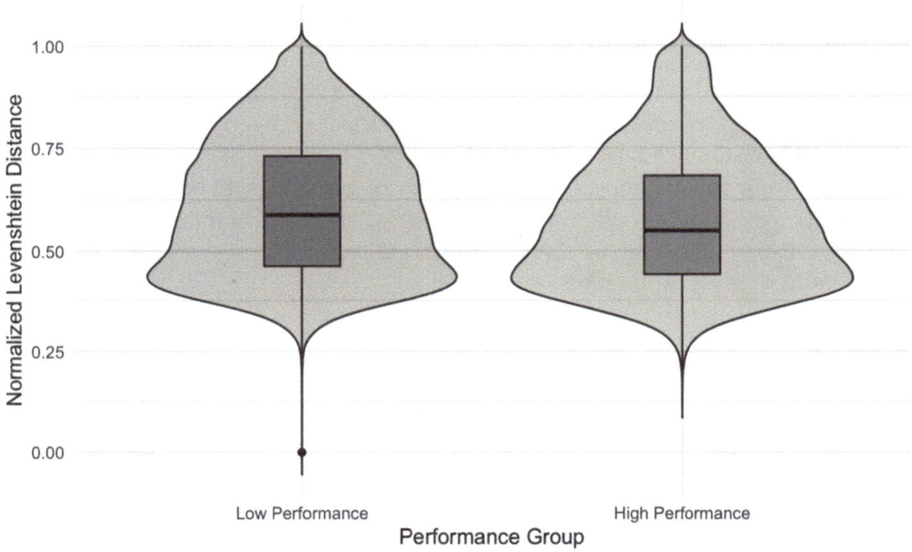


**Fig. 2.** Distribution of normalized Levenshtein distances as a function of performance group (low vs. high). Higher-performing dyads show lower scanpath distances, indicating more similar structural visual exploration patterns and suggesting convergence in visual problem-solving strategies

### 3.4 Individual-Level Analysis

To further examine the relationship between scanpath similarity and performance, scanpath distances were aggregated symmetrically at the participant level across both dyad roles. As illustrated in Fig. 3, a regression analysis revealed a significant negative association between mean scanpath distance and overall performance (BIS_total; $\beta$_*std* = −0.31, $R^2 = .094$, $p = .008$), indicating that participants whose scanpaths were more similar to those of others achieved higher overall performance. This finding extends the dyadic results to the individual level and suggests that convergence in visual exploration is not only a relational property between observers but also reflects an individual tendency toward more shared or efficient task-related visual strategies.

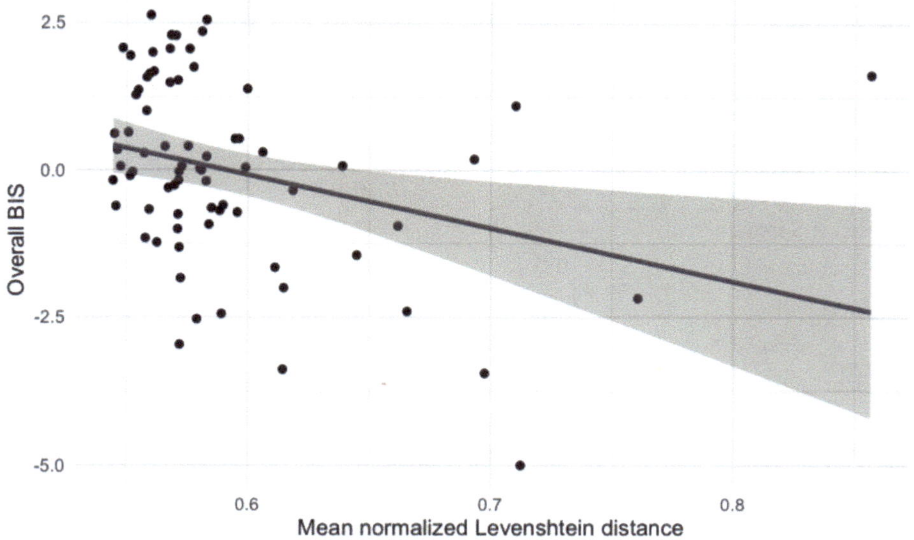


**Fig. 3.** Relationship between mean normalized Levenshtein distance and overall performance (BIS). Each point represents one participant. The regression line indicates that greater average scanpath distance was associated with lower overall performance

### 3.5 Robustness to Scanpath Representation

To verify that the findings were not an artifact of run-length compression, the full mixed model was re-estimated using the full, non-compressed scanpath representation (N = 68,357), which preserves repeated AOI visits and fixations outside defined AOIs. The main qualitative pattern was preserved. Item-specific performance difference (BIS_item_diff) remained the dominant predictor of scanpath divergence and was virtually unchanged across representations (β_std = 0.26 in both; $t = 69.7$, $p < .001$ in the full-scanpath model). As in the compact analysis, neither rotational axis, stimulus type, nor their interaction reached significance (all $p > .05$). The full-scanpath model accounted for a somewhat larger share of variance (conditional $R^2 = .40$, marginal $R^2 = .13$) than the compact model (conditional $R^2 = .28$, marginal $R^2 = .09$).

Some smaller, non-significant coefficients changed in magnitude between representations (e.g., the standardized estimates for rotational axis and stimulus type; see Table 2), as expected when temporal and dwell-time information is retained rather than collapsed. Crucially, however, the two conclusions on which the present interpretation rests were stable across both representations: the stimulus factors remained non-significant, and item-specific performance difference remained the strongest predictor of scanpath divergence. This indicates that the association between scanpath divergence and item-specific performance differences does not arise from the compression procedure.

**Table 2.** Standardized coefficients (β_std) and partial $\eta^2$ for the full mixed model using the **raw/full** scanpath representation

| Predictor | β_std | 95% CI | partial $\eta^2$ |
|---|---|---|---|
| Rotation axis (3D) | 0.21 | [−0.03, 0.46] | – |
| Stimulus type (abstract) | 0.14 | [−0.10, 0.39] | – |
| Rotation × Stimulus type | −0.05 | [−0.42, 0.32] | – |
| BIS_layer_mean | 0.00 | [−0.02, 0.01] | – |
| BIS_layer_diff | 0.07 | [0.06, 0.08] | .004 |
| BIS_item_mean | −0.08 | [−0.09, −0.08] | .006 |
| BIS_item_diff | 0.26 | [0.26, 0.27] | .066 |

***Note.*** Results based on the full, non-compressed scanpath representation ($N = 68{,}357$). Partial $\eta^2$ (from drop1 F-tests) reported only for predictors significant at $p < .001$. Stimulus factors were non-significant in both representations.

## 4 Discussion

The present study investigated inter-individual scanpath similarity in a mental-rotation task using a dyadic framework. A consistent pattern emerged across all analyses: scanpath similarity was not systematically influenced by stimulus features such as rotational axis or stimulus type, but was reliably associated with performance-related variables, particularly item-specific performance differences.

### 4.1 Scanpath Convergence and Shared Visual Strategies

The finding that scanpath similarity appears to be more strongly linked to performance convergence than to stimulus properties has important implications for theories of visual cognition. While classical accounts emphasize the role of stimulus-driven factors, more recent work [e.g. 21] highlights the dominance of top-down, task-dependent processes in guiding eye movements. Specifically, individuals who solve a problem in a similar way, reflected in comparable performance levels, also exhibit more similar patterns of visual exploration. This interpretation is consistent with research on individual differences in spatial cognition, which distinguishes between holistic transformation strategies and more analytical, feature-based comparison strategies [3, 4]. This pattern can be interpreted in light of more fine-grained cognitive mechanisms. One plausible account is that individuals solving mental-rotation tasks identify salient anchor points within the stimuli, distinctive features that serve as reference markers, and then engage in iterative comparisons between corresponding features of the figures [22]. The number and order of these comparison operations are likely to depend on how efficiently the individual can maintain and transform spatial information in working memory [1].

From this perspective, scanpath similarity between two individuals on a given item may reflect that they relied on comparable reference features and engaged in similar sequences of comparison operations, which in turn is associated with similar performance levels on that item. Importantly, the present findings do not imply that performance itself directly causes scanpath convergence. Rather, similar scanpaths and similar performance are more likely to reflect a shared underlying mode of task processing. Participants who understand and solve a given item in a similar way may also converge on similar visual exploration patterns.

This interpretation aligns with the finding that performance differences on the item level (BIS_item_diff) were the strongest predictor of scanpath divergence and further underscores the adaptive nature of visual strategies. Smaller but significant effects at the layer level suggest that convergence also operates at a more general level of task demands, although these effects were clearly weaker than the item-specific effects. The present findings extend this perspective by showing that such strategic differences are not only observable at the individual level but also manifest systematically in the similarity structure between individuals.

Scanpath convergence can thus be interpreted as an observable marker of shared visual strategies. Importantly, the strongest effect was observed for item-specific performance differences (BIS_item_diff), suggesting that convergence is dynamically modulated at the level of individual problem instances. This supports the view that visual exploration is adaptively regulated in response to momentary task demands and strategy implementation, rather than reflecting fixed, trait-like strategies.

This pattern is also compatible with previous work showing that successful visual task performance is associated with more systematic and less idiosyncratic gaze behavior. Research on expertise and scanpath structure suggests that more successful or more experienced observers tend to display more consistent visual exploration patterns, whereas less successful observers show greater variability [13, 24]. More generally, eye-tracking research has also emphasized that structurally similar scanpaths can reflect comparable modes of visual processing, and that sequence-based approaches are particularly informative for capturing such similarities beyond simple spatial overlap [5, 6].

While the present study does not directly model the underlying cognitive mechanisms, the observed relationship between performance convergence and scanpath similarity provides an empirical basis for future research investigating how shared visual strategies, task understanding, and successful problem-solving routines jointly shape structural patterns of visual exploration. From a spatial cognition perspective, this suggests that successful mental rotation is not simply a matter of general visuospatial ability, but involves the dynamic deployment of item-specific visual strategies and that scanpath convergence provides a window into when and for whom such strategies are effectively engaged.

## 4.2 Limited Role of Stimulus-Driven Factors

Although classical mental-rotation research demonstrates strong effects of stimulus properties on response times, the present findings suggest that such effects do not necessarily translate into differences in scanpath structure. While stimulus characteristics may influence processing time or task difficulty, they did not substantially alter the sequential organization of visual exploration captured by scanpath similarity in the present study.

This is consistent with Tatler et al. [21], who argue that in goal-directed tasks, gaze behavior is primarily governed by task demands and expected information gain rather than by low-level stimulus saliency. One possible interpretation is that participants adopt relatively stable task-specific visual routines that generalize across the stimulus conditions examined here.

### 4.3 The Dyadic Framework and Methodological Contribution

A central contribution of this study is the dyadic framework, which conceptualizes scanpath similarity as a relational construct emerging from pairwise comparisons between observers rather than as a property of individuals. This enables the integration of individual- and item-level predictors within a unified mixed-effects model and provides a scalable approach for analyzing inter-individual variability in visual behavior. The use of Levenshtein distance as the similarity metric is well established in eye-tracking research and has been applied productively to identify distinct gaze-strategy clusters in problem-solving contexts [16]. Although most standardized coefficients were small in magnitude, which is typical for behavioral data, their consistency across dyadic and individual-level analyses, combined with the large number of observations ($N = 68{,}357$), indicates robust and theoretically meaningful relationships. The moderate effect of BIS_item_diff is particularly noteworthy, as it accounts for a substantial proportion of the variance explained by fixed effects.

### 4.4 Limitations and Future Directions

The compact AOI sequence representation emphasizes structural order but reduces temporal and spatial detail; AOI discretization may also introduce boundary-related artifacts when fixations occur near AOI borders [6]. Future research should complement this approach with continuous or vector-based scanpath methods. The sample was homogeneous, consisting primarily of young female psychology students, which limits the generalizability of the findings. Future research should examine whether similar patterns hold in more diverse samples with respect to age, gender, and domain expertise.

The dyadic framework can be extended to other task domains such as visual search or scene perception and combined with multimodal data sources including EEG or physiological measures. The relational nature of dyadic data also lends itself to network-based analyses, allowing researchers to identify clusters of individuals sharing similar visual strategies. Such approaches may be particularly informative for studying expertise development, learning processes, or adaptive changes in visual behavior over time.

### 4.5 Conclusion

The present study demonstrates that structural scanpath similarity in mental rotation, measured as Levenshtein distance between AOI sequences, was more strongly associated with item-specific performance convergence than with stimulus features. Participants who processed a given item in a similar and successful way tended to show more similar scanpaths, suggesting that scanpath convergence may reflect shared task-related visual strategies. Beyond its methodological contribution, this work implies that the quality of visual exploration, specifically the degree to which it converges with that of successful peers, may serve as a behavioral indicator of strategy effectiveness in spatial problem solving. By introducing a dyadic perspective, the present approach provides a useful framework for analyzing visual behavior as a relational phenomenon and for linking structural gaze convergence to spatial problem solving.

**Disclosure of Interests.** The first author is the developer of the Iriscope and PeriTag software used in this study, which is proprietary and commercially licensed. The authors have no other competing interests to declare.

## References


1. Baddeley, A.D., Hitch, G.J.: Working memory. In: Bower, G.H. (ed.) The Psychology of Learning and Motivation, pp. 47–89. Academic, New York (1974). https://doi.org/10.1016/S0079-7421(08)60452-1
2. Cristino, F., et al.: ScanMatch: a novel method for comparing fixation sequences. Behav. Res. Methods. **42**(3), 692–700 (2010). https://doi.org/10.3758/BRM.42.3.692
3. Hegarty, M.: Chapter 7 - Components of Spatial Intelligence. In: Psychology of Learning and Motivation. pp. 265–297 Academic Press (2010). doi:10.1016/S0079-7421(10)52007-3.
4. Hegarty, M., Waller, D.A.: Individual differences in spatial abilities. In: The Cambridge Handbook of Visuospatial Thinking, pp. 121–169. Cambridge University Press, New York, NY, US (2005). https://doi.org/10.1017/CBO9780511610448.005
5. Holmqvist, K., et al.: Eye Tracking: a Comprehensive Guide to Methods and Measures. Oxford University Press, Oxford (2011)
6. Jarodzka, H. et al.: A vector-based, multidimensional scanpath similarity measure. In: Proceedings of the 2010 Symposium on Eye-Tracking Research & Applications, pp. 211–218 Association for Computing Machinery, New York, NY, USA (2010). doi:10.1145/1743666.1743718.
7. Just, M.A., Carpenter, P.A.: Eye fixations and cognitive processes. Cogn. Psychol. **8**(4), 441–480 (1976). https://doi.org/10.1016/0010-0285(76)90015-3
8. Kenny, D.A. et al.: Dyadic data analysis (2006).
9. Kosel, C., et al.: Identifying expert and novice visual Scanpath patterns and their relationship to assessing learning-relevant student characteristics. Front. Educ. **5** (2021). https://doi.org/10.3389/feduc.2020.612175
10. Lennon-Maslin, M., et al.: Under my skin: reducing bias in STEM through new approaches to assessment of spatial abilities considering the role of emotional regulation. Soc. Sci. **12, 6**, 356 (2023). https://doi.org/10.3390/socsci12060356
11. Levenshtein, V.I.: Binary codes capable of correcting deletions. Insertions Reversals. Soviet Phys. Doklady. **10**, 707 (1966)
12. Liesefeld, H.R., Janczyk, M.: Combining speed and accuracy to control for speed-accuracy trade-offs(?). Behav Res. **51**(1), 40–60 (2019). https://doi.org/10.3758/s13428-018-1076-x
13. McIntyre, N.A., Foulsham, T.: Scanpath analysis of expertise and culture in teacher gaze in real-world classrooms. Instr. Sci. **46**(3), 435–455 (2018). https://doi.org/10.1007/s11251-017-9445-x
14. Nazareth, A., et al.: Strategy selection versus flexibility: using eye-trackers to investigate strategy use during mental rotation. J. Exp. Psychol. Learn. Mem. Cogn. **45**(2), 232–245 (2019). https://doi.org/10.1037/xlm0000574

15. Noton, D., Stark, L.: Scanpaths in eye movements during pattern perception. Science. **171**(3968), 308–311 (1971)
16. Omarbakiyeva, Y., et al.: Relationship between the cognitive load and the learning success in applying force diagrams: eye-tracking study. Front. Educ. **10**, 1451020 (2025). https://doi.org/10.3389/feduc.2025.1451020
17. Salvucci, D.D., Goldberg, J.H.: Identifying fixations and saccades in eye-tracking protocols. In: Proceedings of the symposium on Eye tracking research & applications - ETRA '00. pp. 71–78 ACM Press, Palm Beach Gardens, Florida, United States (2000). doi:10.1145/355017.355028.
18. Saunders, M.: Iriscope (version 1.0.0) [computer software]. Zenodo. (2026). https://doi.org/10.5281/zenodo.20510528
19. Saunders, M.: PeriTag (version 1.0.0) [computer software]. Zenodo. (2026). https://doi.org/10.5281/zenodo.20510209
20. Shepard, R.N., Metzler, J.: Mental rotation of three-dimensional objects. Science. **171**, 701–703 (1971)
21. Tatler, B.W., et al.: Eye guidance in natural vision: reinterpreting salience. J. Vis. **11, 5, 5** (2011)
22. Tversky, B.: Functional significance of visuospatial representations. In: Miyake, A., Shah, P. (eds.) The Cambridge Handbook of Visuospatial Thinking, pp. 1–34. Cambridge University Press, Cambridge (2005). https://doi.org/10.1017/CBO9780511610448.002
23. Vandenberg, S.G., Kuse, A.R.: Mental rotations, a group test of three-dimensional spatial visualization. Percept. Mot. Skills. **47**(2), 599–604 (1978). https://doi.org/10.2466/pms.1978.47.2.599
24. Wang, F.S., et al.: An algorithmic approach to determine expertise development using object-related gaze pattern sequences. Behav. Res. Methods. **54**(1), 493–507 (2022). https://doi.org/10.3758/s13428-021-01652-z

# Comparing Externalization Methods for Perceived Distance and Slant on Sloped Terrain

Yuzhe Che[1](✉), Tianyi Xiao[2](✉), Yunan Yang[3], Ece Beren Genc[4], Diah Iraw[5], and Martin Raubal[2]

[1] Department of Architecture, ETH Zurich, Zurich, Switzerland
yuzche@ethz.ch
[2] Institute of Cartography and Geoinformation, ETH Zurich, Zurich, Switzerland
{xiaoti,mraubal}@ethz.ch
[3] Department of Social Development and Public Policy, Fudan University, Shanghai, China
ynyang22@m.fudan.edu.cn
[4] Biometria Lab, Istanbul, Turkey
genc@biometrialab.org
[5] Technische Hochschule Ingolstadt, Technologietransferzentrum (TTZ), Ingolstadt, Germany
diahayu.irawati@thi.de

**Abstract.** Understanding how people externalize spatial knowledge in sloped terrain is fundamental to modeling navigation behavior in environments with elevation change. Prior research consistently shows that observers overestimate slant across established measurement methods such as verbal estimation and 2D sketch mapping. However, it remains unclear whether these biases arise from perception itself or from limitations of measurement techniques. We conducted a preliminary user study ($N = 12$) comparing three externalization methods: verbal estimation, 2D sketch mapping, and 3D sketch mapping in virtual reality (VR). We evaluated topological fidelity (e.g., route structure), metric accuracy (e.g., distance and slant), and content (e.g., spatial elements and spatial-reference frames). Results indicate that Verbal estimation preserved route order, but it underestimated route length by 40–91%. 2D sketch maps produced the lowest distance bias (+11.6%), whereas projected 3D sketch maps showed substantially greater overestimation (+52.2%) in route segment length. In addition, 3D sketch maps provide the most complete representation of route segments and turns (73.1%). 3D sketch mapping uniquely captured the elevation information compared to other externalization methods, but it showed a 5.48× slant exaggeration and individual variability. Our findings present key insights for the development of adaptive navigation aids in sloped terrains.

**Keywords:** Distance perception · Slant perception · Spatial cognition

Y. Che and T. Xiao: These authors contributed equally.


E. Farran et al. (Eds.): Spatial Cognition 2026, LNAI 16785, pp. 77–91, 2027.
https://doi.org/10.1007/978-3-032-36716-7_6

## 1 Introduction

Understanding how people acquire spatial knowledge, particularly perceptions of distance and slant, is fundamental to modeling navigation in environments with elevation changes [9,13,32]. During navigation, people develop internal spatial representations of landmarks, topological relationships and terrain characteristics [12,33,34]. These internal spatial representations are conceptualized as cognitive maps, which provide structured knowledge of the environment [40]. Because cognitive maps cannot be observed directly, researchers have developed diverse methods, such as verbal reports and sketch mapping [42], to externalize them and examine how people encode, structure, and communicate spatial information through these external representations.

Spatial perception is subject to systematic distortions. Slant is consistently overestimated [29,39], and distance estimates are highly susceptible to distortion [22,31]. However, measured distortions may not arise solely from perceptual processes; they may also result from constraints imposed by the medium through which spatial knowledge is externalized [42]. For instance, traditional sketch maps are typically created with pen and paper, requiring users to mentally transform three-dimensional (3D) spatial information into a two-dimensional (2D) representation. This dimensional reduction imposed by conventional methods may introduce additional cognitive demands and potential distortions, particularly when vertical spatial relationships are relevant [18,20,41]. This becomes critical on sloped terrain because perceived steepness directly influences route selection, anticipated physical effort, and judgment [26]. Additionally, it remains unclear whether the well-documented overestimation of slant and distortion of distance reflects a perceptual bias or and artifact of the used medium.

Recent advances in VR enable individuals to externalize their spatial knowledge directly within three-dimensional virtual environments. This technique, known as 3D sketch mapping, offers a novel means of examining the relationship between perceptual processes and the representational constraints that shape spatial cognition [19,41]. To address the research gap identified above, this study proposes the following overarching research question (RQ0): How do different externalization methods (e.g.,verbal estimation, 2D sketch mapping, and 3D sketch mapping) externalize spatial knowledge acquired during navigation on sloped terrain? The RQ0 can be further divided into the following sub-questions:

**RQ1.** Which externalization method shows the lowest bias in distance and slant estimates?
**RQ2.** How do verbal estimation, 2D and 3D sketch mapping differ in the spatial information they preserve?

The corresponding hypotheses (H) are:

**H1.** 3D sketch mapping yields lower distance bias than verbal estimation and 2D sketch mapping.
**H2.** 3D sketch mapping preserves a more comprehensive integration of vertical structure and metric information compared to verbal estimation and 2D sketch mapping.

To address RQs, we conducted a preliminarily user study ($N = 12$) on a university campus route consisting of segments with varying slant angles and walking directions. Participants first navigated a predefined outdoor route, and then they externalized their perceived slant and distance using verbal estimation, 2D sketch mapping, and 3D sketch mapping. We found that verbal estimation emphasizes egocentric topological information (e.g., turns), 2D sketch mapping emphasizes allocentric metric information, and 3D sketch mapping integrates both types of information while additionally preserving vertical structure. Compared with other methods, 3D sketch mapping provides a more comprehensive externalization of spatial knowledge related to sloped terrain and enables the measurement of perceptual biases, such as the downhill illusion. Overall, this study provides empirical and methodological insights into how different externalization methods reveal and distort spatial knowledge in environments containing elevation changes and demonstrates the potential of 3D sketch mapping as a tool for investigating perceived distance and slant.

## 2 Related Work

Understanding spatial perception is a fundamental step in explaining navigation and spatial learning [2,16,30,44]. Cognitive maps, or "cognitive collages" [40], refer to the mental representation of spatial environments that are used to guide navigation [37], yet they are subject to systematic cognitive distortions [24]. Sketch mapping is an intuitive method for externalizing cognitive maps, typically asking a person to draw on paper using a pen [35]. Lynch identifies several fundamental elements commonly represented in sketch maps, including paths, edges, districts, nodes, and landmarks [23]. Although this framework was originally developed to characterize perceptions of urban environments, subsequent studies have adapted its elements to other navigational contexts, including campuses [3], virtual environments [6], and public spaces [38]. In this work, we extend this framework to sloped terrain by adapting its elements to terrain-related regions and environmental features.

The conventional sketch mapping method poses a significant challenge in representing vertical information, as translating three-dimensional space onto a planar surface imposes substantial cognitive load and introduces distortions and errors [7,19,42]. Recent advances in VR have enabled immersive 3D sketching in virtual environments, leading to the development of 3D sketch mapping. Tools such as VResin [42], Sketch2Terrain [41], and CoMap [43] reduce the dimensionality-reduction penalty of 2D sketch mapping, allowing users to externalize elevation changes and 3D spatial relationships more intuitively. 3D sketch mapping has been widely used in indoor [5,21] and outdoor spaces [8], providing the opportunity to evaluate whether it produces intrinsically more reliable representations of slant and distance than established methods.

Distance perception is highly susceptible to topographic and contextual distortions [22,31]. Uphill and downhill routes, for example, are often overestimated due to the physical effort associated with ascent and the caution required during descent [26]. Such distortions may be amplified by the need to integrate egocentric sensory input with allocentric, map-like representations during navigation [27,35], particularly in complex 3D environments [20]. Nevertheless, qualitative spatial topology can remain relatively stable in externalized maps despite discrepancies between perceived 3D configurations and traversed 2D path distances [20,35].

Slant perception is similarly shaped by methodological and contextual factors. In virtual environments, slant is often underestimated [15]. Most psychophysical studies examine the slant of currently visible surfaces, whereas navigation tasks require the reconstruction of previously experienced terrain. Creem and Proffitt [10] showed that remembered geographical slant judgments differ from immediate perceptual judgments, with verbal estimates becoming increasingly exaggerated after memory delays as judgments converge toward an explicit memory representation. Thus, slant estimates obtained through verbal reports or sketch maps should be interpreted as externalizations of remembered spatial knowledge rather than direct measures of perceptual slant alone.

## 3 Methods

**Study Design.** We employed a within-subjects design with measurement method as the primary independent variable, comprising three conditions: verbal estimation (C1), 2D sketch mapping (C2), and 3D sketch mapping (C3). To mitigate learning and order effects, the order of the conditions was counterbalanced. The study protocol was approved by the ETH Zurich Ethics Commission.

**Stimuli.** We employed a 1260-meter outdoor route on the ETH Zurich Honggerberg campus, with segments selected following [4] for metric extent, uniform surface morphometry, and accessibility. The detail of the route is shown in Fig. 1.

**Apparatus and Interface.** We tracked participant movement and ground-truth (GT) elevations using a high-accuracy GPS module. The experiment utilized three interfaces: (C1) a smartphone-based voice recorder; (C2) a paper canvas printed with a compass rose, a scale, and a starting point; and (C3) a VR-based 3D sketch-mapping tool deployed on a Meta Quest headset (powered by a laptop: i7-10750H, 16GB RAM). The 3D sketch-mapping tool, adapted from [41], supports mid-air sketching, stroke management (color, erase, undo/redo), and reference images as the base canvas.

**Tasks and Procedure.** The procedure of the study consists of three phases, shown as follows:

*Briefing (10 min):* Participants signed informed consent forms, completed demographic surveys and spatial ability assessments, and received instruction on how to use the VR system.

*Task 1. Navigation (20 min):* Participants walked a predefined route between two points (A to B or B to A as in Fig. 1(a)(b)). They were instructed to navigate at a

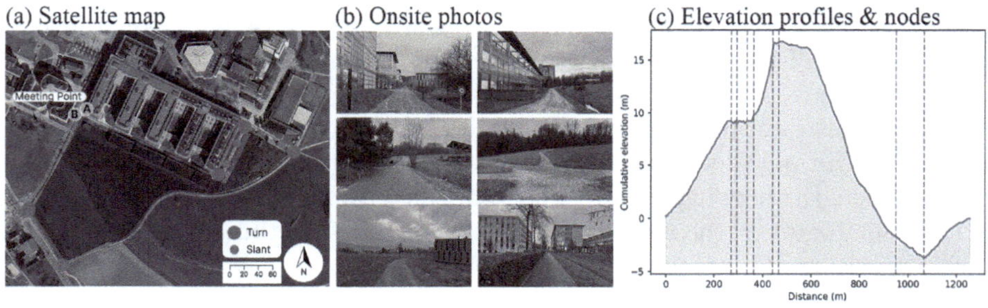


**Fig. 1.** (a) shows a satellite map with two possible starting or ending points (A/B) and the boundaries of each route segment. (b) presents representative on-site photographs taken along the route. (c) shows the elevation profile, including the distance and average gradient of each segment, which were used in the subsequent analysis of distance and slant accuracy.

self-selected pace while attending to route geometry (turns, segments), relative lengths, and slope changes. Elevation profiles are detailed in Fig. 1(c).

textitTask 2. Externalization (25 min): Participants externalized their memory of the route across three conditions:

C1: Participants verbally reported the distance and slant of each route segment.
C2: Participants drew a top-down sketch map on paper, including turns, landmarks, and the length and, where possible, elevation changes of each route segment.
C3: Participants drew a 3D sketch map in VR, including turns, landmarks, and the length and elevation changes of each route segment.

**Participants.** Participants were recruited via an internal research panel and social media. Twelve participants were enrolled and included in the analysis. The final sample comprised 8 female, 3 male, and 1 non-binary participant (mean age = 25.1 years, $SD = 2.5$), all of whom held university degrees and reported regular map use. Mental Rotation Test (MRT) scores were generally high.

**Metrics.** We evaluated externalization results using three complementary dimensions: topological fidelity, metric accuracy, and content analysis. Topological fidelity refers to how completely and correctly participants reproduced the structure of the route. We quantified this using three completeness measures: turn completeness ($C_{\text{turn}}$), slant completeness ($C_{\text{slant}}$), and segment completeness ($C_{\text{seg}}$), each calculated as the proportion of GT features reproduced in the externalization. To assess whether participants preserved the correct sequence of route elements, we compared the node order in externalization with the GT node order using Kendall's $\tau$; nodes were considered matched when their cumulative route length differed from the GT position by no more than 10%.

Metric accuracy refers to how accurately participants represented the length of each route segment. Because sketch maps may vary in overall scale, drawn segment lengths were first normalized using a scale factor based on the first segment: $k = \text{GT-Seg}_1/\text{Drawn-Seg}_1$. The normalized distance error for each segment was then calculated as $\text{Error-Seg}_i = [\text{Drawn-Seg}_i \times \text{k} - \text{GT-Seg}_i]/\text{GT-Seg}_i$. Positive values indicate overestimation, whereas negative values indicate underestimation. For 3D sketch maps, we measured both the 3D path length and its projected length, allowing for direct comparison with 2D sketch maps and verbal estimation. Together, these metrics capture both the structural organization and metric precision of externalized route knowledge.

We also conducted a content analysis to examine how route geometry, vertical structure, spatial content, and reference frames were externalized across modalities. The analysis included four metrics. *Turn-Angle Distortion* quantified deviations in represented turn magnitude after coding turn direction, that is, left versus right, separately from angular magnitude. Vertical structure was assessed using two modality-specific measures: *Categorical Slant Accuracy* for C1 and C2, where segments were coded as uphill, flat, or downhill and compared with the ground truth, and *Metric Slant Bias* for C3, where represented slope profiles were compared with the ground-truth slope profile to capture systematic over- or underestimation. *Spatial-Element Distribution* was coded using Lynch's framework [23] to characterize the inclusion of paths, edges, districts, nodes, and landmarks. Finally, each representation was classified by its dominant *Spatial Reference Frame* as egocentric, allocentric, or hybrid; verbal descriptions were categorized based on self-centered versus environment-centered expressions, whereas 2D and 3D sketch maps were evaluated based on map type, orientation, route knowledge, topology, and shape accuracy.

## 4 Results

Example artifacts produced by participants are shown in Fig. 2. Before analysis, data from the three conditions were processed as follows. Verbal reports produced in C1 were transcribed and analyzed using Condens [1]. For the 2D sketch maps produced in C2, each paper map was digitized and manually traced as a polyline in Rhino 8. Nodes were placed at turns and segment boundaries to define individual route segments. For the 3D sketch maps produced in C3, stroke data were exported from the VR environment as 3D tubular meshes and imported into Rhino 8. These meshes were converted into polylines and further analyzed in Python. For each 3D route segment, two length measures were extracted: the *3D path length*, measured along the original three-dimensional stroke, and the *projected length*, obtained by collapsing the $z$-axis onto the horizontal plane.

### 4.1 Topological Fidelity

All responses were scored against the GT route, which consisted of 5 turns, 5 slant nodes, and 6 segments. Scoring followed the shared coding scheme described in Sect. 3. Inter-rater reliability was high, with ICC(2,1) = 1.00 for

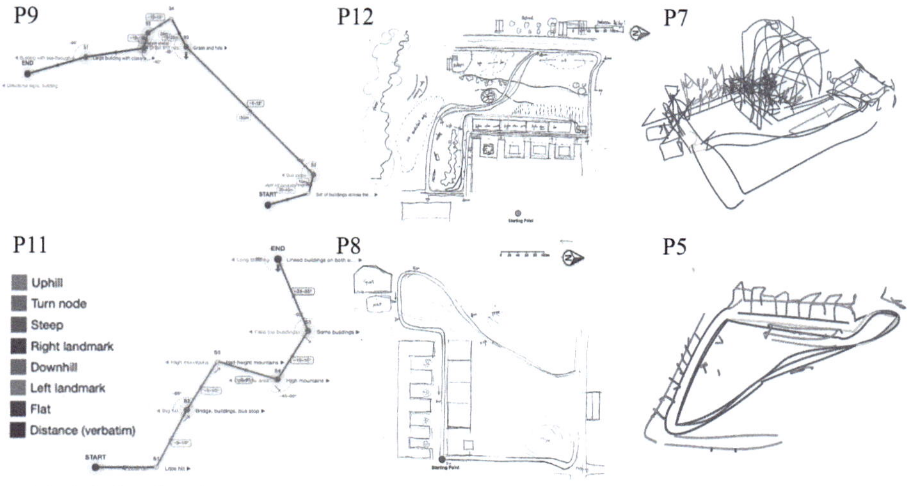


(a) Verbal estimation (b) 2D sketch maps (c) 3D sketch maps

**Fig. 2.** Example artifacts produced in the experiment.

$C_{\text{turn}}$ and $C_{\text{slant}}$ and ICC(2,1) = 0.96–0.98 for $C_{\text{seg}}$. Full values for each condition are reported in Table 1.

$C_{\text{turn}}$ increased progressively from C1 to C2 to C3, while $C_{\text{seg}}$ was highest in C3. In C3, $C_{\text{slant}}$ ($M = 0.420$) was substantially lower than $C_{\text{turn}}$ ($M = 0.900$), indicating that participants reproduced turns more completely than slant-related features. Node ordering was consistently high across all conditions (Kendall's $\tau \approx 0.93$), suggesting that the serial structure of the route [25] was preserved regardless of externalization medium.

**Table 1.** Topological accuracy by condition ($N = 12$).

| Measure | C1 | C2 | C3 |
|---|---|---|---|
| Turn completeness ($C_{\text{turn}}$) | 0.690 | 0.880 | 0.900 |
| Slant completeness ($C_{\text{slant}}$) | – | – | 0.420 |
| Segment completeness ($C_{\text{Seg}}$) | 0.639 | 0.600 | 0.731 |
| Node order (Kendall $\tau$) | 0.930 | 0.838 | 0.943 |

### 4.2 Metrics Accuracy

We first assessed the normality of per-participant mean distance errors using Shapiro–Wilk tests. Normality assumptions were met for all comparisons (all $W > .92$, $p > .05$). We then conducted three a priori paired $t$-tests based on our hypotheses, applying Holm–Bonferroni correction for multiple comparisons.

***C1:*** Only 7 of 12 participants reported any distance value, and none estimated all route segments. Therefore, C1 was not included in inferential testing. Among the four participants for whom a total-route estimate could be approximated, all underestimated the ground-truth route length (GT = 1259.7 m) by 40%–91%. This pattern is therefore treated as exploratory.

***C2:*** Participants reproduced, on average, 87.5% of the target segments. Most participants (8/12) showed net overestimation. A one-sample $t$-test confirmed a significant positive distance bias ($M = +11.6\%$, $SD = 16.3\%$, $p = .031$), indicating that distances were modestly overestimated in C2. This was the smallest distance bias across the three conditions.

***C3:*** Seven participants overestimated total distance and five underestimated it, with individual errors ranging from −217% to +211%. A one-sample $t$-test showed no significant group-level bias for 3D path length ($M = +6.7\%$, $SD = 102.5\%$, $p = .825$). Projected length were significantly overestimated ($M = +52.2\%$, $SD = 57.0\%$, $p = .009$).

The paired $t$-tests with HolmBonferroni correction were conducted between different conditions (see Table 2). The comparison between C2 and the projected length was significant: the projected length showed larger overestimation than the 2D sketch maps.

**Table 2.** Planned pairwise comparisons of distance error.

| Comparison | Mean difference (%) | $p_{adj}$ | Cohen's $d$ | Sig. |
|---|---|---|---|---|
| C2 vs Projected length | −40.6 | .012 | −0.87 | * |
| C2 vs 3D path length | +4.9 | .863 | 0.05 | *ns* |
| Projected length vs 3D path length | +45.5 | .105 | 0.51 | *ns* |

*Note.* Mean difference was calculated as the first condition minus the second condition. Positive values indicate larger distance error in the first condition.
$^*p < .05$; *ns* = not significant

Taken together, C2 showed the smallest distance bias ($M = +11.6\%$), the projected length of C3 showed the largest overestimation ($M = +52.2\%$), and C3 showed high individual variability ($SD = 102.5\%$).

### 4.3 Content Analysis

**Turn-Angle Distortion.** We distinguish turn *direction*, the egocentric left/right sense of each turn, from turn *magnitude*, its angular size. Absolute orientation, such as compass bearing, was not evaluated because it was not consistently available across modalities. Left/right direction was preserved with high fidelity (C2: $M = 0.903$; C3: all recalled turns correct), but angular magnitude was distorted or unreported. In C1, no participant gave a numeric angle, and in C2 over-sharp errors ($M = 0.528$) exceeded under-sharp ones ($M = 0.272$). This pattern of correct left/right direction without metric precision parallels the slant findings reported next.

**Categorical Slant Accuracy.** In C1, participants selectively encoded gradient changes: flat segments were largely omitted (mean capture rate 49%, with 11/12 participants under-reporting flatness), whereas sloped segments were retained as salient wayfinding events. An uphill–downhill asymmetry mirrored the perceptual "downhill illusion": participants under-reported the two uphill segments ($M = 1.08$ mentions) while over-attributing the single downhill segment ($M = 1.25$ mentions), suggesting that exaggerated descents are more readily encoded into memory. Furthermore, 42% of participants intensified slopes with unwarranted descriptors such as "steep" or "peak." In C2, slope was annotated by only 8/12 participants; the drawn direction matched GT on 47.5% of sloped segments, and the mean slope hit rate was 0.32. Across both modalities, the qualitative directional sign, that is, up versus down, was partly preserved, whereas ordinal intensity was not, aligning with Tversky's cognitive-collage theory [40] and the category-adjustment model [17]: spatial memory stores categorical slant knowledge, but not ordinal or metric slant knowledge.

**Metric Slant Bias.** For C3, slant bias was computed for each route segment as the signed difference between the Gaussian-smoothed 3D sketch slant ($\sigma \approx n/80$) and the GT slope profile. Segments were grouped by GT slope type: uphill (GT $> +2.5\%$), downhill (GT $< -2.5\%$), and flat ($|\text{GT}| \leq 2.5\%$). *Universal slant overestimation.* All 12 participants over-steepened the slope, drawing it on average 5.48× steeper than GT ($M = +8.61\%$; all $p < .001$; large effects). The overestimation was systematic in both directions, with uphill segments exaggerated upward (+14.47%) and downhill segments exaggerated downward (−16.85%). This far exceeds the 2 to 3 times exaggeration reported for geographical-slant perception [28], suggesting that 3D sketch externalization amplifies slope beyond perception alone, plausibly through a cascade of perceptual, memorial, and motor sources. The opposing signs of the uphill and downhill bias indicate a consistent exaggeration away from horizontal rather than a uniform directional shift. Every participant preserved slope sign, yet the per-participant Pearson correlation between 3D sketch map and GT segment slant did not differ from zero ($\bar{r} = 0.076$, $p = .30$; significant for only 4 of 12 participants). Thus, participants preserved whether a segment went up or down, but not which segment was steeper than which (Table 3). The large slant bias in C3 therefore reflects not lower fidelity, but the fact that 3D is the only medium in which slope becomes metrically measurable, exposing a perceptual overestimation that 2D and verbal externalization leave invisible.

**Distribution of Spatial Elements.** Using Lynch's framework [23], we quantified the distribution of spatial elements across modalities via Jensen–Shannon (JS) divergence. The two graphical modalities produced nearly identical distributions ($\text{JS}_{2\text{D},3\text{D}} \approx 0.002$), with paths dominant (44%) and landmarks underrepresented (14%). By contrast, verbal externalizations (JS $\approx 0.054$) prioritized landmarks (32.6%) and districts (9.2%). This suggests that the graphical–linguistic distinction shapes spatial externalization more strongly than the 2D–

**Table 3.** Metric slant bias of C3 against GT ($N = 12$; one-sample $t$-tests).

| Measure | $M$ | $SD$ | $p$ | Sig. |
|---|---|---|---|---|
| Overall slant bias (%) | +8.61 | 4.86 | $< .001$ | *** |
| Uphill bias (%) | +14.47 | 6.88 | $< .001$ | *** |
| Downhill bias (%) | −16.85 | 8.30 | $< .001$ | *** |
| Z-exaggeration (×, vs. 1) | 5.48 | 2.40 | $< .001$ | *** |
| C3–GT slant $r$ | +0.08 | 0.24 | .30 | ns |

*** $p < .001$; ns = not significant. The slope correlation is the per-participant Pearson $r$ between C3 and GT segment slant

3D format. We further categorized each representation as egocentric, allocentric, or hybrid. C1 was predominantly egocentric (75%), consistent with the absence of a drawing medium encouraging first-person route reporting. C2 was predominantly allocentric (75%), whereas C3 produced an equal split (50/50), confirming their role as a hybrid modality.

## 5 Discussion

We want to answer our RQs first.

**RQ1.** *Which externalization method shows the lowest bias in distance and slant estimates?* For *distance*, C2 showed the smallest systematic bias ($M = +11.6\%$), C1 systematically underestimated, and C3 showed no reliable group-level direction but very large individual variability. For *slant*, all media overestimated slope, and C3 showed the largest angular bias because it is the only method that can expresses slant metrically. H1 is therefore assessed separately by metric: for distance, it is *not supported*, as C2 rather than C3 showed the smallest bias; for slant, it is *reframed rather than confirmed*, as C3 did not minimize bias but was the only medium able to express slant metrically.

**RQ2.** *How do verbal estimation, 2D and 3D sketch mapping differ in the spatial information they preserve?* Regarding RQ2, while verbal estimation prioritizes egocentric, sequential route information, 2D sketch mapping preserves horizontal layout and distance within an allocentric frame, and 3D sketch mapping achieves the highest $C_{\text{seg}}$ and $C_{\text{turn}}$, uniquely translating elevation and slant into measurable geometry. H2 is therefore partially supported: 3D sketch mapping preserves a more comprehensive spatial representation than verbal or 2D methods, particularly for vertical structure.

**Topological Structure is Robustly Preserved Across Externalization Methods.** Across all three conditions, topological fidelity metrics were consistently high: $C_{\text{turn}}$ ranged from 0.690 to 0.900, $C_{\text{seg}}$ from 0.600 to 0.731, and node ordering from $\tau = 0.838$ to 0.943. Together, these results indicate that the sequential structure of the route–the order of turns, path segments, and junctions—was preserved regardless of output format. These results are consistent with the view that primary spatial knowledge is organized as a labeled place graph [14], in which topological connectivity is robustly encoded while metric information is not embedded in a geometrically consistent structure.

**Representational Constraints and the Limits of Single-Metric Comparison.** Prior work demonstrated that manual and proprioceptive methods generally reduce the exaggeration observed in verbal estimation, yet systematic overestimation remains even when haptic information is available [11,36]. Similarly, our results show that changing the externalization medium does not eliminate spatial bias. Instead, each medium preserves different aspects of spatial knowledge while introducing modality-specific distortions. However, unlike traditional slant perception studies that evaluate judgments of currently perceived surfaces, our task required participants to reconstruct previously experienced terrain. This distinction is important because remembered spatial representations are influenced by memory transformation and task demands. Creem and Proffitt [10] showed that delayed judgments increasingly reflect explicit memory representations rather than immediate perceptual experience. Therefore, the biases observed in our study should be interpreted as distortions in the externalization of cognitive spatial representations, which arise from the interaction between perception, memory, and the constraints of the representation medium.

**Implications for Navigation Design.** Our findings present key insights for the development of adaptive navigation aids in complex terrain environments. Because 2D sketch mapping prioritizes horizontal metric relationships and 3D sketch mapping uniquely captures vertical structure, we propose a hybrid display design for future navigation interfaces: a conventional 2D map for general orientation combined with an 3D elevation profile to explicitly visualize slant. Furthermore, since our results indicate that 3D sketch mapping makes perceptual bias measurable, future VR systems could integrate an adjustment feature to calibrate visual steepness, thus serving to normalize the perceived incline and mitigate the downhill illusion. Finally, given that users naturally encode spatial information through categorical landmark associations rather than precise metrics, navigation aids should prioritize context-aware, landmark-based instructions over strictly distance-based reporting in high-slope terrain.

**Limitations**: We acknowledge that our sample size ($N = 12$) is modest; however, the study is intended as an exploratory, high-fidelity comparison across three demanding externalization modalities. To support implicit rigor, all pairwise condition contrasts used paired $t$-tests with HolmBonferroni correction to control the family-wise error rate. We also acknowledge that distance underestimation is a known phenomenon in VR. By utilizing a within-subjects design and comparing a 3D sketch mapping to 2D sketch mapping, we aimed to isolate the relative accuracy of the medium rather than absolute distance estimation. Furthermore, regarding the verbal estimations, missing data points were handled via listwise deletion, a common practice in spatial cognitive studies where participants may occasionally fail to recall or articulate specific segment distances.

## 6 Conclusion

This study shows that 3D sketch mapping captures terrain more comprehensively than 2D sketch mapping. Although 3D sketches reveal greater slant error, this is a methodological strength: unlike 2D maps, which flatten terrain and can obscure slope misperception, 3D sketches make vertical biases measurable. Verbal reports remain useful for sequential turns and landmarks but cannot capture metric slope or distance accuracy. Thus, 3D sketch mapping turns hidden perceptual errors into quantifiable data, supporting the design of safer navigation tools for high-altitude terrain. Future work should extend these findings to broader use cases and interactive VR scenarios.

**Acknowledgments.** This study is part of a Sinergia project called "3D Sketch Maps" (No. 202284), funded by the Swiss National Science Foundation (SNSF). This work was conducted as part of an initial exploratory study on spatial cognition in humanmachine interaction and was supported by the Technology Transfer Center (TTZ) for Unmanned Aerial Systems.

## References

1. Condens (condens.io). https://app.condens.io/. Accessed: 28 June 2026
2. Ahmadpoor, N., Shahab, S.: Spatial knowledge acquisition in the process of navigation: a review. Curr. Urban Stud. **7**, 1–19 (2019). https://doi.org/10.4236/cus.2019.71001
3. Alptekin, O.: A reading attempt of the urban memory of Eskisehir Osmangazi university Meselik campus via cognitive mapping. IOP Conf. Ser.: Mater. Sci. Eng. **245**, 052016 (2017). https://doi.org/10.1088/1757-899X/245/5/052016
4. Bhalla, M., Proffitt, D.R.: Visual-motor recalibration in geographical slant perception. J. Experim. Psychol. Hum. Percep. Perform. **25**(4), 1076–1096 (1999). https://doi.org/10.1037/0096-1523.25.4.1076
5. Bock, O.: Cognitive representations of multilevel buildings: two- or three-dimensional? Exp. Brain Res. **243**, 202 (2025). https://doi.org/10.1007/s00221-025-07136-2
6. Bruns, C.R., Chamberlain, B.C.: The influence of landmarks and urban form on cognitive maps using virtual reality. Landsc. Urban Plan. **189**, 296–306 (2019). https://doi.org/10.1016/j.landurbplan.2019.05.006, https://www.sciencedirect.com/science/article/pii/S0169204618303104
7. Ceriotti, M., Tribello, G.A., Parrinello, M.: Simplifying the representation of complex free-energy landscapes using sketch-map. Proc. Natl. Acad. Sci. U.S.A. **108**(32), 13023–13028 (2011). https://doi.org/10.1073/pnas.1108486108
8. Cheng, Y., et al.: Computer-assisted terrain sketch mapping that considers the geomorphological features in a loess landform. Geomorphology **364**, 107169 (2020). https://doi.org/10.1016/j.geomorph.2020.107169
9. Chrastil, E.R., Warren, W.H.: Active and passive spatial learning in human navigation: acquisition of survey knowledge. J. Exp. Psychol. Learn. Mem. Cogn. **39**(5), 1520–1537 (2013). https://doi.org/10.1037/a0032382

10. Creem, S.H., Proffitt, D.R.: Two memories for geographical slant: separation and interdependence of action and awareness. Psych. Bulletin Rev. **5**(1), 22–36 (1998). https://doi.org/10.3758/BF03209455
11. Durgin, F.H., Hajnal, A., Li, Z., Tonge, N., Stigliani, A.: Palm boards are not action measures: an alternative to the two-systems theory of geographical slant perception. Acta Physiol. (Oxf) **134**(2), 182–197 (2010). https://doi.org/10.1016/j.actpsy.2010.01.009, https://www.sciencedirect.com/science/article/pii/S0001691810000181
12. Egenhofer, M.J., Shariff, A.R.B.M.: Metric details for natural-language spatial relations. ACM Trans. Inf. Syst. **16**(4), 295–321 (1998). https://doi.org/10.1145/291128.291129
13. Egorova, E., Tenbrink, T., Purves, R.S.: Where snow is a landmark: Route direction elements in alpine contexts. In: Fabrikant, S.I., Raubal, M., Bertolotto, M., Davies, C., Freundschuh, S., Bell, S. (eds.) Spatial Information Theory, pp. 175–195. Springer International Publishing, Cham (2015). https://doi.org/10.1007/978-3-319-23374-1_9
14. Ericson, J.D., Warren, W.H.: Probing the invariant structure of spatial knowledge: support for the cognitive graph hypothesis. Cognition **200**, 104276 (2020)
15. Erkelens, C.J.: Virtual slant explains perceived slant, distortion, and motion in pictorial scenes. Perception **42**(3), 253–270 (2013). https://doi.org/10.1068/p7328
16. Gillner, S., Mallot, H.A.: Navigation and acquisition of spatial knowledge in a virtual maze. J. Cogn. Neurosci. **10**(4), 445–463 (1998). https://doi.org/10.1162/089892998562861
17. Huttenlocher, J., Hedges, L.V., Duncan, S.: Categories and particulars: prototype effects in estimating spatial location. Psychol. Rev. **98**(3), 352–376 (1991). https://doi.org/10.1037/0033-295X.98.3.352
18. Kim, K.G., et al.: 3D Sketch Maps: concept, potential benefits, and challenges. In: Ishikawa, T., Fabrikant, S.I., Winter, S. (eds.) 15th International Conference on Spatial Information Theory (COSIT 2022). Leibniz International Proceedings in Informatics (LIPIcs), vol. 240, pp. 14:1–14:7. Schloss Dagstuhl – Leibniz-Zentrum für Informatik, Dagstuhl, Germany (2022). https://doi.org/10.4230/LIPIcs.COSIT.2022.14
19. Kim, K.G., Kwok, T.C., Zhong, S., Kiefer, P., Raubal, M.: Can You Sketch in 3D? Exploring perceived feasibility and use cases of 3D sketch mapping. LIPIcs, vol. 315, COSIT 2024 **315**, 3:1–3:17 (2024). https://doi.org/10.4230/LIPICS.COSIT.2024.3
20. Kim, M., Doeller, C.F.: Adaptive cognitive maps for curved surfaces in the 3D world. Cognition **225**, 105126 (2022). https://doi.org/10.1016/j.cognition.2022.105126
21. Li, H., Giudice, N.A.: Assessment of between-floor structural and topological properties on cognitive map development in multilevel built environments. Spatial Cognit. Comput. **18**(3), 138–172 (2018). https://doi.org/10.1080/13875868.2017.1384829
22. Li, H., Mavros, P., Krukar, J., Hölscher, C.: The effect of navigation method and visual display on distance perception in a large-scale virtual building. Cogn. Process. **22**(2), 239–259 (2021). https://doi.org/10.1007/s10339-020-01011-4
23. Lynch, K.: The Image of the City. MIT Press, Cambridge, Mass (1960)
24. Manley, E., Filomena, G., Mavros, P.: A spatial model of cognitive distance in cities. Int. J. Geogr. Inf. Sci. **35**(11), 2316–2338 (2021). https://doi.org/10.1080/13658816.2021.1887488

25. Montello, D.R.: A new framework for understanding the acquisition of spatial knowledge in large-scale environments. Spatial Temporal Reason. Geograph. Info. Syst. **1**, 143–154 (1998)
26. Mottet, M., Eccles, D.W., Saury, J.: Navigation in outdoor environments as an embodied, social, cultural, and situated experience: an empirical study of orienteering. Spatial Cogni. Comput. **16**(3), 220–243 (2016). https://doi.org/10.1080/13875868.2016.1166229
27. Pappalardo, L., Manley, E., Sekara, V., Alessandretti, L.: Future directions in human mobility science. Nat. Comput. Sci. **3**(7), 588–600 (2023). https://doi.org/10.1038/s43588-023-00469-4
28. Proffitt, D.R., Bhalla, M., Gossweiler, R., Midgett, J.: Perceiving geographical slant. Psych. Bulletin Rev. **2**(4), 409–428 (1995)
29. Proffitt, D.R., Creem, S.H., Zosh, W.D.: Seeing mountains in mole hills: geographical-slant perception. Psychol. Sci. **12**(5), 418–423 (2001). https://doi.org/10.1111/1467-9280.00377, pMID: 11554677
30. Proulx, M.J., Todorov, O.S., Taylor Aiken, A., de Sousa, A.A.: Where am i? who am i? The relation between spatial cognition, social cognition and individual differences in the built environment. Front. Psychol. **7**, 64 (2016). https://doi.org/10.3389/fpsyg.2016.00064
31. Renner, R.S., Velichkovsky, B.M., Helmert, J.R.: The perception of egocentric distances in virtual environments - a review. ACM Comput. Surv. **46**(2), 23:1–23:40 (2013). https://doi.org/10.1145/2543581.2543590
32. Richardson, A.E., Montello, D.R., Hegarty, M.: Spatial knowledge acquisition from maps and from navigation in real and virtual environments. Memory Cogn. **27**(4), 741–750 (1999). https://doi.org/10.3758/BF03211566
33. Sadalla, E., Burroughs, W., Staplin, L.: Reference points in spatial cognition. J. Experim. Psychol. Hum. Learn. Memory **6**, 516–28 (1980). https://doi.org/10.1037/0278-7393.6.5.516
34. Schultheis, H., Carlson, L.A.: Spatial reasoning. In: Reisberg, D. (ed.) The Oxford Handbook of Cognitive Psychology, pp. 719–732. Oxford University Press (2013). https://doi.org/10.1093/oxfordhb/9780195376746.013.0045
35. Schwering, A., Wang, J., Chipofya, M., Jan, S., Li, R., Broelemann, K.: SketchMapia: qualitative representations for the alignment of sketch and metric maps. Spatial Cognit. Comput. **14**(3), 220–254 (2014). https://doi.org/10.1080/13875868.2014.917378
36. Shaffer, D.M., Taylor, A., Thomas, A., Graves, P., Smith, E., McManama, E.: Pitching people with an inversion table. Attention Percept. Psychophys. **78**, 700–706 (2016). https://doi.org/10.3758/s13414-015-1019-x
37. Simonet, M., Vater, C., Abati, C., et al.: Probing mental representations of space through sketch mapping: a scoping review. Cognit. Res.: Principl. Impl. **10**, 59 (2025). https://doi.org/10.1186/s41235-025-00667-w
38. Stadler, J., Dugmore, C., Venables, E., MacPhail, C., Delany-Moretlwe, S.: Cognitive mapping: using local knowledge for planning health research. BMC Med. Res. Methodol. **13**, 96 (2013). https://doi.org/10.1186/1471-2288-13-96
39. Stefanucci, J.K., Proffitt, D.R., Clore, G.L., Parekh, N.: Skating down a steeper slope: fear influences the perception of geographical slant. Perception **37**(2), 321–323 (2008)
40. Tversky, B.: Cognitive maps, cognitive collages, and spatial mental models. LNCS **716/1993**, 14–24 (1993). https://doi.org/10.1007/3-540-57207-4_2

41. Xiao, T., et al.: Sketch2Terrain: AI-driven real-time terrain sketch mapping in augmented reality. In: Proceedings of the 2025 CHI Conference on Human Factors in Computing Systems, pp. 1–24 (2025)
42. Xiao, T., et al.: VResin: externalizing spatial memory into 3D sketch maps. Int. J. Hum Comput Stud. **190**, 103322 (2024). https://doi.org/10.1016/j.ijhcs.2024.103322
43. Xiao, T., Zhong, S., Kiefer, P., Mizuki, M., Toups Dugas, P.O., Raubal, M.: CoMap: a collaborative 3D sketch mapping game to engage spatial communication in search and rescue. In: Proceedings of the 2026 CHI Conference on Human Factors in Computing Systems, pp. 1–22 (2026)
44. Zisch, F.E., et al.: Real and virtual environments have comparable spatial memory distortions after scale and geometric transformations. Spatial Cognit. Comput. **24**(2), 115–143 (2024). https://doi.org/10.1080/13875868.2024.2303016

# Context-Aware Personalized Routing: Learning User Preferences Through Geographic Features

Leon Preusker(✉) and Mina Karimi(✉)

Department of Geography and Regional Research, University of Vienna, Vienna, Austria
a12244061@unet.univie.ac.at, mina.karimi@univie.ac.at

**Abstract.** The selection of routes in a road network is often determined by distance alone, particularly in route finding applications. However, humans rely on experience, familiarity, and implicit preferences when navigating space. In this study, we revisit personalized routing from a spatial cognitive perspective by examining how past movement patterns can be understood as expressions of cognitive spatial behavior. We address the cold start problem, where insufficient behavioral data limits model performance, by introducing geographic features into the Behavior-based Route Recommendation ($BR^2$) framework. In particular, we utilize Geographic Peer Frequencies (GPF), which transfer behavioral patterns between spatially similar road segments. We use two large-scale GPS trajectory datasets (Geolife and CyclePhilly) and features extracted from OpenStreetMap (OSM) to evaluate the influence of GPFs on route prediction. Our results show modest improvements in prediction accuracy, while also revealing trade-offs related to congestion and route diversity. Our framework thus demonstrates a data-driven method for capturing spatial generalization of preferences, bridging personalized routing with cognitive notions of spatial and environmental familiarity.

**Keywords:** Route Finding · Personalized Routing · Geographic Features · Spatial Cognition

## 1 Introduction

Routing is a task humans are faced with every day and requires their full attention in an unfamiliar place. About 20–25% of destinations are places that a person has never visited before, and a person visits about four new places per week [10]. Humans do not always choose the shortest path. Instead, their navigation is shaped by familiarity, habits, and subjective preferences that emerge over time. These behaviors reflect underlying cognitive processes that structure how people perceive, remember, and use space. For example, cyclists usually take routes, which are on average longer than the shortest path [21] to ride on bicycle


E. Farran et al. (Eds.): Spatial Cognition 2026, LNAI 16785, pp. 92–107, 2027.
https://doi.org/10.1007/978-3-032-36716-7_7

paths and through green spaces or avoid main roads with traffic [34], noise pollution, or steep roads. In addition, land use and time of day have a significant impact on Pedestrians' route choice [5].

Traditional routing algorithms mostly consider objective criteria such as distance or travel time, often ignoring user preferences and experiences. Personalized routing addresses this limitation by incorporating preferences derived from historical movement data. Major navigation providers still use traditional routing algorithms such as Dijkstra and A* as well as real-time traffic data to detect congestion and do not provide personalized routing to any significant degree. Personalized routing is usually based on two types of human feedback, explicit and implicit [20]. In explicit feedback, users directly provide the preferences through a menu option, survey, or rating. While in implicit feedback, user behavior is simply observed and information is derived from it. In the context of routing, user's previously taken routes are the implicit feedback. In this approach, the amount of available feedback is much larger and the mathematical model has greater potential to capture the many preferences of users.

This paper revisits personalized routing from a spatial cognition perspective by treating users' historical movements as representations of latent cognitive maps of the road network. Specifically, we build on the Behavior-based Route Recommendation ($BR^2$) framework [32], which models each user's travel history as frequencies of behavior patterns and applies an implicit-feedback matrix approach to predict missing behaviors via Random Walk with Restart (RWR) [25]. We extend $\mathrm{BR}^2$ by introducing Geographic Peer Frequencies (GPF). When a user has no observed data for a given segment, we infer their likely behavior frequency from geographically similar segments (e.g., similar road type, slope, or surrounding land use). From a cognitive perspective, this approach captures how users generalize spatial preferences to unfamiliar but analogous parts of the road network. **The main contributions of this study are fourfold:**

- We expand the ($BR^2$) framework for personalized routing by considering the user's behavior frequencies that integrates geographic feature similarity to mitigate the item cold-start problem.
- We introduce the GPF as a proxy to use the existing behavior frequencies of geographically similar road segments for computing and smoothing usersegment frequencies.
- We test our framework on large-scale GPS datasets: Geolife and CyclePhilly, which they are treated separately.
- We consider several techniques and various combinations of geographic properties to calculate the GPF and evaluate results using precision, recall, congestion, diversion.

The remainder of this study is structured as follows: In Sect. 2, we review the literature and the background methods in personalized route finding. In Sect. 3 we introduce our framework. Section 4 presents the results of our analysis. Section 5 discusses our findings and limitations. Finally, we conclude the study in Sect. 6.

# 2 Background

## 2.1 Literature

The most well-known routing method is Dijkstra's algorithm, which finds the path between a start and destination in a weighted graph such that the total cost is minimized. These weights can represent distance, travel time, or other quantities, while in our framework they are derived from learned behavior rather than physical measures [14]. Another important algorithm is A*, an extension of Dijkstra that uses heuristics to speed up the search [22]. For large-scale road networks, which can contain millions of nodes and edges [30], more advanced methods such as Transit Node Routing have been developed to improve efficiency by exploiting the hierarchical structure of roads [4]. These approaches work with a graph, which differs from public transport systems that are schedule-based and better modeled as timetables rather than networks [3]. In such cases, specialized methods such as RAPTOR are used [13]. However, they are general route finding algorithms and do not incorporate users' preferences.

[18] developed a new bicycle routing algorithm by defining four criteria including travel time, comfort, quietness, and flatness. Each road segment has a value for these as well as a weight profile for each user, determining how much each criteria matter to them. Then, Djikstra is used for the actual routing. These four criteria were considered the important ones for cycling and others (like number of traffic lights) ignored. Later, this framework was expanded to support true multicriteria routing [19]. Instead of combining different criteria into a single weight, multicriteria routing aims to optimize several criteria simultaneously. This problem is often addressed using the Multi-Criteria Label-Setting (MLS) algorithm [24], an extension of Dijkstra that produces a set of Pareto-optimal routes. Each route in this set is optimal in at least one criterion compared to all others, which allows users to choose based on their preferences. However, this approach requires users to actively select a route each time and does not learn from their behavior, and the choice of criteria still depends on assumptions made by the researchers.

Early research on implicit feedback in routing relied on how to learn user preferences without directly changing how routes are generated. For example, several alternative routes are suggested to users, and their choices based on features such as travel time, distance, and familiarity are used to update a decision tree [27]. However, it is limited to a fixed set of predefined features and does not truly personalize the routes. Other frameworks, such as TURAS [25], rely on connecting segments from a user's past trips, which makes them simple and intuitive but unable to generalize well to unfamiliar areas. Extensions such as CCBR [16] attempt to address this by borrowing information from similar users, but the main idea is based on recombining existing trajectories rather than learning deeper behavioral patterns.

With the availability of GPS trajectory data, more advanced methods began to model user behavior directly from movement traces. The TRIP framework [23], for instance, introduces an inefficiency ratio to show users' willingness to deviate from the shortest path. Later work [11] models preferences using distributions over multiple criteria such as time and fuel consumption. More recent approaches, such as [8,9], move closer to the idea behind the $BR^2$ framework by estimating preferences at the level of individual road segments through appearance and transition behaviors. These methods represent a shift toward viewing routing as a probabilistic and behavior-driven problem. However, they still face limitations, particularly in handling unseen parts of the network and incorporating geographic context. Our work builds on this line of research by extending the $BR^2$ framework and explicitly addressing these gaps, especially the cold start problem. To our knowledge, no prior work solves the cold start problem in personalized routing using geographic features of road segments. This study contributes to improving personalized routing under incomplete data and to better integrating geographic information into such frameworks.

### 2.2 The $BR^2$ Framework for Personalized Routing

The core idea of $BR^2$ is to treat personalized routing like a recommendation system. A recommendation system consists of a set of users and a set of items. Some users have rated some of these items, and the system tries to find good recommendations based on these ratings. Recommendation systems are divided into content-based approaches and collaborative filtering approaches. The former suggests items similar to items that a user already liked, while the latter recommend items liked by other users with similar history of behavior (e.g., ratings, appearances, purchase history) [1]. Collaborative filtering does not depend on domain-specific similarity measures, which makes it flexible across applications. However, it deals with the cold start problem, where items with no interaction history cannot be recommended. Hence, hybrid systems were developed. Our framework follows a similar idea: we primarily use collaborative (implicit) feedback via RWR, but when it cannot predict a user's behavior for a segment, we fall back on a content-based strategy by averaging frequencies of geographic peers (segments similar in features).

The items of the recommendation system in the $BR^2$ case are the behaviors, of which there are two kinds. An *appearance behavior* describes if a user has been at a certain road segment, a *transition behavior* if they have transitioned from one segment to an adjacent one. Both types of behaviors also include time of day. The ratings are the *behavior frequencies* (how often a user is associated with a behavior). The behaviors and behavior frequencies encode the movement patterns of users. These behavior frequencies are extracted from a set of GPS trajectories tracking users movements through the road network.

After counting all behavior frequencies based on a dataset of users and GPS trajectories, most frequencies will still be 0, since most users will not have visited all parts of the road network at all parts of the day. Even if a complete dataset of all user movements would be available, a user should also be recommended good routes in parts of the road network they have actually never been before. The "recommendation" of the $BR^2$ framework is to predict the missing behavior frequencies. The RWR algorithm is used for this. The RWR algorithm is a collaborative filtering method that represents the relationships between users and items through a graph structure [31]. It suffers from the cold start problem.

### 2.3 Cold Start Problem

The cold start problem refers to the difficulty of making recommendations without an initial set of ratings [6]. It is typically divided into two types: user cold start and item cold start [35]. Content-based systems can often handle new items through their attributes, while collaborative approaches struggle when no prior interaction data exists. This issue is often addressed by integrating additional information, such as user profiles or initial feedback. For example, some methods cluster users based on demographic or behavioral attributes and recommend items that are popular within the groups [26], while other methods use active learning approaches that ask new users to provide initial ratings [12]. However, these approaches may not always be practical since they depend on the availability and reliability of external information.

In personalized routing, most existing work has focused on the user cold start problem. Frameworks such as FAVOUR [7] address this by collecting initial user preferences through questionnaires and simple route comparisons. This allows the system to estimate an initial preference model that is later refined through observed choices. Follow-up work further improves this by clustering users using latent class models [29]. However, these approaches still rely on explicit input and do not personalize the routing process itself, but rather the ranking of predefined routes. In contrast, the item cold start problem, such as unseen road segments, has received little attention in the literature, which is where this work aims to contribute. In our case, some behaviors $b_i$ may not be associated with any user, meaning certain road segments have never been visited. As a result, RWR assigns a frequency of 0 to these behaviors for all users, preventing them from being recommended. While this could indicate undesirable segments, it is more likely due to incomplete data, as many movement datasets contain sparsely observed regions. To address zero frequencies, the $BR^2$ framework applies Laplace smoothing with a parameter $\alpha$. However, this assigns the same small value to all unseen segments, which is not ideal. We therefore aim to improve the model by more effectively addressing the cold start problem in personalized routing.

### 2.4 Congestion and Diversion

Congestion can be understood and measured in different ways, depending on whether one focuses on real-time traffic conditions or patterns derived from historical data. Some studies use detailed GPS traces to identify congestion zones by comparing observed speeds to free-flow conditions across time and space, which is useful for urban planning but relatively complex [15]. Simpler measures such as the Gini coefficient [33] show uneven distribution of travel times among users, which indicates congestion through inequality. In our setting, however, the goal is slightly different: rather than measuring actual travel delays, we are interested in how routing recommendations distribute users across the network. This can be seen as a question of road segment utilization—whether traffic is concentrated on a few segments or spread more evenly. Since we do not have real-time traffic data, we adopt a simplified approach inspired by the Gini coefficient to evaluate how balanced the usage of the network is. Related work has also explored optimizing traffic distribution directly by minimizing the maximum load on any road segment [2] or by generating diverse alternative routes to reduce overlap [17], both of which point to possible extensions of our framework.

# 3 Methodology

This section present our framework, including the datasets, prepossessing, and methodology. Our goal is to compute, for each user $u$ and each road segment $e$, an estimated behavior frequency $f(u, b)$ for every behavior $b$ (appearance or transition), reflecting how often $u$ performs $b$. Based on these estimates, we derive behavior probabilities and ultimately generate personalized routes. The overall approach consists of the steps illustrated in Fig. 1.

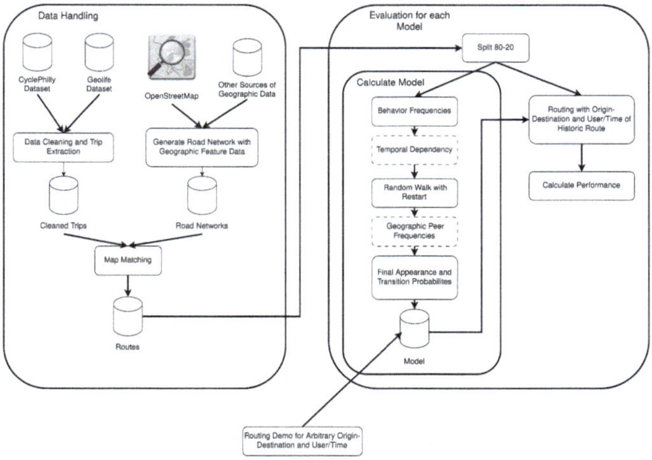


**Fig. 1.** The structure of our framework.

## 3.1 Datasets

The analysis is based on two large-scale GPS trajectory datasets: Geolife and CyclePhilly. Geolife contains GPS trajectories in Beijing, while CyclePhilly contains bicycle trips in Philadelphia. Both datasets require substantial preprocessing before being used within this framework. They are imbalanced, with some users having significantly more trajectories than others. We remove the bottom 10% of users (all with only one trajectory), as well as the top 4 users in Geolife and the top user in CyclePhilly (who accounts for half of the trajectories).

The road network is created by converting OSM nodes and ways into a navigable graph using `NetworkX` via the `OSMnx` Python library. An overview of the datasets is provided in Table 1. Geolife contains GPS tracks of 182 users (mostly drivers) over several years, resulting in about 110,000 trajectories. The road network of central Beijing consists of 98,759 road segments and 43,302 vertices. CyclePhilly comprises bike trips from 300 users in Philadelphia, with a network of 178,093 segments and 71,447 nodes.

Next, we apply map matching to align cleaned GPS trajectories with the road network. For both datasets, we split each user's trips into a training set (80%) and a validation set (20%). We then enrich each road segment with OSM attributes, including road class (motorway, primary, residential, etc.), presence of bike lanes, surface type, speed limit, and traffic lights. We also extract surrounding OSM features within a 200 m buffer to determine whether segments pass near water or green spaces. Finally, for CyclePhilly, the features are further enriched with Open Government Data from the *PennDOT Spatial Data Portal*[1], which provides elevation data. The list of geographic features is shown in Table 2. These features form the basis for defining geographic similarity (i.e., the GPFs) between segments.

**Table 1.** Data overview.

| Dataset | Users | Trajectories | Segments | Graph vertices |
|---|---|---|---|---|
| Geolife | 182 | 110,000 | 98,759 | 43,302 |
| CyclePhilly | 300 | 11,000 | 178,093 | 71,447 |

### 3.2 Proposed Approach

The first step is behavior extraction. From the training GPS data matched to the road network, we identify all appearance behaviors $b = (e, t)$, meaning that user $u$ visited segment $e$ during hour $t \in \{0, \ldots, 23\}$. We count the frequency $f(u, b)$ for each $u$. Similarly, transition behaviors $b_{e \to e'} = ((e, e'), t)$ represent moving from segment $e$ to an adjacent segment $e'$ at time $t$. These counts form a sparse user-behavior matrix $UB$. For example, the CyclePhilly $UB$ matrix has a usual sparsity of 99.98%. The $UB$ matrix can also be represented as a bipartite graph with user nodes on one side and behavior nodes on the other (appearance and transition), where an edge $(u, b)$ has weight $f(u, b)$. The RWR iteratively propagates user preferences over this graph; an optimized version called the Optimized Random Walk with Restart is used due to spacial and time complexity

[1] https://data-pennshare.opendata.arcgis.com.

improvements [28]. The output is an estimated frequency $\widehat{f}(u, b)$ for almost every user-behavior pair, including unseen ones. The RWR only fails if a behavior node has no connection to any user node, or a user node has no connection to any behavior node, which are the item and user cold start problem respectively. An equivalent formulation is to say a column of the $UB$ matrix consists of all zeros (item cold start) or a row of the $UB$ matrix consists of all zeros (user cold start). The GPFs alleviate the item cold start problem.

**Table 2.** Geographic Attributes of Road Segments

| CyclePhilly | | Geolife | |
|---|---|---|---|
| Name | Meaning | Name | Meaning |
| *bi_inf* | Bicycle Infrastructure | *highway* | Road type |
| *highway* | Road type | *green* | Adjacent Green Space |
| *green* | Adjacent Green Space | *water* | Adjacent Water Space |
| *water* | Adjacent Water Space | *trafSignal* | Traffic Signal |
| *surface* | Surface Type | | |
| *trafSignal* | Traffic Signal | | |
| *traffic_calming* | Traffic calming measures | | |
| *slope* | Slope | | |

For an edge $e$, let $N(e)$ be the set of geographic peer segments, i.e. a set of the geographically most similar segments, based on a feature vector of the geographic attributes listed in Table 2. Two road segments are geographically similar if their attribute values are equal. Let $N'(e)$ be the set of all geographically similar road segments of $e$. To find $N(e)$ from $N'(e)$, we considered four different methods described in Table 3: closest distance, $k$-nearest neighbors (by Euclidean distance in feature space) or density-based clustering (DBSCAN/OPTICS). For any behavior $b_e$ where $\forall u \in U : \widehat{f}(u, b_e) = 0$, we estimate:

$$\widehat{f}_{\mathrm{GPF}}(u, b_e) = \frac{1}{(d(e, N(e)) + 1)^2} \cdot \frac{1}{|N(e)|} \cdot \sum_{e' \in N(e)} \widehat{f}(u, b_{e'}) \tag{1}$$

where $d(e, N(e))$ is the distance measure between $e$ and its peer segments $N(e)$ (in meters), which depends on the method used and is listed in Table 3. The process works similar for transition behaviors: for $b_{e \to e'}$, we consider the geographic features of both adjacent road segments and find $N(e, e')$, finding similar adjacent road segment pairs. Since distance measures are well defined on points, we consider the *centroid* of a road segment as it's geographical representation. A transition is represented by the point where the two segments touch. Let $d_\epsilon(a, b)$ be the euclidean distance between two points. Let $e_c$ be the centroid of road segment $e$ and $\zeta_c$ be the centroid of a cluster $\zeta$. Table 3 now gives the techniques for calculating the GPF.

**Table 3.** Techniques for calculating the GPF

| Name | $N(e)$ | $d(e, N(e))$ |
|---|---|---|
| *nearest* | $N(e) = e' \in N'(e)$ so that $d_\epsilon(e_c, e'_c)$ minimal. | $d_\epsilon(e_c, e'_c)$ |
| *kNN* | $N(e) = \{k$ closest $e'$ to $e$ for $e' \in N'(e)\}$ | $d_\epsilon(e_c, N(e)_c)$ |
| *DBSCAN* | $N(e) = \zeta \in DBSCAN(N'(e))$ so that $d_\epsilon(e_c, \zeta_c)$ minimal. | $d_\epsilon(e_c, \zeta_c)$ |
| *OPTICS* | Same as above, but with OPTICS. | Same as above. |

In summary, a user's frequency for $b_e$ or $b_{e \to e'}$ is found by averaging their frequencies on similar segments, analogous to content-based inference in recommender systems. Parameters (e.g., $k$ or distance thresholds) are tuned experimentally. Then, we convert all frequencies into probabilities with Laplace smoothing, as in $BR^2$. These probabilities indicate how likely $u$ is to visit segments or move between adjacent segments at each time. For each user $u$, appearance behavior $b_{e_i}$ and set of all appearance behaviors $B_a$:

$$P(b_{e_i}|u) = \frac{\widehat{f}(u, b_{e_i}) + \alpha}{\sum_{b \in B_a} \widehat{f}(u, b) + |B_a| \cdot \alpha} \tag{2}$$

where $\alpha$ is a small smoothing parameter. If there is still a $\widehat{f}(u, b) = 0$ (after GPF), we assign $\alpha$ to avoid zero probabilities. For transition behaviors:

$$P(b_{e_i \to e_j}|u) = \frac{\widehat{f}(u, b_{e_i \to e_j}) + \alpha}{\sum_{k=1}^{m} \widehat{f}(u, b_{e_i \to e_k}) + m \cdot \alpha} \tag{3}$$

where $m$ is the number of possible transitions from road segment $e_i$. The final edge weight is defined as:

$$w_{u,b} = -ln(P(b|u)) \tag{4}$$

Since a transition behavior weight represents the probability of going from one edge to an adjacent one, we cannot use these with the normal road network $G$ because there, the weights lie on the edges. Routing is done on the linegraph $L(G)$ of $G$. In $L(G)$, every edge in $G$ becomes a node and two nodes are connected by an edge if the respective edges in $G$ share a node (i.e., are connected). So, every edge in $L(G)$ represents a transition between edges in $G$, and these edges take the respective weights of the transition behaviors.

For a routing query $(u, o, d, t)$ (user, origin, destination, departure time), we first insert all transition behavior weights for $u$ and $t$ into $L(G)$. We then insert the special nodes $o$ and $d$ into $L(G)$. $o$ is connected to every node in $L(G)$ that was an edge $(o, w)$ in $G$, and every node in $L(G)$ that was an edge $(v, d)$ in $G$ is connected to $d$. These new edges from $o$ and to $d$ are given the appearance behavior weights of edges $(o, w)$ and $(v, d)$. Then Dijkstra finds the minimum-cost path from $o$ to $d$. The resulting path is the personalized recommended route from $o$ to $d$ for user $u$.

### 3.3 Evaluation Metrics

Precision and recall are standard measures of model performance. Consider a user $u_1$ whose route is contained in the dataset. The recommended route should closely match the actual route, as it is assumed to reflect the user's preferences. We evaluate this similarity using precision and recall, which measure how well the algorithm reproduces observed behavior. Precision compares the number of correct predictions to the total number of predicted instances, while recall compares the number of correct predictions to the total number of relevant instances. The comparison between the recommended and actual route can be conducted either by total length or segment by segment. In [32], these measures are defined as follows:

$$Precision_{Segments} = P_S = \frac{S_o}{S_r} \quad \text{and} \quad Precision_{Distance} = P_D = \frac{L_o}{L_r} \tag{5}$$

$$Recall_{Segments} = R_S = \frac{S_o}{S_a} \quad \text{and} \quad Recall_{Distance} = R_D = \frac{L_o}{L_a} \tag{6}$$

where $S_o$ is the number of overlapping segments between the recommended and actual routes. $S_r$ and $S_a$ denote the total number of segments in the recommended and actual routes. Similarly, $L_o$ is the total length of overlapping segments, and $L_r$ and $L_a$ denote the total lengths of the routes.

Beyond accuracy, we examine two additional aspects of personalized routing: congestion and diversion. Congestion reflects how traffic is distributed across the network. If many users are guided along the same roads, traffic jams may occur, especially when a navigation system is widely used. We therefore investigate whether personalized routing alleviates or exacerbates congestion. For this purpose, we assume all recommended routes are taken simultaneously. Each road segment is then associated with the number of routes passing through it; the more uneven this distribution, the higher the congestion. We quantify this imbalance using the Gini coefficient. The second aspect concerns detours. The goal of this framework is not to recommend the shortest path, as observed routes are assumed acceptable to users. However, if a recommended route is significantly longer than the actual route, this becomes problematic. We therefore define a detour as a substantial deviation in length from the true route. While related to low precision, the average detour length (i.e., the mean difference in length between recommended and actual routes) provides an additional useful metric.

# 4 Results

In this section, we present the result of our framework. The evaluation results are shown in Tables 4 and 5, which have been collected over 5 trials. Different parameters were also tried for the four methods of calculating the GPF, the ones listed in the tables are representative and lead to the best results in case of

**Table 4.** The results for the CyclePhilly dataset.

| | Precision | | Recall | | Gini | | Diversion |
|---|---|---|---|---|---|---|---|
| | Seg. | Dist. | Seg. | Dist. | All RS | Used RS | |
| Only RWR ($\epsilon = 5^{-5}$, $p = 0.5$) | 0.743 | 0.744 | 0.728 | 0.728 | 0.979 | 0.658 | 68.83 |
| + Nearest | **0.746** | **0.748** | 0.728 | **0.730** | 0.980 | 0.665 | 131.74 |
| + KN ($k = 10$) | 0.624 | 0.623 | 0.662 | 0.659 | **0.977** | **0.648** | −312.24 |
| + DBSCAN ($\varepsilon = 100$, $min = 5$) | **0.744** | **0.745** | **0.729** | **0.729** | 0.979 | 0.661 | 70.39 |
| + OPTICS ($min = 5$) | **0.744** | **0.745** | **0.730** | **0.730** | 0.979 | 0.661 | 93.96 |
| + temporal dep. ($t = 2$) | 0.733 | 0.733 | 0.723 | 0.723 | 0.978 | 0.648 | −12.14 |
| + temporal dep. ($t = 4$) | 0.748 | 0.749 | 0.737 | 0.737 | 0.978 | 0.648 | −7.85 |
| + temporal dep. ($t = 6$) | 0.744 | 0.743 | 0.734 | 0.734 | 0.978 | 0.648 | −18.49 |
| + Shortest Path | 0.484 | 0.488 | 0.428 | 0.434 | 0.979 | 0.650 | 1062.76 |

DBSCAN and OPTICS. For KN, higher $k$ leads to worse results. Numbers in bold are cases when the GPF improve on the RWR.

We can observe that adding the GPF improves precision and recall of the algorithm in some cases. In particular, the Nearest method gives the best overall improvement, improving both precision and recall. Although, the improvements are consistent across both cases and multiple trials, they remain small (in the range of 0.4%). Since the Nearest method has the advantage of being parameter-free and the least computationally intensive, and the model only has to be calculated once, this improvement might still be worth implementing, especially as it appears to improve precision more than recall. DBSCAN and OPTICS lead not only to improvements in the Philadelphia case, but also never worsen performance compared to the pure RWR model. Interestingly, KN performs worse than the pure RWR and deteriorates further for higher values of $k$.

A lower Gini coefficient indicates lower congestion. Contrary to our expectations, personalized routing does not reduce congestion but slightly worsens it, as seen more clearly when considering only non-empty road segments. Congestion increases by up to 1% in Philadelphia and up to 3% in Beijing. If many users are routed along the same small set of roads, personalized routing may lead to a less balanced distribution than shortest-path routing. It is also notable that adding GPF slightly worsens congestion compared to the standard RWR. The only method that reduces congestion compared to RWR is KN, which also performs worse in terms of precision and recall. This supports the idea that personalization and congestion may be in conflict.

In Philadelphia, diversion fluctuates between positive and negative values but mostly remains within ±100 m. In contrast, the shortest path is on average 1000 m shorter than the true route. The diversion produced by our models is therefore much smaller in magnitude. The only notable negative outlier is KN, where the recommended route is on average about 300m longer than the true route, which coincides with its lower precision and recall. In Beijing, all models

**Table 5.** The results for the GeoLife dataset. Routes with transport labels car and None were considered.

| | Precision | | Recall | | Gini | | Diversion |
|---|---|---|---|---|---|---|---|
| | Seg. | Dist. | Seg. | Dist. | All RS | Used RS | |
| Only RWR ($\epsilon = 5^{-5}$, $p = 0.5$) | 0.875 | 0.882 | 0.690 | 0.697 | 0.922 | 0.627 | 993.48 |
| + Nearest | **0.879** | **0.885** | **0.691** | **0.698** | 0.925 | 0.630 | 1036.71 |
| + KN ($k = 10$) | 0.657 | 0.692 | 0.630 | 0.634 | **0.914** | 0.633 | 769.14 |
| + DBSCAN ($\varepsilon = 100$,$min = 5$) | 0.875 | 0.882 | 0.690 | 0.697 | 0.922 | 0.627 | 997.86 |
| + OPTICS ($min = 5$) | 0.875 | 0.882 | 0.690 | 0.697 | 0.923 | 0.628 | 1002.20 |
| + temporal dep. ($t = 2$) | 0.864 | 0.872 | 0.686 | 0.693 | 0.917 | 0.624 | 932.26 |
| + temporal dep. ($t = 4$) | 0.870 | 0.877 | 0.689 | 0.696 | 0.919 | 0.624 | 964.03 |
| + temporal dep. ($t = 6$) | 0.871 | 0.879 | 0.690 | 0.697 | 0.919 | 0.625 | 976.19 |
| + Shortest Path | 0.842 | 0.851 | 0.609 | 0.612 | 0.918 | 0.605 | 1164.44 |

produce routes that are about 1000m shorter than the true route. This aligns with precision being consistently higher than recall across all models.

Precision and Recall measure the accuracy of a model, but even high precision and recall can sometimes produce unsatisfying results. A visual inspection of recommended routes was also conducted to spot imperfect behaviors. Figure 2 shows an example of querying for the same origin destination nodes but different users showing distinctly different recommended routes.

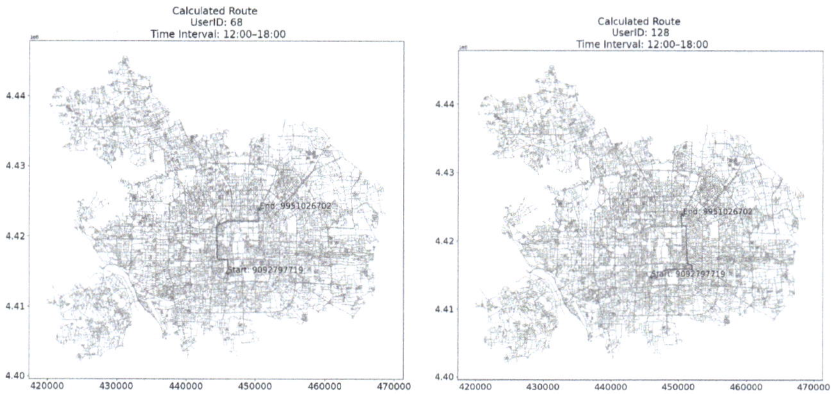


(a) Route of User 68.

(b) Route of User 128.

**Fig. 2.** Route finding in Beijing at time 12:00–18:00.

However, behavior as seen in Fig. 3 was also observed occasionally. It occurs because Dijkstra's algorithm is applied to the line graph $L(G)$, where the weights are transition probabilities. If the combined transition probabilities $a \rightarrow b$, $b \rightarrow c$, and $c \rightarrow d$ are lower than the direct transition probability $a \rightarrow d$, such minor diversions occur. This is an inherent issue with transition probabilities as used in [32]. It does not significantly affect precision and recall, as these phenomena are usually small "appendixes", but it would impact real-world navigation usage of the framework. Improving the algorithm in this regard would be an interesting area for future research.

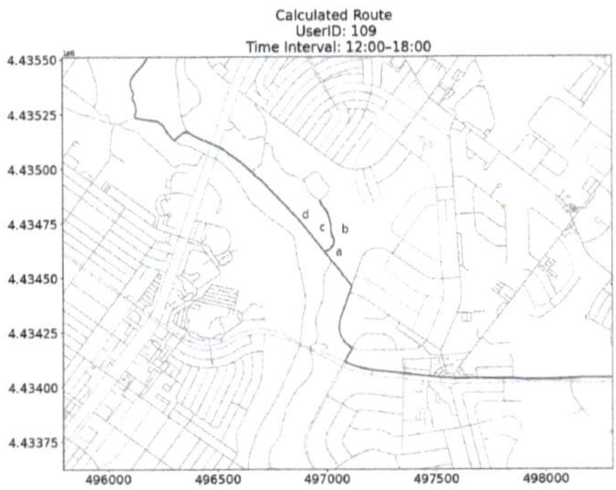


**Fig. 3.** A route with a strange diversion at the labeled road segments $a, b, c, d$.

## 5 Discussion

The results show incorporating geographic similarity into the $BR^2$ model slightly increases the accuracy and users' personalized routes align better with actual behavior. This supports the intuition that people generalize their spatial preferences: a cyclist who likes a neighborhood street may also like a similar unvisited street. The GPF method provides a principled way to approximate that generalization from data. However, these benefits come with trade-offs. The higher Gini index for $BR^2$+GPF indicates more concentrated traffic patterns: by aligning each user's route more closely with typical usage, the model increases route overlap. While this is consistent with spatial cognition theories in which familiar routes become more popular, it also highlights the need for diversity-aware extensions in the case of urban congestion. One possible extension is to introduce a diversity objective, for example by penalizing high-use segments [16] or incorporating surprise/diversity mechanisms (e.g., TANGENT) during route selection [22].

From a spatial cognition perspective, these findings are reasonable. Cognitive map theory suggests people rely on salient features (e.g. road type, scenery) to infer unfamiliar routes. Our method mimics this by using segment features. However, human navigators might also consider the risk of congestion or novelty.

Future models could introduce a "surprise" factor (favoring less-used alternatives).

One limitation of this study is the reliance on historical, static data and fixed graph. Real-world routing systems typically incorporate live congestion information and dynamically reroute users away from congested areas. Our framework could be extended with a dynamic layer that downweights heavily used roads in real time. Another limitation is that OSM-derived features serve only as a coarse proxy for cognitive similarity. Future work could incorporate richer semantic information, such as landmarks or points of interest, or learned embeddings from street-level imagery to better capture how users perceive roads. Finally, while this study focuses on user–segment cold-start scenarios, similar ideas could be extended to user-level cold start by clustering similar users, as in approaches such as FAVOUR [7].

## 6 Conclusion

We have presented a personalized routing framework that uses both behavior frequencies and geographic similarity. By interpreting past GPS trajectories through the $BR^2$ framework, and filling gaps through Geographic Peer Frequencies, our method strikes a balance between data-driven personalization and cognitive plausibility. Experiments on diverse datasets confirm that geographic context can modestly improve route prediction accuracy, at the cost of greater route overlap. This work opened a new avenue for richer models of how people generalize spatial knowledge, in particular personalized route finding, by incorporating spatial cognition ideas into computational recommendation techniques. Future work can focus on integrating semantic features and real-time feedback for optimizing routes for both personal and societal outcomes (e.g. congestion).

**Disclosure of Interests.** The authors have no competing interests to declare.

## References


1. Adomavicius, G., Tuzhilin, A.: Toward the next generation of recommender systems: a survey of the state-of-the-art and possible extensions. IEEE Trans. Knowl. Data Eng. **17**(6), 734–749 (2005). https://doi.org/10.1109/TKDE.2005.99
2. Angelelli, E., Arsik, I., Morandi, V., Savelsbergh, M., Speranza, M.: Proactive route guidance to avoid congestion. Transp. Res. Part B: Methodol. **94**, 1–21 (2016). https://doi.org/10.1016/j.trb.2016.08.015
3. Bast, H., et al.: Route planning in transportation networks (2015). https://arxiv.org/abs/1504.05140
4. Bast, H., Funke, S., Sanders, P., Schultes, D.: Fast routing in road networks with transit nodes. Science **316**(5824), 566–566 (2007). https://doi.org/10.1126/science.1137521
5. Basu, N., Oviedo-Trespalacios, O., King, M., Kamruzzaman, M., Haque, M.: What do pedestrians consider when choosing a route? The role of safety, security, and attractiveness perceptions and the built environment during day and night walking. Cities **143** (2023). https://doi.org/10.1016/j.cities.2023.104551

6. Bobadilla, J., Ortega, F., Hernando, A., Gutiérrez, A.: Recommender systems survey. Knowl.-Based Syst. **46**, 109–132 (2013). https://doi.org/10.1016/j.knosys.2013.03.012
7. Campigotto, P., Rudloff, C., Leodolter, M., Bauer, D.: Personalized and situation-aware multimodal route recommendations: the favour algorithm. IEEE Trans. Intell. Transp. Syst. **18**(1), 92–102 (2017). https://doi.org/10.1109/TITS.2016.2565643
8. Cui, G., Luo, J., Wang, X.: Personalized travel route recommendation using collaborative filtering based on GPS trajectories. Int. J. Digit. Earth **11**, 1–24 (2017). https://doi.org/10.1080/17538947.2017.1326535
9. Cui, G., Wang, X.: Map2R: a personalized maximum probability route recommendation method using GPS trajectories, pp. 168–180 (2017). https://doi.org/10.1007/978-3-319-57529-2_14
10. Cuttone, A., Lehmann, S., González, M.C.: Understanding predictability and exploration in human mobility (2016). https://arxiv.org/abs/1608.01939
11. Dai, J., Yang, B., Guo, C., Ding, Z.: Personalized route recommendation using big trajectory data. In: 2015 IEEE 31st International Conference on Data Engineering, pp. 543–554 (2015). https://doi.org/10.1109/ICDE.2015.7113313
12. De Pessemier, T., Willems, B., Martens, L.: Active learning algorithm for alleviating the user cold start problem of recommender systems. Sci. Rep. **15** (2025). https://doi.org/10.1038/s41598-025-09708-2
13. Delling, D., Pajor, T., Werneck, R.: Round-based public transit routing. Transp. Sci. **49** (2012). https://doi.org/10.1287/trsc.2014.0534
14. Dijkstra, E.W.: A note on two problems in connexion with graphs. Numer. Math. **1**, 269–271 (1959). https://doi.org/10.1007/BF01386390
15. Erdelić, T., Carić, T., Erdelić, M., Tišljarić, L., Turković, A., Jelušić, N.: Estimating congestion zones and travel time indexes based on the floating car data. Comput. Environ. Urban Syst. **87**, 101604 (2021). https://doi.org/10.1016/j.compenvurbsys.2021.101604
16. Ginty, L.M., Smyth, B.: Collaborative case-based reasoning: applications in personalised route planning. In: Aha, D.W., Watson, I. (eds.) ICCBR 2001. LNCS (LNAI), vol. 2080, pp. 362–376. Springer, Heidelberg (2001). https://doi.org/10.1007/3-540-44593-5_26
17. Häcker, C., Bouros, P., Chondrogiannis, T., Althaus, E.: Most diverse near-shortest paths. SIGSPATIAL '21, pp. 229–239. Association for Computing Machinery, New York, NY, USA (2021). https://doi.org/10.1145/3474717.3483955
18. Hrncir, J., Song, Q., Zilecky, P., Nemet, M., Jakob, M.: Bicycle route planning with route choice preferences, vol. 263 (2014). https://doi.org/10.3233/978-1-61499-419-0-1149
19. Hrnčíř, J., Žilecký, P., Song, Q., Jakob, M.: Practical multicriteria urban bicycle routing. IEEE Trans. Intell. Transp. Syst. **18**(3), 493–504 (2017). https://doi.org/10.1109/TITS.2016.2577047
20. Hu, Y., Koren, Y., Volinsky, C.: Collaborative filtering for implicit feedback datasets, pp. 263–272 (2008). https://doi.org/10.1109/ICDM.2008.22
21. Krenn, P., Oja, P., Titze, S.: Route choices of transport bicyclists: a comparison of actually used and shortest routes. Int. J. Behav. Nutr. Phys. Activity **11**, 31 (2014). https://doi.org/10.1186/1479-5868-11-31
22. Kuznetsov, O.: The A* algorithm. In: Intelligent Systems: From Theory to Applications. Cognitive Technologies, pp. 167–188. Springer, Cham (2026). https://doi.org/10.1007/978-3-032-00044-6_8

23. Letchner, J., Krumm, J., Horvitz, E.: Trip Router with Individualized Preferences (TRIP): Incorporating Personalization into Route Planning, vol. 2 (2006)
24. Martins, E.Q.V.: On a multicriteria shortest path problem. Eur. J. Oper. Res. **16**(2), 236–245 (1984). https://doi.org/10.1016/0377-2217(84)90077-8
25. McGinty, L., Smyth, B.: Personalised route planning: a case-based approach. In: Blanzieri, E., Portinale, L. (eds.) EWCBR 2000. LNCS, vol. 1898, pp. 431–443. Springer, Heidelberg (2000). https://doi.org/10.1007/3-540-44527-7_37
26. Panteli, A., Boutsinas, B.: Addressing the cold-start problem in recommender systems based on frequent patterns. Algorithms **16**(4) (2023). https://doi.org/10.3390/a16040182
27. Park, K., Bell, M., Kaparias, I., Bogenberger, K.: Learning user preferences of route choice behaviour for adaptive route guidance. IET Intel. Transp. Syst. **1**, 159–166 (2007)
28. Rahimi, S.M., de Oliveira e Silva, R.A., Far, B., Wang, X.: Optimized random walk with restart for recommendation systems. In: Meurs, M.J., Rudzicz, F. (eds.) Advances in Artificial Intelligence, pp. 320–332. Springer, Cham (2019)
29. Rudloff, C., Leodolter, M.: Personalization of routing services – user classification as a method to overcome the cold start problem for personalized models. Transp. Res. Rec. J. Transp. Res. Board **2666** (2018)
30. Schultes, D., Sanders, P.: Dynamic Highway-node Routing, pp. 66–79 (2007). https://doi.org/10.1007/978-3-540-72845-0_6
31. Semage, L.: Recommender systems with random walks: a survey (2017). https://doi.org/10.48550/arXiv.1711.04101
32. Silva, R., Cui, G., Rahimi, M., Wang, X.: BR2: a travel behavioral approach to personalized route recommendation based on GPS trajectories (2020). https://ceur-ws.org/Vol-2578/BMDA4.pdf
33. Soong Bong, L., Lee, S., Lee, K.Y.: A gini coefficient based evaluation on the reliability of travel time forecasting. J. King Saud Univ. - Eng. Sci. **31** (2017). https://doi.org/10.1016/j.jksues.2017.12.001
34. Tarkkala, K., Vosough, S., West, J., Roncoli, C.: Evaluating the influence of cyclists' route choices incorporation into travel demand modelling: a case study in greater Helsinki. Transport. Res. Interdisc. Perspect. **27**, 101224 (2024). https://doi.org/10.1016/j.trip.2024.101224
35. Yuan, H., Hernandez, A.: User cold start problem in recommendation systems: a systematic review. IEEE Access (2023). https://doi.org/10.1109/ACCESS.2023.3338705

# Evaluating Large Language Models' Ability to Reason About Anatomical Spatial Relations

Maria Tsourma[1,4](✉), Robert E. Blackwell[2], Anthony G. Cohn[2,3], Anastasios Drosou[4], and Manolis Koubarakis[1]

[1] Department of Informatics and Telecommunications, National and Kapodistrian University of Athens, Athens, Greece
[2] School of Computer Science, University of Leeds, Leeds, UK
[3] The Alan Turing Institute, London, UK
[4] Centre for Research and Technology Hellas, Information Technologies Institute, Thessaloniki, Greece
mtsourma@iti.gr

**Abstract.** We investigate the ability of large language models to reason about spatial relations in human anatomy. First, we define a synthetic, graph-based dataset based on the ontology Foundational Model of Anatomy. Then, we evaluate the capabilities of eight large language models on the problem of answering single and multi-hop spatial questions. Our results show that performance varies substantially across models and relation types. While top-tier models achieve near-perfect performance across most relations, all models exhibit systematic weaknesses on more abstract spatial relations, such as medial and lateral. Furthermore, we find that reasoning performance does not degrade monotonically with increasing hop count; instead, accuracy is influenced by the interaction between reasoning depth and the structural properties of relational chains. Qualitative analysis reveals distinct reasoning strategies across models, with larger models demonstrating more stable compositional reasoning, while smaller models rely more heavily on heuristic shortcuts and local interpretations. Finally, we identify cases of over-alignment in instruction-tuned models, where strong language models may accept incorrect premises rather than critically evaluating them, highlighting a trade-off between reasoning capability and alignment behavior. To better understand the emergence of these capabilities, we conducted comparative experiments across model families of varying parameter scales using the same dataset. This allowed us to identify a specific performance cutoff, or "emergence threshold", where models show a marked transition in benchmark performance, suggesting an improved ability to approximate relational spatial entailment in anatomically grounded queries.

## 1 Introduction

Since understanding human anatomical structures and reasoning about them is inherently spatial and requires the interpretation of relative positions, orienta-


E. Farran et al. (Eds.): Spatial Cognition 2026, LNAI 16785, pp. 108–130, 2027.
https://doi.org/10.1007/978-3-032-36716-7_8

tions, and functional relationships between structures, there have been recent works that investigate how multi-modal models perform in e.g., 3D anatomical reasoning [10], radiology interpretation [8], and anatomy education [15]. There are a few studies [5] that explore the performance of large language models (LLMs) in the anatomy domain; however, there is a gap in spatial anatomy-related research where this paper makes original contributions.

We first define a graph-based dataset based on the ontology Foundational Model of Anatomy (FMA)[1]. The dataset models the anatomical structure of the human body through a qualitative directional reasoning framework, where anatomical entities are represented in terms of their relative positions along the three principal body planes (transverse, sagittal, and coronal). The dataset is then used to construct a graph consisting of six subgraphs, one for each directional relation in a principal body plane. Then, we evaluate the capabilities of eight LLMs on the problem of answering single and multi-hop spatial questions on this graph.

The contributions of the paper are the following: (i) construction of a graph-based benchmark derived from the Foundational Model of Anatomy, representing anatomical entities and qualitative spatial relations between them, (ii) definition of a controlled set of single-hop and multi-hop Yes/No spatial reasoning questions based on graph-defined relational entailment; (iii) detailed experiments that show how eight LLMs perform in answering spatial questions about anatomy, (iv) comparative experiments on open-weight model (Qwen 3.5) sizes to identify the performance cut-off (emergence threshold) necessary for reliable anatomical reasoning. The questions are formulated using the graph and can be single-hop or multi-hop. Our experiments show that model behavior varies not only in terms of overall accuracy but also in how spatial knowledge is represented and utilized during inference. In particular, models differ in their ability to maintain consistent reference frames, compose relational information across steps, and handle directionally versus reference-dependent relations. We further observe that increasing reasoning depth exposes distinct failure modes, including inconsistent intermediate representations and reliance on implicit assumptions. Finally, our analysis provides evidence that model scale and training objectives influence not only performance but also the underlying reasoning strategies employed to solve spatial tasks.

Human anatomy is not only a biomedical knowledge domain, but also a structured spatial domain. Anatomical entities are described through their relative positions within a stable body-centered reference frame, using relations such as superior, inferior, anterior, posterior, medial, and lateral. This makes anatomy an appropriate testbed for studying qualitative spatial reasoning in language models. In this paper, we therefore use anatomical spatial questions not merely as factual biomedical questions, but as controlled probes for examining whether LLMs can approximate qualitative spatial entailments involving reference frames, directional relations, and relational composition.

[1] https://bioportal.bioontology.org/ontologies/FMA.

## 2 Related Work

The problem of identifying human anatomical structures in a spatial context has traditionally been addressed within the domain of computational anatomy, which focuses on modeling biological form and variability using imaging and text data [12]. Recent advances in LLMs (especially, reasoning models, LRMs [19]) have demonstrated that these models are capable of certain forms of reasoning, e.g., about arithmetic, logic, etc. Studies have also demonstrated that large language models (LLMs) can encode domain-specific factual knowledge and perform inference tasks without task-specific training [14]. This has motivated interest in their application to domains requiring relational understanding, including scientific reasoning and spatial cognition. However, spatial reasoning remains a known limitation of transformer-based architectures. In this context, recent research has begun to systematically examine whether LLMs and LRMs can infer spatial relationships between entities described in language. Cohn and Blackwell [6,7] and Gardelakos et al. [11] evaluated the ability of LLMs and LRMs to reason about topological and cardinal relations, highlighting both their potential and their limitations in relational inference. Their findings suggest that while LLMs and LRMs can approximate spatial reasoning through pattern recognition, they often fail when deeper relational consistency is required. These results are particularly relevant to anatomy, where understanding is fundamentally relational, and structures are defined not only by identity, but also by their position relative to others.

Parallel work in cognitive science–inspired AI has emphasized that spatial understanding is not simply a matter of memorizing relationships, but requires the construction of internal representations of relative positioning [9]. In language-based systems, such representations must emerge implicitly through training rather than explicit geometric modeling. Consequently, while LLMs may correctly identify anatomical entities in isolation, their ability to reason about spatial arrangements remains uncertain.

Anatomy provides a particularly challenging domain for LLMs because spatial relationships, such as medial–lateral positioning, containment, and adjacency, are central to conceptual understanding. Recent research has concentrated on multi-modal models for anatomy understanding, e.g., 3D anatomical reasoning [10], radiology interpretation [8], and anatomy education [15].

Several studies have looked at LLM ability to answers anatomical questions (for example [2,22,24]), and indeed Chaba-Karnaś et al. [5] showed that LLMs are capable of passing anatomy examinations intended for medical students. However, to the best of our knowledge, there is no study that systematically explores the performance of LLMs in spatial anatomy.

## 3 Experimental Design

### 3.1 Dataset Preparation

To evaluate the spatial anatomical reasoning capabilities of LLMs, we constructed a *graph-based dataset grounded in the ontology FMA*. The dataset oper-

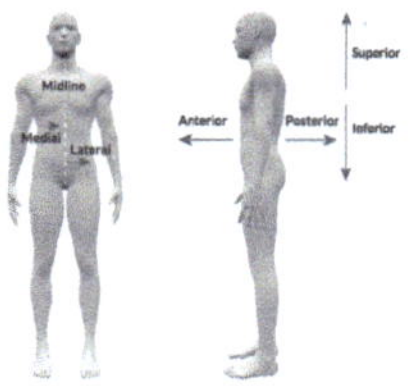


**Fig. 1.** Spatial anatomical terminology.

**Table 1.** Directional relations and tokens

| Plane (Axis) | Relation | Tokens |
|---|---|---|
| Transverse (Z-axis) | Superior (SUP) | 18172 |
| | Inferior (INF) | 18228 |
| Sagittal (Y-axis) | Anterior (ANT) | 14346 |
| | Posterior (POS) | 17308 |
| Coronal (X-axis) | Medial (MED) | 15950 |
| | Lateral (LAT) | 15950 |

ationalizes human anatomy through a qualitative directional reasoning framework, where anatomical entities are represented in terms of their relative positions along the three principal body planes. The benchmark is defined around six strict directional relations (Fig. 1), corresponding to the three anatomical axes presented in Table 1: transverse (Z-axis), sagittal (Y-axis), and coronal (X-axis). For each plane, the table lists the associated directional relations, along with the corresponding dataset tokens used to represent them. These tokens were calculated using the `tiktoken` library [20].

These relations form the basis for evaluating whether models can perform transitive inference over anatomical space. Specifically, a query of the form *R(A, C)* is labeled as *True* if and only if entity *C* is reachable from entity *A* within the relation-specific graph via transitive closure. First, we performed semantic normalization by mapping heterogeneous spatial properties into six canonical directional relations. This involved translating synonymous terms to ensure consistency, such as mapping 'ventral' to 'anterior' and 'dorsal' to 'posterior', thereby standardizing the anatomical descriptions while preserving their qualitative spatial meaning.

The benchmark follows a qualitative spatial reasoning abstraction. Each anatomical relation is represented as a directed relation between two anatomical entities, and each relation type is modelled through a separate directed graph. Under this representation, a spatial statement R(A, C) is considered true when C is reachable from A in the relation-specific graph for relation R. The task therefore corresponds to graph-defined relational entailment.

Next, we constructed a task-specific anatomical graph, where: (a) *Nodes* represent anatomical entities (e.g., organs or major structures), and (b) *Edges* represent normalized directional relations between entities. The graph was decomposed into six subgraphs, one for each directional relation. Each subgraph functions as a directional backbone for a single anatomical axis. For example, the 'MED' subgraph represents a directed flow toward the midline, while its 'LAT' counterpart represents directed flow towards the side of the body.

Filtering of bidirectional and contradictory relations was essential to transform FMA from a descriptive medical resource into a logically sound reasoning benchmark. These inconsistencies primarily stem from annotation noise in the ontology and the spatial complexity of anatomical structures, in which curvilinear entities (e.g., blood vessels) may overlap across multiple axes. By removing cases of mutual reachability and inverse relation overlaps (e.g., an entity being simultaneously labeled as Anterior and Posterior to another), we ensured that each subgraph maintains a strict partial ordering. This pruning step is crucial for evaluating LLMs, as it eliminates ambiguous ground truths that would otherwise penalize a model for logical inferences that are formally valid but contextually contradictory.

After filtering, we computed the transitive closure of each relation-specific subgraph. This closure defines the ground-truth reasoning space: if $C$ is reachable from $A$ through a path in the graph, then $R(A, C)$ is considered logically entailed. To explicitly evaluate transitive spatial reasoning, we constructed both single-hop and multi-hop query instances. For each reachable node pair $(A, C)$, we computed the shortest-path distance in the original relation-specific graph and used it as the *reasoning hop depth.* Pairs connected by a single edge correspond to *single-hop* relations, while pairs requiring paths of length greater than one correspond to *multi-hop* relations that require chaining intermediate anatomical entities (Fig. 2). The maximum number of hops we created was 4.

The hop depth is used as an operational measure of graph-defined relational distance. It is computed as the shortest-path distance between two entities in the original relation-specific graph. A two-hop query requires one intermediate entity, a three-hop query requires two intermediate entities, and so on. However, hop depth should not be interpreted as a direct measure of human cognitive difficulty or as a complete measure of task complexity. It is a structural measure of the benchmark graph. Model difficulty may also depend on relation type, anatomical salience, entity familiarity, and the stability of the relevant spatial reference frame.

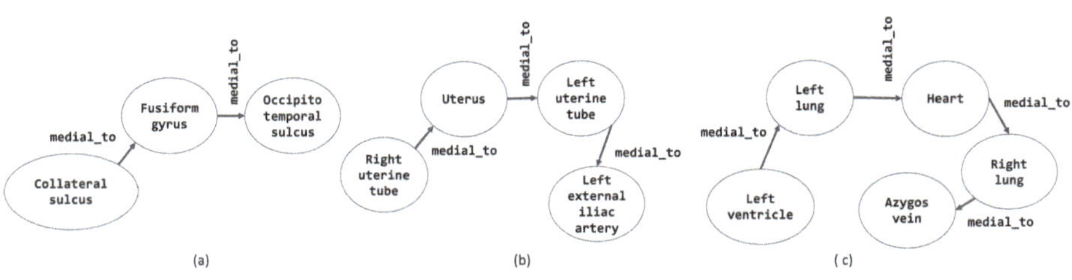


**Fig. 2.** Representative examples of multi-hop spatial reasoning paths in the anatomical graph. The diagrams illustrate relational chains across increasing complexity levels: (a) a 2-hop sequence connecting the collateral sulcus to the occipitotemporal sulcus; (b) a 3-hop sequence traversing uterine and iliac structures; and (c) a 4-hop sequence tracking a spatial path from the left ventricle through the thoracic cavity to the azygos vein.

Using this structure, we generated a synthetic dataset by sampling: (a) *Positive examples* from node pairs whose relation is entailed by the transitive closure, including both direct and multi-hop entailments, and (b) *Negative examples* from logically guaranteed false cases, primarily inverse relations in the relation-specific graph. Each dataset instance was annotated with: (a) the relation type (e.g.

*ANT*), and (b) the reasoning hop depth required to infer the relation using the graph. This design enables systematic evaluation of model performance across increasing levels of transitive-reasoning complexity, isolating the ability of LLMs to perform multi-step spatial inference from anatomical knowledge.

Finally, these graph queries were converted into Yes/No controlled natural-language prompts. During the evaluation, the LLMs were tested in a closed-book setting, without access to the underlying graph, ensuring that the performance reflects internal reasoning rather than retrieval. To support transparency, we have made the complete dataset publicly available at: [THE LINK WILL BE MADE AVAILABLE ONCE THE PAPER IS ACCEPTED, DUE TO BLIND REVIEW REQUIREMENTS]. In total, the created dataset includes:

- Number of anatomical entities (Table 2): 313 of 18 main organs
- Number of directional relations after normalization: 6 (ANT, INF, SUP, POS, MED, LAT)
- Total benchmark queries: 1996
- Positive examples: 998
- Negative examples of inverse relations: 998
- Hop distribution (in total): (a) 2-hop: 940, (b) 3-hop: 636, (c) 4-hop: 420
- Relation's distribution (in total): (a) ANT: 400, (b) INF: 400, (c) SUP: 400, (d) POS: 382, (e) MED: 400, (f) LAT: 14

### 3.2 Methodology

In this paper, our focus is on answering the following research questions: (a) How well each individual model performs on the dataset presented above, and why? (b) Do the number of parameters and architecture play an important role in their reasoning capabilities? (c) Do models answer better on the single or multi-hop questions? (d) Based on our experimental analysis of performance across different model sizes, is there an optimal parameter cut-off that balances efficiency and reasoning performance, and what does this reveal about the minimum effective size of an LLM for this task?

To answer these research questions, we experimented with eight LLMs (i.e., DeepSeek-r1:14B, Magistral:24B, Gemma 3:27B, Qwen 3:32B, Qwen 3.5:35B, Llava, GPT-OSS:120B, GPT-5.2 Thinking). For the proprietary models, the exact number of parameters is not publicly disclosed. We evaluated a diverse selection of both closed-weight proprietary APIs and open-weight models across varying parameter scales to investigate how model capacity influences spatial reasoning performance. The inclusion of open-weight architectures was specifically intended to ensure scientific reproducibility. We selected Qwen-3:32B and Qwen-3.5:35B due to their strong capabilities in structured and multi-step reasoning, which are essential for accurately modeling anatomical relations. Their similar scale but different versions also allow us to examine the impact of training improvements on domain-specific reasoning performance.

The above models have different architectures and different numbers of parameters, allowing us to investigate if the size of a model and its architecture affect its capabilities. In general, the size of models directly impacts their ability to understand the task at hand and generate an answer, as larger models tend to demonstrate better performance in contextual understanding and the preparation of more coherent answers [13]. However, the benefits of increasing size are not always linear: performance may plateau on some tasks, and the computational cost grows significantly with model scale. Therefore, understanding how performance scales with size in current experiments is crucial for assessing trade-offs between efficiency and accuracy.

Beyond standard text-based architectures, we included LLaVA (Large Language-and-Vision Assistant) to evaluate the impact of multimodal pre-training on abstract spatial reasoning. As a multimodal model like GPT-5.2 Thinking, LLaVA is trained to align linguistic concepts with visual features via a vision encoder, a process that potentially fosters a more robust internal "world model" regarding physical orientations [1]. Given that human anatomy is a fundamentally visual and structural domain, we sought to determine if this visual-spatial grounding provides a competitive advantage over text-pure models when navigating graph-based directional relations. We used the LlaVa model to investigate the extent to which spatial intuitions developed through image-text alignment can be effectively transferred to logical, zero-shot anatomical inference in a strictly textual format. This inclusion allows for a comparison between models optimized for linguistic patterns and those designed to bridge the gap between language and physical reality. Since we were not interested in the creative aspects of the tested models but only in the generation of correct answers, temperature was set to 0.0 with a fixed seed. The experiments on OpenAI's model are performed using OpenAI's API [23].

### 3.3 Prompting

To evaluate the spatial anatomical reasoning capabilities of the models in a controlled setting, we designed a minimal and standardized prompting scheme. Each prompt begins with the contextual statement "In standard human anatomical position:", ensuring that spatial relations are interpreted according to the conventional reference orientation used in anatomy. The standard human anatomical position is the universal, upright reference posture used for consistent anatomical description, regardless of the body's actual orientation. It features the body standing erect, facing forward, with arms at the sides, palms facing forward (supinated), and feet slightly apart and parallel [3]. This is important because directional terms such as anterior, posterior, superior, and inferior are defined relative to this canonical posture.

Then comes the core question, which asks whether a directional relation holds between two entities $A$ and $C$. Specifically, each one of the graphs created per relation were converted into a natural-language question following a defined template *"Is the < label_A> < relation> the < label_C>?"*, aiming to form questions that ask whether there is a specific directional relation between two anatomical entities. Direction labels from the structured dataset (e.g., anterior, superior) were converted into natural language by replacing underscores with spaces (e.g., Is the stomach anterior to the pancreas?). The prompt format was intentionally kept concise and constrained to reduce ambiguity and simplify automatic evaluation.

The final instruction in the prompt explicitly restricts the response format to "Yes" or "No", which serves two purposes. It ensures that model outputs can be reliably parsed and evaluated as binary classifications. A sample prompt is: *"In standard human anatomical position: Is Right uterine tube medial to Left external iliac artery? Answer with "Yes" or "No" only."* and the expected answer is "Yes" in this case.

### 3.4 Evaluation Metrics

To assess the spatial anatomical reasoning capabilities of the evaluated models, we employ a set of metrics designed to capture both overall performance and performance variations across different reasoning conditions. Since the task is formulated as a binary question-answering problem (Yes/No), all metrics are computed based on classification accuracy, defined as the proportion of correctly predicted answers over the total number of queries.

- *Overall Accuracy:* measures the percentage of queries for which the model produces the correct Yes/No answer, providing an indication of the model's ability to correctly identify whether a spatial anatomical relation between two entities is logically entailed.
- *Accuracy by Hop Depth:* evaluates the models' ability to perform multi-step transitive reasoning. Hop depth corresponds to the length of the shortest path between two entities in the relation-specific graph and measures how performance changes as the number of intermediate reasoning steps increases, providing information on the models' ability to perform multi-hop spatial inference.
- *Accuracy by Relation Type:* computes the accuracy for each plane (aka relation type). This analysis allows us to identify whether certain directional relations are systematically easier or harder for the models to reason about, and whether performance varies across anatomical axes.

## 4 Results

The evaluation results are presented in Fig. 3 which includes 4 charts where the first shows the overall accuracy (%) for each model across the six relation categories, giving a general performance snapshot, and the remaining three show the breakdown of these results by reasoning complexity: hop-2, hop-3, and hop-4, where each "hop" represents the number of relational steps required to arrive at an answer. We did not explicitly report hop-1 results because hop-1 corresponds to standard single-edge (direct relation) predictions, which are typically much easier and are well covered by conventional link prediction evaluations. Our focus was on the more challenging multi-hop (compositional) setting, hence the emphasis on hops more than two. Together, these diagrams allow us to observe not only how models perform across different spatial relations, but also how their accuracy changes as the reasoning chains become longer and potentially more complex.

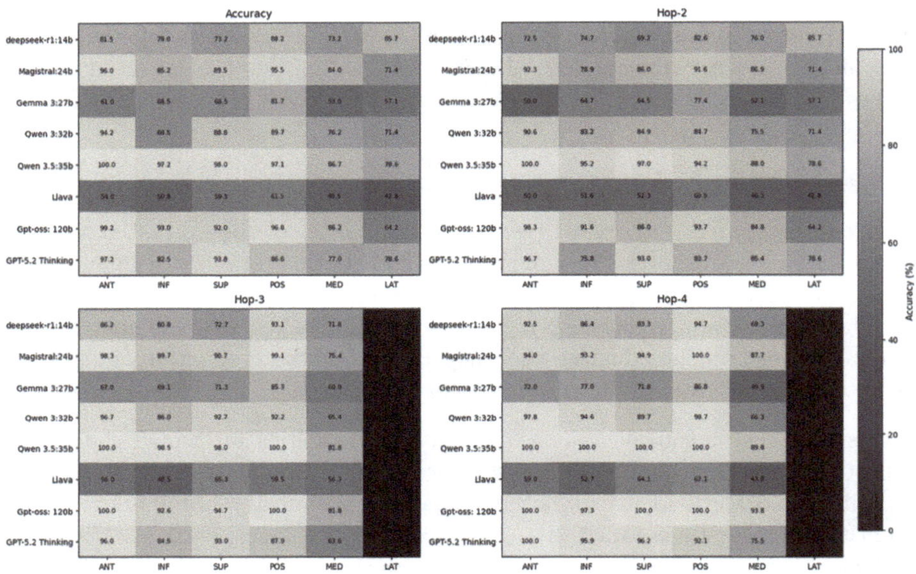


**Fig. 3.** Comparison of model performance across anatomical relation prediction tasks.

Figure 4 summarizes how performance varies by relation type and reasoning depth. Across all settings, POS, ANT, and SUP consistently achieve the highest accuracy, indicating that these relations are generally easier for models to learn and predict. In contrast, INF and MED show lower performance, suggesting greater difficulty and variability across models. The LAT relation remains comparatively lower and exhibits limited variation across hops. Interestingly, performance tends to improve slightly with increasing hop count for several relations (e.g., ANT, SUP, POS), indicating that models capable of multi-step reasoning can maintain or even enhance performance in more compositional settings. However, this trend is not uniform, as some relations (e.g., MED) show fluctuations, reflecting sensitivity to reasoning complexity. Overall, the figure highlights both the relative difficulty of relation types and how multi-hop reasoning impacts model performance.

The overall accuracy results reveal a clear stratification of model performance across the evaluated spatial relations. The strongest performance is achieved by Qwen 3.5:35B, and next comes GPT-OSS:120B, which attains near-perfect accuracy in several relation categories, followed closely by GPT-5.2 Thinking. These

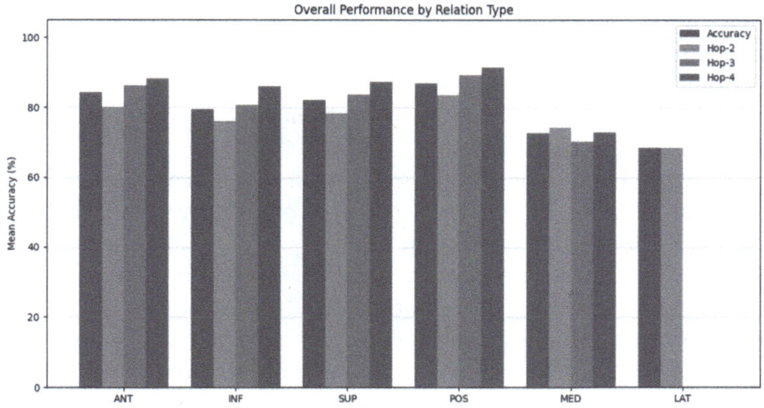


**Fig. 4.** Overall performance by relation type across reasoning hops. Bars show mean accuracy (%) for each relation type (ANT, INF, SUP, POS, MED, LAT), averaged across all models.

models demonstrate both high accuracy and consistency across all relation types. This might occur because these models are good at recalling standard textbook relationships. A second tier of models, including Qwen 3:32B and Magistral:24B, also performs well, generally achieving accuracy in the high 80% to mid-90% range, albeit with slightly greater variability.

In contrast, Gemma 3:27B and DeepSeek-r1:14B exhibit lower overall accuracy, particularly in more challenging relation types, while Llava consistently underperforms relative to all other models. This difference in performance can be attributed to a combination of model scale, training objectives, and reasoning capabilities. Gemma 3:27B and DeepSeek-r1:14B are substantially smaller than the top-performing models, and we suggest that this might limit their capacity to learn rich and stable representations of complex spatial relationships. As a result, while they can handle simple or more common relations reasonably well, they struggle with more challenging relations, such as MED and LAT, which require finer-grained and more abstract spatial reasoning. These relations, unlike relations such as ANT or POS, which can often be interpreted along a single, well-defined axis (front–back), are defined with respect to a reference frame, typically the midline of a structure or body. This means the model must implicitly represent not just two entities, but also an underlying global coordinate system (e.g., what counts as the "center" versus the "side").

Also, the models with lower accuracy appear to have less robust compositional reasoning abilities [16–18, 25, 27]. Multi-hop reasoning requires maintaining intermediate states and correctly chaining relational transformations [21]. Smaller models are more prone to error accumulation, where a mistake in an early step propagates and leads to incorrect final predictions [4, 26]. This becomes particularly evident in relation types that are already difficult, such as MED and LAT, amplifying their performance gap compared to larger models.

Finally, Llava's consistently lower performance might be explained by its different architectural focus and training objective. As a multimodal model designed primarily for vision-language tasks, it is optimized to integrate visual and textual information rather than to perform precise symbolic or relational reasoning in purely textual settings.

To better understand model behavior beyond aggregate accuracy, we analyze the distribution of error types across multiple models by comparing false positives (incorrect "Yes" predictions) and false negatives (incorrect "No" predictions) (Fig. 5). The results reveal a model-dependent bias in error types. Some models, such as deepseek-r1:14b, Gemma 3:27b, and Llava, tend to produce more false positives, meaning they incorrectly predict "Yes" more often than "No" This suggests a bias toward affirming or over-predicting positive outcomes. In contrast, models like Qwen 3.5:35b, Gpt-oss:120b, and GPT-5.2 Thinking show the opposite trend, with more false negatives, indicating a tendency to incorrectly predict "No" and thus behave more conservatively. Overall, this variation suggests that different models have distinct decision thresholds or calibration behaviors, which could significantly impact downstream applications depending on whether false positives or false negatives are more costly.

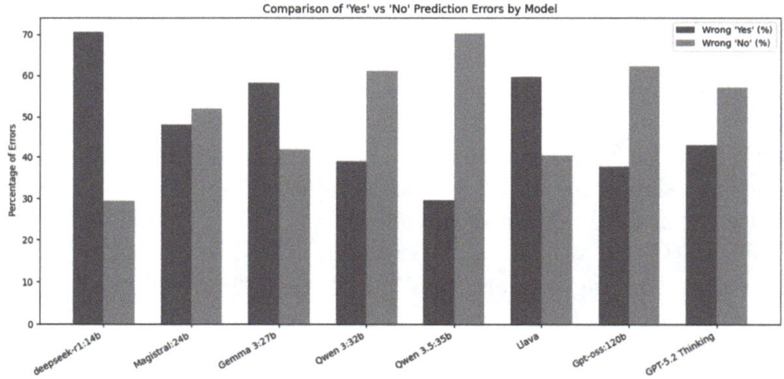


**Fig. 5.** Comparison of "Yes" vs "No" prediction errors by model.

## 4.1 Class Issues Identified

Across all models, a consistent pattern emerges in terms of relation difficulty. Relations such as posterior and anterior are associated with higher accuracy, whereas medial and lateral systematically yield lower performance. This suggests that certain spatial relations are inherently more difficult for models to capture, independent of model size or architecture. From the analysis of the results, it can be concluded that medial and lateral relations achieve the lowest accuracy in all models, compared to the rest of the relations. One interpretation can be that the difference between medial and lateral is often subtle and context-sensitive: two entities can both be on the same general side, yet differ in how close they are to the midline. Capturing this requires the model to encode relative distance and ordering, rather than just categorical direction. In contrast, relations like SUP or inferior often involve clearer, more separable spatial distinctions (up vs. down).

Also, these relations are typically less frequent and less explicitly expressed in natural language data compared to more common directional terms like "above", "below", "in front of", or "behind". Because language models learn from statistical patterns in text, this lower frequency can lead to weaker or less stable representations of these concepts. Thus, these relations are more sensitive to error propagation in multi-step reasoning. Since they depend on maintaining a consistent reference frame across steps, any small misalignment early in the reasoning chain can lead to incorrect conclusions later. This makes them particularly challenging in multi-hop settings.

### 4.2 Multi-hop Performance Comparison

The **hop-2** results, corresponding to shorter reasoning chains, indicate that most models maintain relatively high accuracy under limited compositional demands. The top-performing models (Qwen 3.5:35B, GPT-OSS:120B, and GPT-5.2 Thinking) continue to achieve strong results, typically exceeding 90% accuracy across most relation types. Mid-tier models such as Qwen 3:32B and Magistral:24B also perform robustly, though with a slight reduction compared to overall accuracy. Lower-tier models, including Gemma 3:27B and DeepSeek-r1:14B, exhibit more noticeable declines in performance, indicating sensitivity to even modest increases in reasoning complexity. Furthermore, variability across relation types becomes profound. In particular, relations such as MED show sharp drops in accuracy for certain models, highlighting that performance is influenced not only by reasoning depth but also by the semantical difficulty of specific relations.

At **hop-3**, Qwen 3.5:35B, followed by GPT-OSS:120B maintain near-perfect accuracy in several categories, while GPT-5.2 Thinking remains highly competitive. The gap between top-tier and mid-tier models becomes increasingly evident, where Qwen 3:32B and Magistral:24B show more consistent declines, particularly in relation types that are already challenging. Lower-tier models frequently fall into the 60–80% accuracy range, reflecting reduced robustness to longer reasoning chains. Llava continues to perform significantly worse than all other models, with limited improvement across relation types. Importantly, the effect of relation difficulty is amplified at this stage where easier relations, such as POS remain relatively stable, whereas more difficult ones, including MED and LAT, exhibit larger performance drops. This indicates that errors are more prone in relation types that require more complex spatial reasoning.

The **hop-4** results, corresponding to longer reasoning chains, provide insight into model robustness under increased compositional demands. Notably, performance does not exhibit a uniform decline with increased hop count. Qwen 3.5:35B continues to achieve near-perfect accuracy across most relation types, while GPT-OSS:120B also maintains strong performance with only minor variability. Mid-tier models, including Qwen 3:32B and Magistral:24B, remain competitive, often achieving accuracy in the 90% range. Although some weaknesses persist in relations like MED. Lower-tier models such as Gemma 3:27B and DeepSeek-r1:14B continue to underperform relative to stronger models, although their performance does not deteriorate substantially beyond hop-3, suggesting a degree of stabilization.

A key observation is that increasing the number of reasoning steps does not necessarily lead to decreased performance (Fig. 6). Since the intermediate reasoning chains are not provided to the model at inference time, differences across hop levels cannot be attributed to the availability of additional structural guidance in the prompt. Instead, the results suggest that model accuracy is more strongly influenced by the difficulty of the underlying relation and the model's ability to infer it from its anatomical knowledge. Consistent with previous observations, MED (and LAT, where available) remains among the most challenging relations across all models.

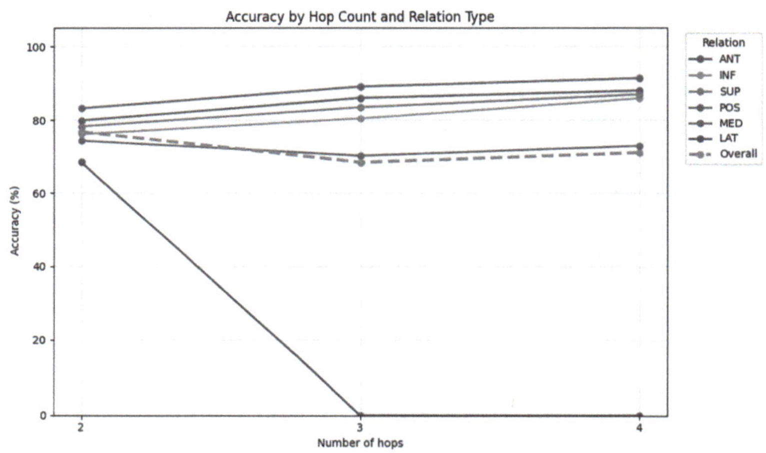


**Fig. 6.** Accuracy as a function of reasoning depth across relation types.

A possible explanation is that graph distance and inferential difficulty are not perfectly aligned. Although hop-4 relations correspond to longer paths in the underlying graph, they may connect entity pairs whose spatial relationship is more salient or more consistently encoded in the model's internal representations. Therefore, some hop-2 relations may involve entity pairs whose direct spatial relationship is more ambiguous, less frequently expressed in the model's training data, or harder to retrieve without additional context. As a result, shorter graph distance does not necessarily imply easier inference.

Another important factor is the distribution of relation types across hops. Even if the dataset is not easier by design, the composition of relations can differ across hop levels. As shown in the results, some relations (e.g., POS and ANT) are consistently easier, while others (e.g., MED) are more difficult. If higher-hop queries disproportionately involve relations that are more reliably encoded or easier to infer, this can lead to improved performance without implying reduced task complexity. This effect is particularly visible for relations such as POS, where many models exhibit a gradual improvement from hop-2 to hop-4. This suggests that certain spatial relations are more robustly represented and can be inferred reliably even when the underlying connection between entities is indirect. In contrast, for relations such as MED, performance remains unstable across hops, indicating that difficulty is driven more by the nature of the relation than by graph distance.

These findings suggest that models do not necessarily perform explicit step-by-step compositional reasoning over the underlying graph structure. Instead, they appear to rely on learned associations or global relational patterns between entities. In this setting, higher-hop queries do not impose additional reasoning steps in the model's inference process, but rather require the retrieval or approximation of an end-to-end relation. Consequently, performance differences across hop levels reflect variation in how well these relations are represented internally, rather than the length of an explicitly executed reasoning chain.

### 4.3 Qualitative Analysis of Model Reasoning Behavior

To gain deeper insight into how models navigate anatomical space, we performed a qualitative analysis of their reasoning traces. For models supporting models that provide an explicit reasoning trace or those with native reasoning capabilities (e.g., "reasoning models"), we explicitly examined the intermediate steps generated before the final answer by requesting that the models also generate justification apart from just Yes or No. This allowed us to distinguish behaviour consistent with compositional reasoning, where a model might arrive at a correct Yes or No answer based on local entity familiarity rather than spatial transitivity. The analysis of these logic paths allowed us to identify specific failure modes, such as when a model correctly identifies the start and end points but fails to maintain the correct directional vector across intermediate anatomical structures. This process occurred manually, and we focused mostly on the misclassified relations. The following analysis has been conducted per model.

Qwen 3:32B demonstrates a strong tendency to ground its reasoning in an explicit reconstruction of the standard anatomical position before attempting to answer spatial queries. In multiple instances, the model begins by recalling the canonical human pose (e.g., upright body, forward-facing orientation, arms at the sides), suggesting that it relies on an internal normalization step to establish a reference frame. This behavior indicates that the model does not treat spatial relations as purely symbolic but instead anchors them in an implicit spatial schema. Notably, the model occasionally adapts this reasoning when context shifts (e.g., fetal anatomy), showing an awareness of domain-specific variations in anatomical orientation. In terms of reasoning structure, Qwen 3:32B consistently follows a chain-of-thought decomposition, breaking down the problem into sequential steps such as identifying the question, recalling anatomical definitions, applying directional terminology, and comparing relative positions. This structured approach reflects a compositional reasoning strategy in which intermediate states are explicitly constructed and evaluated. However, this process is not always uniformly applied. In some cases, the model relies on surface-level cues, such as inferring spatial properties directly from organ names (e.g., "left lung"), without further verification. This suggests a hybrid strategy combining deeper reasoning with heuristic shortcuts.

Additionally, Qwen 3:32B often adopts a progressive reasoning approach, starting from general anatomical principles and incrementally refining its understanding of the specific structures involved. For example, it may first establish the global orientation of the brain before resolving relations between individual regions. The use of domain-specific terminology (e.g., "neuroanatomy" instead of "anatomy") further indicates that the model leverages specialized knowledge representations. Overall, Qwen 3:32B exhibits relatively sophisticated reasoning behavior, but with occasional reliance on heuristics that may limit robustness. However, this case was not noticed by the Qwen 3.5:35B.

Magistral:24B operates at a more conceptual and abstraction-driven level, combining memorized anatomical knowledge with geometric reasoning. Unlike Qwen 3:32B, Magistral tends to implicitly encode spatial relationships and translate them into geometric comparisons. This allows the model to reason about anatomical structures in terms of relative positioning without always explicitly restating the reference frame. For example, when asked whether the interventricular septum is medial to the right ventricular septal wall, a reconstruction-based model might first establish a full anatomical frame (midline → ventricles → septum). In contrast, Magistral can shortcut this process by directly mapping "left-sided septal structures" as more medial than "right-sided" ones, performing a relative geometric comparison without explicitly rebuilding the coordinate system.

The model demonstrates two complementary reasoning modes. First, it relies on stored biological knowledge, recalling the relative locations of anatomical structures as learned facts. Second, it performs logical transformations, mapping these anatomical facts into directional relationships (e.g., anterior vs. posterior) through geometric interpretation. This dual strategy enables relatively stable performance, as it combines factual recall with relational reasoning. However, Magistral's reasoning is generally less explicit and less stepwise compared to Qwen 3. While it achieves similar outcomes, it does not consistently articulate intermediate reasoning steps, which may indicate a more compressed internal reasoning process. This can be advantageous for efficiency but may reduce transparency and make the model more susceptible to subtle errors when relational complexity increases.

Furthermore, to investigate whether model performance varies systematically by anatomical structure, we performed a stratified analysis of accuracy by organ across relations. This analysis was motivated by the hypothesis that organs more frequently represented in training data (e.g., the heart or brain) would yield higher classification accuracy. However, the results indicate that performance differences are not solely explained by presumed exposure frequency. While some highly salient structures such as the brain and craniofacial skeleton achieved consistently high performance (typically 90–100% in superior and posterior relations, and up to 100% in medial relation for several models), the heart showed more moderate and variable accuracy (ranging approximately from 35% to 93% in superior/posterior relation and 48–90% in medial relation). Conversely, certain less commonly emphasized systems, such as the male reproductive organs, reached near-ceiling performance in many cases (often 83–100%). In contrast, anatomically complex or visually heterogeneous regions, including the lung/bronchial tree and musculoskeletal soft tissues, exhibited substantially lower and less stable accuracies (e.g., lung ranging from 0–100% in posterior but often 39–64% in medial relation, and muscles/ligaments as low as 25%). These findings indicate that performance differences are not solely explained by presumed exposure frequency, but are more strongly influenced by visual distinctiveness, structural variability, and viewpoint dependence.

### 4.4 Optimal Model Size and Parameter Cut-Off

To address research question (d), we conduct a series of experiments analyzing model performance across different parameter scales. Our goal is to identify whether there exists an optimal parameter cut-off that balances reasoning performance and computational efficiency. We evaluate Qwen3.5 models of varying sizes on the proposed dataset and examine performance trends as model capacity increases (Fig. 7). In particular, we investigate whether performance improvements saturate beyond a certain scale, indicating a minimum effective model size for this task.

Qwen-3.5:35B demonstrates strong reasoning performance, particularly on multi-step and knowledge-intensive tasks. As such, it is a reliable candidate for near-peak performance within the range of models we evaluate. The selection of this model enables a controlled comparison across a consistent model family, ensuring that observed differences are not driven by drastic architectural changes but rather by scaling and training improvements. Secondly, by treating Qwen-3.5:35B as the upper bound, we can more clearly analyze performance trends across small-to-mid and mid-to-large models, and identify whether improvements saturate before reaching extremely large scales.

The results of our scaling experiments reveal a distinct cut-off threshold for reliable anatomical reasoning. For the more intuitive relations, such as ANT, the performance inflection occurs early, with the 35B parameter scale serving as a saturation point where the model achieves near-perfect accuracy (100%). This suggests that the linguistic and structural patterns associated with anterior-posterior orientation are sufficiently represented in the training data of mid-sized models. However, the Medial (MED) axis demonstrates a significantly wider scaling curve. Accuracy remains almost entirely horizontal between the 4B and 27B scales, indicating that simply increasing parameters within this range is insufficient to overcome the conceptual difficulty of midline-relative spatial logic. The

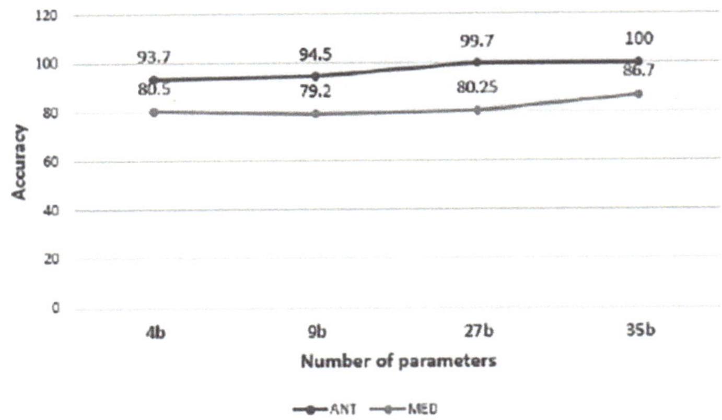


**Fig. 7.** Cut-off experiment identifying the emergence of spatial reasoning across model scales. The graph illustrates accuracy trends for Anterior (ANT) and Medial (MED) relations as a function of parameter count.

identification of this cut-off is critical for the deployment of LLMs in specialized domains like medicine. We observe that while a 9B model might be "good enough" for simple directional tasks, it fails to show any meaningful improvement on abstract relations (MED) until it reaches the 35B parameter mark. This 6.45% jump at 35B represents a transition from stochastic guessing toward the emergence of stable spatial inference. These findings imply that for complex anatomical systems, there is a minimum computational scale required to move beyond local heuristics and achieve the compositional reasoning necessary for multi-hop spatial navigation.

## 5 Discussion and Conclusions

In this work, we presented a systematic evaluation of large language models on spatial reasoning tasks grounded in human anatomy. Using a synthetic dataset and graph derived from the Foundational Model of Anatomy, we assessed the ability of eight models to answer both single-hop and multi-hop spatial queries. Our results demonstrate that, while modern language models exhibit strong performance on many spatial relations, their capabilities are not uniform across relation types or reasoning depths. Qwen 3.5:35B and GPT-OSS:120B exhibit the most structured and systematic reasoning behavior among the evaluated models. They consistently ground their responses in the standard anatomical position, using this as a stable reference frame for all spatial interpretations. Unlike smaller models, they do not appear to "reinterpret" the prompt dynamically; instead, this applies a well-defined internal framework to analyze the problem.

A key characteristic of GPT-OSS:120B is its use of self-generated subquestions to guide reasoning. The model decomposes the task into smaller logical units (e.g., comparing anterior and posterior regions, evaluating relative positions) and resolves each step before concluding. This reflects a highly compositional reasoning strategy, where intermediate states are explicitly constructed and integrated. However, an interesting inconsistency is observed in certain cases where the model produces minimal justifications despite correct answers. For example, when evaluating whether an anterior structure is posterior to another, the model may provide a direct answer without elaborating on the underlying reasoning. This suggests that while the model is capable of deep reasoning, it may sometimes rely on internalized knowledge shortcuts, bypassing full explanation when the answer is deemed trivial. This behavior highlights a distinction between reasoning capability and explanation generation.

An additional behavioral pattern observed in GPT-5.2 Thinking is a tendency toward conservative responses, as reflected by a higher proportion of false negatives compared to false positives. This suggests that the model is more likely to incorrectly reject true statements than to incorrectly affirm false ones. As a result, instead of fully reconstructing the underlying anatomical relationships, the model may rely on surface-level validation of the statement, leading to confidently stated but incorrect answers. This indicates that the model is more likely to reject correct statements than to affirm incorrect ones, rather than systematically agreeing with the prompt. This behavior can be interpreted as a consequence of alignment optimization, where models are trained to be helpful and cautious, sometimes at the expense of fully verifying complex relational claims. While GPT-5.2 demonstrates strong overall reasoning capabilities, this introduces a distinct failure mode: the model may produce coherent and well-structured justifications that nonetheless arrive at an incorrect conclusion due to incomplete validation of the underlying premise. This contrasts with smaller models, which more often fail due to gaps in knowledge or incomplete reasoning processes. Consequently, the limitations observed in larger models such as GPT-5.2 Thinking do not primarily reflect insufficient capacity, but rather a trade-off between cautious decision-making and thorough epistemic verification.

DeepSeek-R1 adopts a reasoning strategy centered on explicit definition recall and perspective setting. The model frequently begins by stating, "Let me recall what these terms mean", indicating a reliance on reconstructing the semantic meaning of spatial terminology before applying it. This reflects a more definition-driven approach, where understanding of directional terms (e.g., anterior, posterior) is treated as a prerequisite for reasoning. The model also demonstrates a tendency to establish a visual or spatial perspective, often describing how the body or brain is oriented (e.g., face forward, feet downward) and how this affects the interpretation of directions. This suggests that DeepSeek attempts to simulate a mental spatial model, though this representation appears less stable and less consistently applied than in larger models. Compared to Qwen 3 and GPT-OSS:120B, DeepSeek's reasoning is less compositional and more step-local, focusing on interpreting individual terms rather than constructing a fully integrated reasoning chain. While this approach can be effective for simpler cases, it is more vulnerable to inconsistencies, particularly in multi-step reasoning scenarios where maintaining intermediate states is critical. The repeated need to "recall definitions" also suggests weaker internalization of spatial relations, which may contribute to lower overall accuracy.

Another important distinction emerging from the results is between stable and brittle reasoning behavior. Larger models display stable performance across both relation types and hop levels, indicating that they can generalize their reasoning strategies effectively. Smaller models, by contrast, are more brittle: their performance varies significantly depending on the relation type and degrades more sharply under increased compositional demands. This brittleness suggests that smaller models may rely more heavily on surface-level patterns or heuristics rather than robust internal representations. As a result, they are less able to recover from intermediate errors or adapt to more complex reasoning chains. Larger models, on the other hand, appear to better integrate information across steps, reducing error propagation.

Finally, the results highlight that reasoning difficulty cannot be attributed solely to hop count. Although hop-4 represents longer reasoning chains, as determined by the FMA induced graph, it does not consistently lead to lower accuracy. Instead, performance appears to depend more strongly on the structure of the reasoning chain and the type of spatial relation involved. In particular, relations such as MED and LAT remain challenging across all hop levels, suggesting that certain forms of spatial reasoning require more complex or less well-represented abstractions. This effect persists regardless of model size, although it is mitigated in larger models. Overall, these findings indicate that while model scale plays a crucial role in enabling robust multi-step reasoning, task characteristics—such as relation type and structural regularity—are equally important in determining performance.

Overall, the findings suggest that LLMs can often approximate anatomical spatial entailments, especially for relations grounded in stable and salient anatomical axes. However, their behaviour remains uneven. Relations such as medial and lateral expose persistent difficulty because they require reference-frame-dependent reasoning with respect to the anatomical midline. Moreover, high accuracy should not be interpreted as proof of explicit symbolic reasoning, since models may rely on a mixture of anatomical recall, learned associations, implicit spatial representations, and partial relational composition. The benchmark therefore provides a controlled diagnostic tool for studying the spatial behaviour of LLMs. Its main contribution is not to show that LLMs possess human-like anatomical spatial understanding, but to identify where their answers align with formal graph-defined spatial entailments and where they fail under relation-specific and reference-frame-dependent demands.

A future step to address the semantic inconsistencies inherent in raw anatomical data concerns the implementation of a systematic translation of anatomical entities into a unified terminology. This process involves translation of diverse synonyms and traditional anatomical relations, for instance, translating 'superior' to 'above' and 'anterior' to 'in front of.' This strategy aims to bridge the gap between specialized medical ontologies and the general-purpose spatial world model that LLMs acquire during pre-training on natural language. Additional further experiments concern the evaluation of the same task on different high or low resource languages.

Future work should also explicitly examine whether the observed variability in organ-level accuracy is associated with differences in representation frequency in training data. In particular, correlating the per-organ performance reported above with independent measures of anatomical term frequency would provide a more rigorous test of this hypothesis. Such an analysis could clarify whether frequency contributes additional explanatory power beyond the effects of visual distinctiveness, structural heterogeneity, and viewpoint dependence identified in the current results (experimentally), and may inform strategies for improving model robustness across underrepresented or anatomically complex systems.

In addition, while the current study utilizes normalized relation names to maintain consistency and evaluate core structural reasoning, a compelling direction for future work involves the introduction of relational synonyms. Real-world knowledge graphs and natural language queries rarely adhere to a strictly controlled vocabulary; therefore, generating problem instances where relations are expressed through diverse lexical variants would significantly increase the challenge. By generating new graph problems that use these different names, we can test if a model still understands the graph structure even when the language changes.

**Acknowledgments.** This project has received funding from the European Union's Horizon Europe research and innovation programme under grant agreement No. 101132389 (project REEVALUATE).

# A Annex I: Anatomical Entities Included in the Dataset

**Table 2.** Grouping of anatomical entities by main organ/system

| Main organ | Entities |
|---|---|
| Thorax | Diaphragm, Endothoracic fascia, Fibrous pericardium, Pericardial sac |
| Non-organ-specific | Rectovesical septum |
| Lung | Left lung, Left main bronchus, Main bronchus, Right lung, Right main bronchus, Root of right lung |
| Pharynx | Laryngo- & Naso-pharynx, Oropharynx, Pharyngotympanic tube, Trachea |
| Esophagus | Abdominal part of esophagus, Cervical part of esophagus, T7-T9 segment of esophagus, Thoracic part of esophagus |
| Digestive system | Ascending part of duodenum, Pancreas, Superior mesenteric artery, Superior mesenteric vein |
| Urinary system | Left kidney, Left ureter, Right ureter, Urinary bladder |
| Female reproductive system | Left uterine tube, Perineal part of vagina, Right greater vestibular gland, Right uterine tube, Uterus, Vagina |
| Endocrine system | Left adrenal gland |
| Male reproductive system | Base of prostate, Collicular part of prostatic urethra, Left seminal vesicle, Prostate, Right seminal vesicle, Seminal vesicle, Subcollicular part of prostatic urethra, Supracollicular part of prostatic urethra |
| Axial skeleton/Thoracic cage/Pelvis | Body of 8th thoracic vertebra, Left 8th rib, Left 5th rib, Left 1st rib, Left 4th rib, Left pubis, Left 2nd rib, Left seventh rib, Left 3rd & 6th rib, Right 1st, 4th, 5th, 8th rib, Right pubis, Right 2nd, 3rd, 6th &7th rib |
| Brain | Angular gyrus & cingulate gyrus & inferior, middle temporal gyri & middle, superior frontal gyri, Superior temporal gyrus (anterior, middle, posterior), Supramarginal gyrus (anterior, posterior), Calcarine sulcus, Callosal sulcus, Central sulcus, Cingulate gyrus (including isthmus, posterior part), Cingulate sulcus, Collateral sulcus, Cuneus, Postcentral gyrus (dorsal, middle, ventral parts), Precentral gyrus (dorsal, middle, ventral parts), Fusiform gyrus, Inferior frontal gyrus (opercular, orbital, triangular, polar parts), Inferior frontal sulcus, Inferior temporal gyrus (middle, posterior, polar parts), Inferior temporal sulcus, Intraparietal sulcus, Lateral occipital gyrus, Lateral orbital gyrus, Lateral sulcus, Lingual gyrus, Longitudinal fissure, Middle frontal gyrus (middle, posterior, polar parts), Middle temporal gyrus (middle, posterior, polar parts), Occipitotemporal sulcus, Paracentral lobule, Parahippocampal gyrus, Parieto-occipital sulcus, Superior frontal gyrus (middle, posterior, polar parts), Superior frontal sulcus, Superior occipital gyrus, Superior parietal lobule, Superior temporal sulcus, Supramarginal gyrus, Precuneus |
| Skull/Craniofacial skeleton | Anterior fontanelle, Coronal suture, Fetal occipital bone, Fetal sagittal suture, Fetal suture, Frontal bone, Frontal process of zygomatic bone, Frontal suture, Frontonasal suture, Frontozygomatic suture, Lambdoid suture, Lateral part of occipital bone, Fetal coronal suture (left, right), Fetal frontal bone (left, right), Fetal lambdoid suture (left, right), Fetal parietal bone (left, right), Parietal bone (left, right), Parietal bone proper (left, right), Parietomastoid suture (left, right), Sphenofrontal suture (left, right), Sphenosquamosal suture (left, right), Squamous suture (left, right), Temporal part of frontal bone (left, right), Zygomaticomaxillary suture (left, right), Mastoid part of petrous part of temporal bone (left, right), Maxillary process of zygomatic bone (left, right), Nasal part of frontal bone, Occipitomastoid suture, Parietal bone proper, Parietomastoid suture, Posterior fontanelle, Right nasal bone, Sphenofrontal suture, Sphenosquamosal suture, Squamous part of temporal bone (left, right), Temporal bone, Temporal part of frontal bone, Temporal part of greater wing of sphenoid (left, right), Zygomatic process of frontal bone, Zygomatic process of maxilla (left, right) |
| Muscles/Ligaments/Bursa | Deep transverse perineal muscle, medial collateral ligament, pes anserinus and bursa (all left, right), psoas major, quadratus lumborum (left). |
| Major vessels | Azygos vein (including T7–T8 part), Inferior vena cava (including valve), Superior vena cava, Thoracic aorta (including T7–T8 and T9 parts), Left external iliac vessels (artery, vein), Duct (T7 part), Pulmonary vein (wall). |
| Heart | Atrioventricular bundle (including ventricular part), Atrioventricular node, Atrioventricular septum, Anterior interventricular branch of left coronary artery (basal zone, zones 1, 7, 13–14, 17), Circumflex branch of left coronary artery (zones 4, 10, 15), Left marginal artery (zones 6, 12, 16–18, 20), Left diagonal artery (zone 7), Chorda tendinea and papillary muscle of left ventricle, Trabecula carnea of left ventricle, Endocardium of left ventricle (anterior wall, free wall), Endocardium of right ventricle (free wall), Endocardium of atria (left, right), Endocardium of interatrial and interventricular septa, Myocardium of left ventricle (apical, basal, mid zones), Myocardium of right ventricle (apical anterior, basal anterior, basal inferior, basal septal, mid anterior, mid inferior, mid lateral zones, septal and free wall), Myocardium of interventricular septum, Myocardial zones 1–20, Interatrial septum (including membranous part), Interventricular septum (including membranous part), Internodal tracts (anterior, posterior), Sinuatrial node, Atria (left, right; including inflow part of right atrium), Ventricles (left, right), Heart (including left and right sides, T7–T9 part), Mitral valve (including fibrous ring), Walls of atria and ventricles (left, right; including left auricle and wall proper of left atrium). |

## References


1. Bigverdi, M., Ikezogwo, W.O., et al.: Medblink: probing basic perception in multimodal language models for medicine. In: 2025 IEEE/CVF International Conference on Computer Vision Workshops (ICCVW), pp. 1234–1244. IEEE (2025)
2. Bolgova, O., Mavrych, V.: Evolution of AI in anatomy education study based on comparison of current large language models against historical ChatGPT performance. Sci. Rep. **15**(1), 37545 (2025)
3. Cameron, M.H., Monroe, L.G.: Physical Rehabilitation-E-Book: Evidence-Based Examination, Evaluation, and Intervention. Elsevier Health Sciences (2007)
4. Cao, S., Lin, H., Gu, Y., Luo, Z., Ma, J.: Diffcot: diffusion-styled chain-of-thought reasoning in llms. arXiv preprint arXiv:2601.03559 (2026)
5. Chaba-Karnaś, W., et al.: Performance of seven large language models on anatomy examination questions. Clin. Anatom. (2026)
6. Cohn, A.G., Blackwell, R.E.: Evaluating the ability of large language models to reason about cardinal directions (short paper). In: COSIT 2024 (2024)
7. Anthony, G., Cohn, R.E., Blackwell: evaluating the ability of large language models to reason about cardinal directions, revisited (2025)
8. Hashmi, A.U.R.: AnatomiX, an Anatomy-Aware Grounded Multimodal Large Language Model for Chest X-Ray Interpretation (2026)
9. Lake, B.M.: Building machines that learn and think like people. Behav. Brain Sci. **40** (2017)
10. Zhao, C.: Towards Scalable Language-Image Pre-training for 3D Medical Imaging (2026)
11. Gardelakos, E.: Can large reasoning models reason about spatial relations? In: ACM SIGSPATIAL International Workshop on AI for Geographic Knowledge Discovery (2025)
12. Cerrolaza, J.J.: Computational anatomy for multi-organ analysis in medical imaging: a review (2018)
13. Kaplan, J.: Scaling laws for neural language models (2020)
14. Singhal, K.: Large language models encode clinical knowledge. Nature **620**(7972) (2023)
15. Elzayyat, M.: Assessing LLM-generated vs. expert-created clinical anatomy MCQs: a student perception-based comparative study in medical education. Med. Educ. Online **30**(1) (2025)
16. Daya, G., Yang, D., Zhang, H., et al.: DeepSeek-R1 incentivizes reasoning in LLMs through reinforcement learning. Nature **645**(8081), 633–638 (2025)
17. Team, G., Kamath, A., F.: Gemma 3 technical report. arXiv preprint arXiv:2503.19786 (2025)
18. Guo, M.-H., Xu, J., et al.: R-bench: graduate-level multi-disciplinary benchmarks for LLM & MLLM complex reasoning evaluation. arXiv preprint arXiv:2505.02018 (2025)
19. Huang, J., Chang, K.C.-C.: Towards reasoning in large language models: a survey. In: Findings of the Association for Computational Linguistics: ACL 2023, pp. 1049–1065 (2023)
20. Jain, S.: tiktoken 0.3.3. https://pypi.org/project/tiktoken/0.3.3/ (2023). A fast BPE tokenizer for use with OpenAI's models. Python package
21. Mavi, V., Jangra, A., Jatowt, A.: Multi-hop question answering. Found. Trends® Inf. Retriev. **17**(4), 457–586 (2024)

22. Mavrych, V., Ganguly, P., Bolgova, O.: Using large language models (ChatGPT, Copilot, PaLM, Bard, and Gemini) in gross anatomy course: comparative analysis. Clin. Anat. **38**(2), 200–210 (2025)
23. Ollama. Get up and running with large language models (2025). https://ollama.com/
24. Ali Salbas and Ebru Kul Baysan: Assessment of large language models in musculoskeletal radiological anatomy: a comparative study with radiologists. Joint Diseas. Relat. Surg. **37**(1), 190 (2025)
25. So, C.C., Sun, Y., et al.: Are large language models capable of deep relational reasoning? Insights from deepseek-r1 and benchmark comparisons. In: 2025 IEEE International Conference on Artificial Intelligence Testing (AITest), pp. 168–177. IEEE (2025)
26. Yoon, J., Cho, H.: Monte Carlo tree diffusion for system 2 planning. arXiv preprint arXiv:2502.07202 (2025)
27. Yue, X., Ni, Y., et al.: MMMU: a massive multi-discipline multimodal understanding and reasoning benchmark for expert AGI. In: Proceedings of the IEEE/CVF Conference on Computer Vision and Pattern Recognition (CVPR) (2024)

# When Correct Is Not Human: Comparing Human and LLM Preferences in Spatial Reasoning

Robert E. Blackwell[1(✉)], Daniel Brand[2], Anthony G. Cohn[1,3], and Marco Ragni[2]

[1] School of Computer Science, University of Leeds, Leeds, UK
r.e.blackwell@leeds.ac.uk
[2] Technische Universität Chemnitz, Chemnitz, Germany
[3] The Alan Turing Institute, London, UK

**Abstract.** Large Language Models (LLMs) are increasingly evaluated in terms of their ability to demonstrate human-like behaviour on tasks inspired by the Turing Test. We examine this evaluation from the perspective of an *Imitation Game* comparing human and LLM performance on spatial reasoning tasks. We use the Region Connection Calculus (RCC-8), a domain in which complex spatial relations can be communicated with few premises yet still requires genuine spatial understanding. While several state-of-the-art LLMs achieve substantially higher logical accuracy than humans, accuracy alone does not fully characterize their suitability as assistant systems. By analysing response distributions, we identify systematic differences between the relations preferred by humans and those preferred by LLMs, even when LLMs are prompted to respond in a human-like manner. These differences show that cognitive adequacy is not met in these tests of spatial cognition in LLMs.

**Keywords:** Spatial Cognition · Reasoning Preferences · Qualitative Spatial and Temporal Reasoning (QSTR) · Large Language Models (LLMs) · Artificial Intelligence (AI)

## 1 Introduction

Large Language Models (LLMs) have demonstrated impressive performance on a range of reasoning tasks leading some researchers to claim that Artificial Intelligence (AI) has now passed the Turing test (e.g. [7]). In the Turing Test (originally known as the Imitation Game), an interrogator attempts to distinguish between a human and a machine solely based on their responses [28]. If it is impossible to tell the difference between a human and a machine, Turing argued, then the machine can reasonably be regarded as intelligent (or at least be capable of - functionally - imitating or simulating human cognitive capacity). While this has been debated for a long time in the philosophical, AI and cognitive literature [19], LLMs can generate human text remarkably well, and have some ability to


E. Farran et al. (Eds.): Spatial Cognition 2026, LNAI 16785, pp. 131–145, 2027.
https://doi.org/10.1007/978-3-032-36716-7_9

reason logically, a stronger test could be, how well they can deal with spatial cognition, namely with topological spatial reasoning that requires some form of spatial representations, going beyond pure syntactical logical operations.

Indeed, some researchers claim that "spatial is special" [10], not only because it reflects questions of embodiment, but that there are mechanisms and representations that are quite special in reasoning, for example, see [26]. We will consider the Region Connection Calculus (with eight relations, RCC-8 for short) which has been well investigated both from a formal and cognitive perspective [3,22]. RCC-8 is a qualitative spatial calculus for representing and reasoning about spatial relations between non-empty regular closed regions of uniform dimension in a topological space.

An interesting aspect of such calculi is their so-called *cognitive adequacy*. This captures whether the 'reasoning mechanism of the calculus is structurally similar to the way people reason' and if 'empirical evidence supports the assumption that a system of relations is a model of people's conceptual knowledge of spatial relationships' [13]. RCC-8 consists of eight relations: DC (Disconnected), EC (Externally Connected), PO (Partially Overlapping), TPP (Tangential Proper Part), NTPP (Non Tangential Proper Part), EQ (Equals), TPPi (the inverse of TPP) and NTPPi (the inverse of NTPP) (Fig. 1). The composition of two relations $R_1(x, y)$ and $R_2(y, z)$ is defined as the set of all relations $R_3(x, z)$ that may hold between $x$ and $z$ given that $R_1$ holds between $x$ and $y$ and $R_2$ holds between $y$ and $z$. Thus the Composition Table (CT) lists all compositions for all the pairs of RCC-8 relations (64 entries). Consider a simple example:

Circle A is disconnected from Circle B
Circle B is disconnected from Circle C

---

What is a possible relation between Circles A and C?

A human reasoner might imagine the three circles (they are taken as prototypical regions, but of course more general regions are possible) A, B, and C, where the two relations between A and B, and, B and C, are known (namely that both are disconnected). By inspecting his mental model, the human reasoner can then infer for instance, that circles A and C are also disconnected (in fact in our experiments this is the most likely response with 43% percent of all human answers including disconnected).

Research shows that humans demonstrate preferences in multiple model cases, i.e., they prefer some relations over the others [14,23].

The overall question now is whether, in terms of the Imitation Game, LLMs demonstrate the same preferences. *If* LLMs can pass the test (as has been claimed), that might allow LLMs to serve as cost-effective proxies or synthetic subjects in social science experiments (e.g. [8]). Researchers are exploring how LLMs can simulate human responses, replicate experimental outcomes, or generate distributions of behaviour. At the same time researchers also debate the limits and risks of this approach [25].

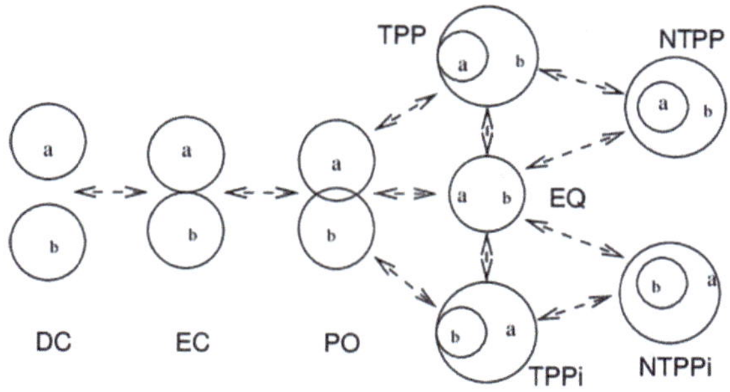


**Fig. 1.** The eight relations of the RCC-8 calculus illustrated in 2D [3]: DC (Disconnected), EC (Externally Connected), PO (Partially Overlapping), TPP (Tangential Proper Part), NTPP (Nontangential Proper Part) and EQ (Equals); TPPi and NTPPi are the inverses of TPP and NTPP respectively since they are asymmetric.

That leads us to the following research question: *To what extent do LLMs win the Imitation Game*? More precisely:

RQ1: How good are LLMs at solving RCC-8 problems compared to humans?
RQ2: How does the reasoning behaviour of LLMs compare to humans?
RQ3: Can LLM answers be distinguished from human answers?

In this paper we ask both human and LLM subjects questions about the RCC-8 CT and their preferred composition relation. By directly comparing distributions of preferred composition relations across humans and LLMs, we aim to shed light on both the cognitive plausibility of LLM spatial reasoning and the nature of human and AI inductive biases in qualitative spatial inference.

## 2 Related Work

Cohn and Blackwell (2025) [4] tested the ability of large language models to reason about RCC-8 compositions and also considered preferred compositions, comparing their results to an earlier human study by Ragni et al. (2007) [21]. The results suggest that humans show strong, consistent preferences but that LLM preferences only weakly align. However, the experiments used RCC-8 terminology that may not be readily accessible to non-technical respondents and the human and LLM experiments were formulated differently, confounding precise comparison.

Liu et al. (2025) [17] surveyed spatial reasoning in multimodal large language models, outlining key tasks, benchmarks, and methods. They highlighted a persistent gap between current models and human-like spatial understanding. Li et al. (2025) [15] used 11Plus-Bench, a spatial reasoning benchmark inspired by human spatial aptitude tests, to assess the spatial reasoning abilities of MLLMs relative to human performance. They found that while some MLLMs exhibit early signs of spatial cognition and share some human-like patterns (e.g., increased effort with higher reasoning complexity), MLLM performance is much less predictable than human performance. Shiri et al. (2024) [27], claim that MLLMs struggle with spatial questions that require a human perspective.

## 3 Experimental Design

We designed two experimental tasks, each consisting of 64 problems. They contain all possible combinations of the respective 8 RCC relations in the two premises.

In the first experimental task we test the ability of a participant to determine *all* compositions of two relations (requiring consideration of all possibilities) by asking the participant to select *every* possible composition via a multiple-choice format. We refer to this as the *spatial relation enumeration* condition. In the second experimental task we ask the participant to select a single, preferred answer, in a single-choice format. Accordingly, we refer to this as the *spatial relation preference* condition.

In the RCC-8 CT, 37 of the 64 tasks have multiple possible answers, while the remaining tasks only have a single logically valid option.

The *spatial relation enumeration* condition allows us to better understand the *spatial relation preference* data, disentangling which responses are chosen as actual *preferences* and which were simply considered to be the only options possible. For both conditions, the experiment starts with task instructions. Each relation is explained with examples and illustrative images, so that the interpretation of the relations is well-defined and clear (see Fig. 2 for examples).

Although the RCC-8 relation names were designed to precisely represent each of the RCC-8 concepts, we choose more informal language to make the task more accessible for human participants with no formal or mathematical education: "Disconnected" for DC, "Touching from the outside" for EC, "Overlapping" for PO, "Equal" for EQ, "Touching from within" for TPP, "Touched from within" for TPPi, "Fully contained within" for NTPP, and "Fully contains" for NTPPi.

### 3.1 Human Experiment

We pose the questions to human participants using Prolific[1]. Participants are randomly assigned to either condition (*spatial relation enumeration* or *spatial relation preference*). After giving consent, they are presented with the respective instructions for their condition. To give their answers, participants in both conditions have to select the respective response options, and then press one of two buttons (*I am confident* or *I needed to guess*) to lock in their response. This allows us to assess their confidence without introducing additional questions that would prolong the experiment. We collected data from 59 participants, with $n = 29$ for the *spatial relation enumeration* condition and $n = 30$ participants for the *spatial relation preference* condition, respectively.

[1] https://www.prolific.com/, retrieved April 2026.

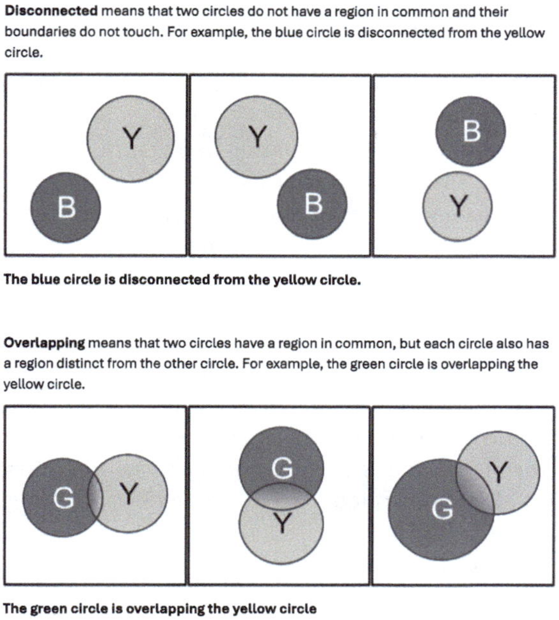


**Fig. 2.** Two examples (DC and PO) of relation descriptions and corresponding illustrative images. The other six relations are described and illustrated similarly.

### 3.2 LLM Experiment

We also pose the questions to a selection of state-of-the-art LLMs via their Application Programming Interfaces (APIs) using Markdown format[2] to enable subheadings and emboldening of text. We remove instructions aimed specifically at humans (e.g. "Please avoid distractions", and "Don't use a smartphone"). We number the answer options from 1 to 8 (in the same order that they appear to human respondents) to facilitate selection, and require output in JSON[3] format for automated evaluation.

The human experiments include diagrams illustrating each of the RCC-8 relations (e.g. Fig. 2), but many LLMs do not have a visual input modality. Vision Language Models (VLMs) extend LLMs with vision encoders so that they can accept images as input in addition to text [16]. There are now many LLMs and VLMs available (e.g. there are 349 models listed on OpenRouter[4]), and it would be infeasible to test them all. We therefore test three representative VLMs - Gemini 3 Flash Preview (*Gemini*), OpenAI GPT-5.2 (*GPT*), and Qwen3-VL-235B-A22B-Instruct (*Qwen*), with and without these illustrative images. We

[2] https://www.markdownguide.org/basic-syntax/, retrieved April 2026.

[3] JavaScript Object Notation, https://www.json.org/json-en.html, retrieved April 2026.

[4] OpenRouter is a popular LLM aggregator, https://openrouter.ai/api/v1/models/count, retrieved April 2026.

also choose three representative LLMs, Claude Sonnet 4.5 (*Claude*), because of its claims to be one of the best models for building AI agents[5], Deepseek V-3.2 (*Deepseek*), a leading Chinese model, and EuroLLM-22B (*EuroLLM*), an emerging European model.

Some models have parameters including *temperature*, *top_p* and a *random seed.* For simplicity, and to avoid favouring one model over another, we accept each model's default parameters. We define *prompt engineering* as the practice of customising a prompt in a model-specific manner to elicit the best results for that model. We avoid prompt engineering and prompt optimisation as far as possible (although we do ask for JSON outputs to facilitate automated analyses, see above), preferring to keep the prompt consistent for all models and as similar as possible to the human experiments. Each question is posed in a separate session to avoid any context or memory effects (this is usual practice for LLM evaluation, although we acknowledge that humans answer the questions sequentially). We first test models with n = 3 experimental repeats to get an overview of accuracy, increasing to n = 30 for the two most accurate models, enabling a more detailed statistical comparison[6].

Burnell et al. [2] call for the routine release of LLM evaluation results and more granular reporting practices to improve transparency and robustness in AI system evaluations. Accordingly, we publish all our experimental data including all prompts and API request/response pairs for all experiments[7].

# 4 Evaluation

## 4.1 Task Performance (RQ1)

We measure the accuracy of the *spatial relation enumeration* condition using strict accuracy where an answer must be precisely correct), and using the Jaccard coefficient (i.e., the size of the overlap between predicted and correct relations divided by the size of their union), which accounts for partially correct answers (i.e., answers where too many or too few relations are specified. See [1] for more information).

Five of the LLMs tested answered RCC-8 *spatial relation enumeration* questions more accurately than humans (see Table 1). While *EuroLLM* gets none of the answers precisely correct, it does get 160/192 partially correct (i.e. Jaccard coefficient > 0). *GPT* and *Gemini* are the best performing models (mean accuracy .99, and .62, n = 3 respectively), whereas humans only answered with .26 mean accuracy (n = 29). Human answers have the highest accuracy standard deviation (.19), with LLMs having a much narrower accuracy standard deviation (the widest being *Claude* and *Qwen*, .02). Humans typically respond with fewer relations (mean 1.99) than LLMs (mean 3.2). Although *Gemini* and

[5] https://www.anthropic.com/news/claude-sonnet-4-5, retrieved April 2026.

[6] Experimental repeats using commercial LLMs can be costly. The confidence intervals for n = 3 are narrow, and so we only increase to n = 30 when direct comparison with human experiments is required.

[7] https://github.com/RobBlackwell/sc2026, accessed June 2026.

*Claude* make errors in roughly 40% of tasks, their high Jaccard coefficients (.84 and .81, respectively) show that their responses still substantially overlap with the correct relations. While human accuracy is only slightly below *Qwen* (.26 vs .28), the Jaccard coefficient is substantially lower (.47 compared to .63). Despite solving a similar number of tasks correctly, human answers deviate further from the correct solution.

LLMs tend to specify too many relations more often than too few (*Claude* 14.6% of the cases, compared to 14.1%; *Deepseek* 22.9% to 20.8%; *EuroLLM* 31.8% to 27.6%; *Gemini* 25.5% to 4.7%; *Qwen* 42.7% to 15.1%; and *GPT* 0.5% to 0.0%). In contrast, humans tend to provide too few relations (27.6%), rather than too many (13.8%).

Including illustrative images in prompts to VLMs has little effect on the accuracy of *spatial relation enumeration* answers compared to purely textual prompts (e.g. *GPT*, 1.00 compared to .995, and *Gemini*, .62 compared to .656) and so we proceed with text only prompting of LLMs.

Overall, LLMs were confident 96% of the time, whereas humans were confident 82% of the time. Most models (*Deepseek*, *EuroLLM*, *Gemini*, and *GPT*) always declared that they were "confident" in all their answers[8]. While the confidence of the human participants seems to be relatively high given the low accuracy, it is likely an effect of the multiple-choice task: On average, humans selected at least a partially correct response in 82.5% of the tasks. Given that they selected too few relations, it is possible that the confidence was indeed high in the relations they selected while simply missing the others.

**Table 1.** *spatial relation enumeration* accuracy. Models are ordered by mean accuracy; *GPT* achieves near-perfect performance, substantially outperforming both humans and other models. Responses is the mean number of relations specified in each answer. Jaccard is a measure of similarity between predicted and correct relations. LLM experiments use $n = 3$, and human $n = 28$ experimental repeats.

| Experiment | Responses | Accuracy | Jaccard |
|---|---|---|---|
| *GPT* | $3.03 \pm 0.02$ | $.99 \pm .01$ | $1.0 \pm .0$ |
| *Gemini* | $3.49 \pm 0.03$ | $.62 \pm .01$ | $.84 \pm .0$ |
| *Claude* | $2.99 \pm 0.09$ | $.58 \pm .02$ | $.81 \pm .0$ |
| *Deepseek* | $2.91 \pm 0.10$ | $.37 \pm .01$ | $.62 \pm .0$ |
| *Qwen* | $3.91 \pm 0.07$ | $.28 \pm .02$ | $.63 \pm .0$ |
| **Human** | $2.27 \pm 1.67$ | $.26 \pm .19$ | $.47 \pm .4$ |
| *EuroLLM* | $2.91 \pm 0.10$ | $.00 \pm .00$ | $.33 \pm .0$ |

[8] Note that this "perceived confidence" of LLMs is purely an artefact of their generation process rather than actual inspection of the final layer output probabilities. Kalai et al. [11] argue that LLMs "hallucinate because the training and evaluation procedures reward guessing over acknowledging uncertainty" – thus acknowledging a lack of confidence is not reinforced during training.

Based on our results, the two most accurate models are *GPT* and *Gemini*. Therefore, we focus on these throughout the following analyses. Although the models are consistent (given the low standard deviation in accuracy, Jaccard coefficient and number of responses) in the *spatial relation enumeration* condition, we increase the number of repeats to $n = 30$ for these two models in the *spatial relation preference* condition to match the number of human participants. All remaining LLMs are tested with $n = 3$ repeats.

Five of the LLMs tested answered with more correct *spatial relation preference* answers than humans (Table 2). *GPT* is the best performing model (63.9/64, 99.8%), whereas human participants only answered with 41.5/64 (64.84%) correct preferences on average. The rank ordering of accuracy is similar in both the *spatial relation enumeration* and *spatial relation preference* condition results (compare Tables 1 and 2).

**Table 2.** *spatial relation preference* accuracy (rows ordered by mean accuracy). A response is accurate if it is one of the possible entries in the actual RCC-8 composition table.

| Preference Experiment | Accuracy |
|---|---|
| *GPT* (n = 30) | .998 ± .005 |
| *Claude* (n = 3) | .99 ± .01 |
| *Gemini* (n = 30) | .976 ± .008 |
| *Deepseek* (n = 3) | .89 ± .03 |
| *Qwen* (n = 3) | .86 ± .02 |
| **Human (n = 30)** | .648 ± .179 |
| *EuroLLM* (n = 3) | .62 ± .02 |

## 4.2 Comparison of Response Behaviour (RQ2)

In the following analysis, we look at *spatial relation preference* in more detail. Given the high accuracy of *GPT*, the corresponding preferences become a more important factor for differentiating LLMs than accuracy alone. Here, comparison with humans is particularly interesting, given that one of the primary use-cases for LLMs is chat-based interaction with human users.

To this end, we tried the instruction "Answer the question as if you were a human" in the preference question prompt. However, the most frequently selected answers (MFA) were largely unaffected: The congruency between the MFA with and without the instruction to give human-like answers was 98.8% for *Gemini* and 96.9% for *GPT*, which correspond to only 1 and 2 different responses, respectively. Furthermore, it had little effect on accuracy either (e.g. *GPT* 1.0 ± .0 (n = 3) compared to .998 ± .005 (n = 30), and *Gemini* .969 ± .0 (n = 3) compared to .975 ± .008 (n = 30). The word "human" is only mentioned in

5 of the available 174 *GPT* reasoning summaries (3%) when the instruction was given and never when the instruction was not given. These results indicate that LLMs pay little attention to the "Answer the question as if you were a human" instruction and so we omit it in subsequent experiments.

Figure 3 compares the respective response behaviour of *GPT* and *Gemini* to human participants. Both LLMs prefer relations that are also preferred by humans, except when these conflict with correctness. However, there are some noteworthy exceptions: *Gemini* made mistakes that are in line with human mistakes in two cases (EC_TPP and TPPi_TPP). Both LLMs select the relation PO, for NTPPi_NTPP– one of the least preferred options for humans – indicating a substantially different approach to this task. Overall, *GPT* showed more variance in its response behaviour, while *Gemini* was more consistent in its preferred responses.

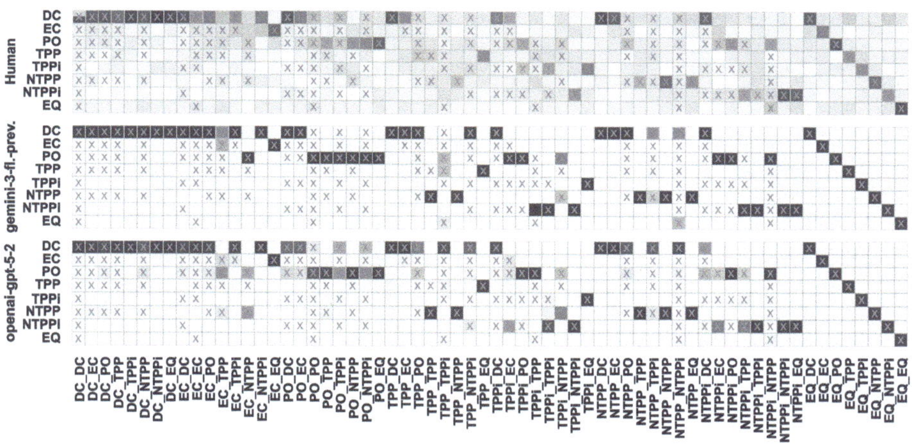

**Fig. 3.** Comparison of human, *GPT* and *Gemini* response patterns for each of the RCC-8 relation compositions (*spatial relation preference* condition). Darker shades of blue indicate higher frequency of response. *X* marks a correct response. (Color figure online)

In order to quantify LLM preference similarity to humans, we compared the patterns based on the congruence of the most frequently selected answer (MFA) and the congruency of all *commonly selected* responses. For this, we used a threshold of 26.6% for determining which of the *spatial relation preference* relations can be considered *commonly selected* (based on a binomial test ensuring a probability of 99% of a non-random result given $n = 30$ observations).

Besides *GPT* and *Gemini*, which have 30 observations for each task, we also included the other LLMs. Note that for the other LLMs (with $n = 3$), the lowest percentage of a selected response is 33.3% (if selected in one of the 3 repeats), which is above our threshold. We only considered tasks where multiple relations were valid solutions in order to focus on preferences by avoiding "forced decisions" due to logical correctness. The results are shown in Table 3.

The *Gemini* model has the most similar preferences to human respondents as measured by MFA, whereas *GPT* has the highest congruency based on the whole response pattern. This is surprising at first glance, since both LLMs are substantially more accurate than humans, yet still respond with similar preferences to humans, whereas LLMs like *Qwen* and *EuroLLM* have a more similar performance to humans. However, after further consideration, it becomes apparent that human performance can be deceptive: when considering the most frequently selected responses across all human participants, accuracy increases to 93.8%, i.e. while humans individually have a low accuracy, they perform similarly well as *GPT* and *Gemini* when evaluated as a collective.

**Table 3.** Most-frequent answer (MFA) congruence and response pattern congruence between the human data and LLMs for the *spatial relation preference* condition.

| Model | MFA | Responses |
|---|---|---|
| *Gemini* | 92.9% | 87.5% |
| *Deepseek* | 92.2% | 85.1% |
| *GPT* | 90.2% | 88.9% |
| *Qwen* | 90.2% | 85.5% |
| *Claude* | 89.5% | 85.5% |
| *EuroLLM* | 82.8% | 77.0% |

We checked if each selected preference is also contained in the corresponding response from the *spatial relation enumeration* condition (if it is not, the result cannot be considered a valid preference). We use the same threshold of 26.6% as for determining which of the relations can be considered to be *commonly selected.* The results are Humans (95.3%), *GPT*(100%) and *Gemini*(100%) showing that preferences are predominantly chosen from the set of valid possibilities.

Investigating the reasoning summaries of *Deepseek* shows a possible explanation: While *Deepseek* does not always provide a reasoning trace, the cases in which it does (41 out of 192) usually show a propensity to determine all possible answers before settling on a preferred answer (although we do not see this for *GPT* perhaps because it only provides a reasoning summary). It is unlikely that humans engage in a similar strategy, since they need a higher median time when selecting multiple responses in the *spatial relation enumeration* condition (35.5 s) compared to the *spatial relation preference* condition (27.1 s).

To gain deeper insight into the preferences and their relation to the *spatial relation enumeration* condition, we investigated whether responses are selected in a manner consistent with the conceptual neighbourhood (CN) shown in Fig. 1. Prior work [12] indicated that, although cross-cultural differences are possible, humans generally appear to first test relations from the left of the CN (i.e., DC) and proceed to the right, that is, to relations with the least overlap (except EQ). For example, they test whether DC is a potential conclusion, followed by EC or EQ, and then PO or NTTPi. We investigate if the selected relations in the *spatial relation enumeration* condition follow a similar pattern of an expanding neighbourhood starting from the respective preferred relation in the *spatial relation preference* condition. To this end, we calculated the respective distances between the relations of both conditions according to the CN. Table 4 shows the rate of occurrence for each distance. In line with the results by [12], humans selected predominantly relations in the closer neighbourhood (with a distance of 1 or 2) to the preferred relation, with a steep decline for distance 3 that then continued to the maximum distance of 4. For all LLMs, the general trend was similar, with *GPT*, *Gemini* and *Claude* being the most similar to humans. For both the human participants and the LLMs, the closer relations are chosen more frequently. However, the effect is more pronounced for humans than for the LLMs. While *GPT* simply reflects the correct solution, *Gemini* and *Claude* still show similar proportions, despite achieving substantially lower accuracies in the *spatial relation enumeration* condition. In this sense, they mimic properties of the correct response behaviour without actually finding the correct responses. For *Deepseek* and *Qwen* the behaviour substantially deviates from humans, with both lacking the decline from the distance of 1 and 2 and showing even a rising proportion of distance 4 relations compared to a distance of 3. Finally, *EuroLLM* deviates from both humans and other LLMs. However, it is most likely an artefact of the poor performance in the *spatial relation enumeration* condition, where it failed to solve a single task fully correctly.

**Table 4.** Rate of occurrence of conceptual neighbourhood graph distances (see Fig. 1). Distances are calculated between relations in the *spatial relation enumeration* condition and the preferred relation.

| Model | 1 | 2 | 3 | 4 |
|---|---|---|---|---|
| *GPT* | 57.81% | 50.00% | 29.69% | 26.56% |
| *Gemini* | 56.25% | 48.44% | 26.56% | 26.56% |
| *Claude* | 65.62% | 53.12% | 21.88% | 20.31% |
| *Deepseek* | 71.88% | 71.88% | 42.19% | 48.44% |
| *Qwen* | 71.88% | 70.31% | 26.56% | 28.12% |
| *EuroLLM* | 79.69% | 89.06% | 56.25% | 45.31% |
| Humans | 67.19% | 54.69% | 29.69% | 23.44% |

To explore whether humans and LLMs expend similar reasoning effort for the *spatial relation preference* and the *spatial relation enumeration* questions, we examine the correlation between human response times and LLM completion tokens. We use *GPT* completion token counts rather than *Gemini* token counts because the *GPT* reported totals include reasoning tokens. The Spearman rank-order correlation coefficient between the completion tokens of *GPT* and the median human response times for each task did not reach significance for the *spatial relation preference* condition ($r_s(62) = .172$, $p = .087$), but for the *spatial relation enumeration* condition ($r_s(62) = .598$, $p < .001$). Thereby, the correlation for the *spatial relation enumeration* condition could be influenced by the number of responses that vary between the tasks (e.g., humans needing more time due to the higher number of clicks when selecting multiple options). However, such effects do not apply to *GPT* and since it solved the task with near-perfect accuracy, it had to at least consider all options for each task. Therefore, the correlation for the *spatial relation enumeration* condition suggests that some tasks are indeed inherently more complex for both humans and LLMs, but it does not necessarily imply that similar solving strategies are used by humans and LLMs. It does suggest that *GPT* uses a strategy and is not relying on merely *recognizing* the answer directly from its training data.

### 4.3 Detecting Human Responses (RQ3)

To determine whether human responses are distinguishable from LLM responses, we train a simple machine learning classifier (a logistic regression model with one-hotencoded categorical features) using 15 stratified random examples (at least two samples from each of the six LLMs) and 15 random examples from human respondents (each example is a set of 64 responses to the *spatial relation preference* questions). We then run the classifier on the remaining data, achieving an accuracy of 95.8% on the test set (training $n = 30$, testing $n = 72$), with an F1-score of 0.90 for the human class and 0.97 for the LLM class. The classifier demonstrates that human and AI respondents are highly distinguishable. Indeed the confusion matrix shows only three mistakes – two where the classifier predicted an LLM response when it was actually a human response and one vice versa.

## 5 Discussion

Our results show that state-of-the-art LLMs such as *GPT* are much more accurate than humans when answering RCC-8 reasoning problems which involve predicting the relationship(s) between x and z when given the relationships between x and y, and y and z. This finding is consistent with reports in the literature of LLMs surpassing human performance across domains, including neuroscience [18] and social science [20]. Critics have argued that the Imitation Game is easily gamed and unsuitable as a test of Artificial General Intelligence [9,19]. We agree, but this is not our focus. Rather, we use the Imitation Game to assess how human-like LLM reasoning currently is, including cases where models are explicitly asked to behave in a human-like manner. While much work focuses on improving correctness, selecting a preference among several valid answers in a human-like manner is also important if LLMs are to be aligned with humans. We therefore consider preference comparison between Humans and LLM evaluation, particularly in settings where accuracy is already high, as a new game.

The theory of *preferred mental models* [14] proposes that humans construct the simplest model consistent with the premises. This explains the preference for models with minimal overlapping complexity and accounts for the prominence of DC observed in our data, consistent with earlier findings in syllogistic and spatial reasoning [21]. We have shown that LLM RCC-8 CT preferences differ from human preferences, even when models are prompted to "answer as if you were a human." In our tests, a simple classifier is sufficient to discriminate LLM responses from human responses in 95.8% of cases, showing that higher logical accuracy does not imply human-like reasoning. Our results further highlight the continued need for sampling human subjects.

This observation aligns with the large-scale replication study of [5], who found that while LLMs achieved high replication rates for main effects, they consistently produced larger effect sizes than human studies. Together, these findings suggest that LLMs cannot currently replace human participants when the structure of human responses is of interest. Inspection of reasoning traces of *Deepseek* reveals a potential explanation: it often determines all possible answers before selecting a preferred one, whereas the differences in response times between selecting a preferred relation and all possible options suggest that humans do not reason in this way.

A possible limitation of RCC-8 as an evaluation framework is that its relations admit a direct symbolic and set-theoretic interpretation, meaning that LLM performance may reflect retrieval and recombination of formal relations rather than genuinely spatial reasoning. Consequently, differences between human and LLM behaviour may arise from fundamentally different strategies, visuospatial mental models in humans versus symbolic reasoning in LLMs.

We did not explicitly measure cognitive load or fatigue effects across trials and thus cannot formally assess whether human performance changes over the course of the experiment. Nevertheless, we did not find evidence of systematic performance drift between earlier and later items in the dataset. LLMs are, of course, not subject to cognitive load or fatigue effects in the same way as humans.

We observed little improvement in overall accuracy when illustrative images were included in the prompt compared to text-only prompts. While others have reported weaknesses in current vision–language models [6], text-only LLMs already show a remarkable capacity for reasoning about RCC-8 relations, and multimodal capability may improve this in the future.

The question remains as to why LLM preferences differ from human preferences. One possibility is that training data increasingly incorporate synthetic content and may no longer fully reflect human behaviour, although this cannot be verified. More likely, the difference reflects a fundamental difference in how humans and LLMs approach reasoning tasks. Humans are well known to build mental models, whereas it is unclear whether LLMs do so (e.g. [24]).

**Disclosure of Interests.** The authors have no competing interests to declare that are relevant to the content of this article.

## References


1. Brand, D., Ragni, M.: Effect of response format on syllogistic reasoning. In: Goldwater, M., Anggoro, F.K., Hayes, B.K., Ong, D.C. (eds.) Proceedings of the 45th Annual Conference of the Cognitive Science Society, pp. 2408–2414 (2023)
2. Burnell, R., et al.: Rethink reporting of evaluation results in AI. Science **380**(6641), 136–138 (2023)
3. Cohn, A.G., Bennett, B., Gooday, J., Gotts, N.M.: Qualitative spatial representation and reasoning with the region connection calculus. GeoInformatica **1**(3), 275–316 (1997)
4. Cohn, A.G., Blackwell, R.E.: Can large language models reason about the region connection calculus? (2024). https://arxiv.org/abs/2411.19589
5. Cui, Z., Li, N., Zhou, H.: A large-scale replication of scenario-based experiments in psychology and management using large language models. Nat. Comput. Sci. **5**(8), 627–634 (2025)
6. Dahou, Y., Huynh, N.D., Le-Khac, P.H., Para, W.R., Singh, A., Narayan, S.: SalBench: vision-language models can't see the obvious. In: Proceedings of the IEEE/CVF International Conference on Computer Vision (ICCV) (2025). https://salbench.github.io
7. Gibney, E.: AI language models killed the Turing test: do we even need a replacement? Nature (2025). https://doi.org/10.1038/d41586-025-03386-w. https://www.nature.com/articles/d41586-025-03386-w. News article
8. Grossmann, I., Feinberg, M., Parker, D.C., Christakis, N.A., Tetlock, P.E., Cunningham, W.A.: AI and the transformation of social science research. Science **380**(6650), 1108–1109 (2023)
9. Halpern, M.: The trouble with the Turing test. New Atlantis **11**, 42–63 (2006)
10. Ishikawa, T., Newcombe, N.S.: Why spatial is special in education, learning, and everyday activities. Cogn. Res. Principles Implications **6**(1), 20 (2021)
11. Kalai, A.T., Nachum, O., Vempala, S.S., Zhang, E.: Why language models hallucinate (2025). https://arxiv.org/abs/2509.04664
12. Knauff, M., Ragni, M.: Cross-cultural preferences in spatial reasoning. J. Cogn. Cult. **11**(1–2), 1–21 (2011)
13. Knauff, M., Rauh, R., Renz, J.: A cognitive assessment of topological spatial relations: results from an empirical investigation. In: Hirtle, S.C., Frank, A.U. (eds.) COSIT 1997. LNCS, vol. 1329, pp. 193–206. Springer, Heidelberg (1997). https://doi.org/10.1007/3-540-63623-4_51
14. Knauff, M., Rauh, R., Schlieder, C.: Preferred mental models in qualitative spatial reasoning: a cognitive assessment of Allen's calculus. In: Proceedings of the Seventeenth Annual Conference of the Cognitive Science Society, pp. 200–205 (1995)
15. Li, C., et al.: 11plus-bench: demystifying multimodal LLM spatial reasoning with cognitive-inspired analysis (2025). https://arxiv.org/abs/2508.20068
16. Liu, H., Li, C., Wu, Q., Lee, Y.J.: Visual instruction tuning. In: Advances in Neural Information Processing Systems, vol. 36, pp. 34892–34916 (2023)
17. Liu, W., Xue, Q., Wang, H., Yin, X., Yang, B., Gao, W.: Spatial reasoning in multimodal large language models: a survey of tasks, benchmarks and methods (2025). arXiv preprint arXiv:2511.15722
18. Luo, X., et al.: Large language models surpass human experts in predicting neuroscience results. Nat. Hum. Behav. **9**(2), 305–315 (2025)
19. Mitchell, M.: The Turing Test and our shifting conceptions of intelligence. Science **385**(6710), eadq9356 (2024)

20. Mittelstädt, J.M., Maier, J., Goerke, P., Zinn, F., Hermes, M.: Large language models can outperform humans in social situational judgments. Sci. Rep. **14**(1), 27449 (2024)
21. Ragni, M., Tseden, B., Knauff, M.: Cross-cultural similarities in topological reasoning. In: Winter, S., Duckham, M., Kulik, L., Kuipers, B. (eds.) COSIT 2007. LNCS, vol. 4736, pp. 32–46. Springer, Heidelberg (2007). https://doi.org/10.1007/978-3-540-74788-8_3. http://geosensor.net/cositprivate/65.pdf
22. Randell, D., Cui, Z., Cohn, A.G.: A spatial logic based on regions and connection. In: 3rd International Conference on Knowledge Representation and Reasoning, vol. 92, pp. 165–176 (1992)
23. Renz, J., Rauh, R., Knauff, M.: Towards cognitive adequacy of topological spatial relations. In: Freksa, C., Habel, C., Brauer, W., Wender, K.F. (eds.) Spatial Cognition II. LNCS (LNAI), vol. 1849, pp. 184–197. Springer, Heidelberg (2000). https://doi.org/10.1007/3-540-45460-8_14
24. Robertson, C., Wolff, P.: LLM world models are mental: output layer evidence of brittle world model use in LLM mechanical reasoning (2025). arXiv preprint arXiv:2507.15521
25. Rossi, L., Harrison, K., Shklovski, I.: The problems of LLM-generated data in social science research. Sociologica Int. J. Sociol. Debate **18**(2), 145–168 (2024)
26. Shepard, R.N., Metzler, J.: Mental rotation of three-dimensional objects. Science **171**(3972), 701–703 (1971)
27. Shiri, F., Guo, X.Y., Far, M.G., Yu, X., Haf, R., Li, Y.F.: An empirical analysis on spatial reasoning capabilities of large multimodal models. In: Al-Onaizan, Y., Bansal, M., Chen, Y.N. (eds.) Proceedings of the 2024 Conference on Empirical Methods in Natural Language Processing, pp. 21440–21455. Association for Computational Linguistics, Miami, Florida, USA (2024)
28. Turing, A.M.: Computing machinery and intelligence. Mind **59**(236), 433–460 (1950). https://doi.org/10.1093/mind/LIX.236.433

# Reliability of Spatial Cues Modifies Entorhinal-Hippocampal Functional Connectivity

Maayan Merhav[1,2](✉)

[1] German Center for Neurodegenerative Diseases (DZNE), Aging and Cognition Research Group, Leipziger Str. 44, 39120 Magdeburg, Germany
merhavmaa@telhai.ac.il
[2] Education Department, Tel Hai College, Upper Galilee 1220800, Israel

**Abstract.** When navigating, humans and other species rely on landmarks and on self-motion cues to infer their position in space. It is suggested that in cue-integration processes, reliable cues are highly weighed, compared to less reliable ones. Yet, the neural circuits that underlie weighting of navigational cues are not fully understood. The current study explores the role of the entorhinal-hippocampal connections in weighting navigational cues. High resolution, functional images (7 t fMRI) were acquired while participants performed a navigational task, subjected to modified reliability levels of landmarks and self-motion cues. The findings indicate that shifts in spatial-cue reliability are associated with modifications in functional connectivity from the entorhinal cortex to the CA3 hippocampal-subfield. The findings suggest a neural mechanism which entailed in the weighting of landmark and self-motion cues during wayfinding.

**Keywords:** Navigation · Cue-Integration · Cue Reliability · Entorhinal Cortex · Hippocampus · Functional-Connectivity

## 1 Introduction

Navigation relies on integrating information from external landmarks and self-motion cues to estimate one's position in space [1, 2]. Landmark information is derived from stable features in the environment [3, 4], whereas self-motion cues arise from internal signals - including vestibular, proprioceptive, and visual (optic-flow) inputs - that support path integration [5, 6]. A large body of behavioral work suggests that humans combine these sources of information in a statistically optimal manner, weighting each cue according to its reliability to reduce uncertainty and improve navigational accuracy [7–10].

Despite substantial progress in characterizing behavioral aspects of cue integration, the neural mechanisms underlying how the brain dynamically weights navigational cues remain incompletely understood [11, 12]. In humans, neuroimaging studies have consistently implicated the medial temporal lobe, particularly the hippocampus and entorhinal


E. Farran et al. (Eds.): Spatial Cognition 2026, LNAI 16785, pp. 146–156, 2027.
https://doi.org/10.1007/978-3-032-36716-7_10

cortex (EC), in spatial navigation and the integration of spatial information from multiple sources [13–15]. These regions have been shown to support representations of spatial layout, distance, and goal direction, and to contribute to both landmark-based navigation and path integration [16, 17].

A growing body of research has further suggested functional differentiation within the entorhinal cortex. In rodents, medial and lateral subdivisions of the entorhinal cortex have been associated with self-motion-related and object-related processing [18]. Translating this organization to humans, it has been proposed that posterior entorhinal cortex (pEC) preferentially supports spatial and self-motion-related computations, whereas anterior entorhinal cortex (aEC) is more involved in processing object- and landmark-related information [11, 19, 20]. However, this proposed dissociation remains under active debate in the human neuroimaging literature. Empirical findings have been mixed, and the extent to which rodent medial-lateral distinctions map onto the human anterior-posterior axis is not fully resolved [15, 17]. Moreover, entorhinal representations may be flexible and task-dependent rather than strictly segregated.

Within this framework, interactions between the entorhinal cortex and hippocampal subfields may play a key role in integrating navigational information. The hippocampus has long been associated with spatial representations, including place-cell activity originally described in rodents [21, 22]. More recent work, however, emphasizes the role of hippocampal subfields, particularly CA3, in pattern completion and the integration of spatial information under uncertainty [23, 24]. In humans, fMRI studies have also implicated hippocampal subfields in navigation-related computations, although resolving their specific contributions remains challenging [11, 25].

One possible mechanism by which navigational cues are weighted is through dynamic modulation of functional connectivity within the entorhinal-hippocampal network. Studies in other domains of multisensory integration have shown that cue reliability can modulate connectivity between brain regions, strengthening pathways associated with more reliable information and weakening those associated with less reliable inputs [26–28]. Applying this framework to navigation, it is plausible that the relative weighting of landmark and self-motion cues is reflected in changes in connectivity between entorhinal subregions and hippocampal subfields.

In the present study, we tested this hypothesis using high-resolution (7 T) fMRI during a virtual navigation task in which the reliability of landmark and self-motion cues was experimentally manipulated. Based on the proposed (but debated) functional differentiation of the entorhinal cortex, we hypothesized that increases in landmark reliability would be associated with stronger connectivity between anterior entorhinal cortex and hippocampal subfields, whereas increases in self-motion reliability would be associated with stronger connectivity involving posterior entorhinal cortex. More broadly, we aimed to examine whether cue reliability modulates entorhinal-hippocampal functional connectivity, thereby providing insight into the neural mechanisms underlying adaptive weighting of navigational information in humans.

## 2 Methods

### 2.1 Participants

The study included 22 participants (13 males); 26.85 ± 0.92 years old, all right-handed, with normal or corrected-to-normal vision, and no history of neurological disease. The participants were recruited via advertisements at the authors' affiliated academic institution, received €45 compensation, and submitted their informed consent to partake in the study. The research was approved by the local Ethics Committee of the author's affiliated academic institution.

### 2.2 Stimuli and Apparatus

The task took place in a non-immersive virtual reality environment displayed on a screen. The graphics were generated using Vizard software (WorldViz, version 5, Santa Barbara, CA). Participants provided input using a joystick. The virtual environment featured a "dotted floor" with a dark grey background consisting 1,000 white dots. These dots appeared at random locations, remaining visible for up to one second before repositioning. This design offered optic-flow cues while minimizing reliance on fixed reference points [14]. Additionally, the virtual environment contained four buildings, each positioned in a corner of an 18.4 x 18.4 virtual meter square. Each building stood 13 virtual meters from the centre, serving as stable landmark and providing consistent reference point (Fig. 1A).

### 2.3 Behavioral Paradigm

The experimental paradigm and the virtual environment stimuli of both practice and experimental phases were identical to the those in Merhav, 2024 [29]. Here, the experimental phase took place within the MRI scanner. Thus, during the MRI scanning, the virtual environment was projected onto a screen at the end of the MRI bed and reflected onto an IR-reflecting, first-surface mirror. The participants responded to the task via an MRI-compatible joystick.

Practice Session:

Before starting the experimental task, participants completed a practice session to become familiar with the virtual environment, joystick controls, and the homing task. Notably, during the practice session only, two additional circular planes (one small and one large) appeared at the centre between the four landmarks. The smaller circle had a radius of 3 virtual meters, while the larger one measured 10 virtual meters (Fig. 1A). Participants were instructed to pay attention to these circles, which did not appear in the actual experimental task.

The practice session began with a minute of free exploration. Then, participants were instructed to "visit" three specific locations within the virtual environment. Subsequently, participants practiced the homing task over 30 trials, each comprising an outbound and an inbound phase. In the outbound phase, participants were passively moved forward through the virtual environment. Afterward, they were automatically rotated 180° to face their starting point. During the inbound phase, participants used the joystick to return to their original position, having to cover the same distance as the outbound path.

The practice trials were structured as follows: In the first 10 trials, the correct starting position was marked, enabling participants to reach it by following the marker. At the next 10 trials, the marker was removed, but participants received feedback at the end of each trial as the distance error (in virtual meters) was displayed, and they were automatically moved back to the original starting point. At the final 10 trials, no markers or feedback were provided, as in the upcoming experimental task. The practice trajectories and distances differed from those in the experimental task. The practice session lasted between 15 to 20 min.

Homing Task: The experiment involved 120 homing-task trials, each consisting of an outbound and inbound phase. In the outbound phase, participants were passively transported through the virtual environment at a speed of 4 m/s along one of five distances, in a randomized mixed order: 8.5, 12, 15, 18, or 21 virtual m (Fig. 1B). Movement always began from the centre and extended outward towards the periphery. After reaching the endpoint, participants were rotated 180° to face their starting point and asked to return to it using the joystick. The return speed varied randomly between 3.5 m/s and 4.5 m/s. To prevent participants from using a time-based strategy to estimate distances, they were explicitly informed that the return speed would differ from the outbound speed. Additionally, landmarks were visible only during the inbound return phase, eliminating the possibility of using them as spatial reference points during the outbound journey. The 120 trials lasted between 35 to 40 min.

Manipulating Landmark Reliability: Two levels of landmark reliability ('high' and 'low') were tested in separate experimental blocks. Participants received prior information about the starting area via images and text before each block (Fig, 1A). In high-reliability blocks, landmarks provided a more precise positional cues regarding the origin of the paths, while in low-reliability blocks, the landmarks were less informative, requiring participants to rely more on self-motion cues. Thus, although landmarks remained constant, their spatial relationship with the starting area differed between reliability conditions.

Manipulating Self-Motion Reliability: Self-motion reliability was modified by altering the noise level of the optic flow, generated by flickering white dots on the virtual ground. These dots provided a visual cue for motion, appearing stationary (0 m/s) thus moving opposite to the participants' forward direction. To vary the reliability of this cue, at the high optic-flow reliability, a small standard deviation (SD = 0.2 m/s) was applied to the optic flow speed, while in the low optic-flow reliability, a large standard deviation (SD = 3.5 m/s) was applied, introducing significant noise and reducing motion reliability. See supplementary videos A and B.

## 2.4 Experimental Design

The experiment consisted of a within-subjects, 2 × 2 factorial design, examining two levels each of landmark reliability and optic-flow reliability (Fig. 1C). Four conditions were formed by combining these reliability levels: Low landmarks, low optic-flow reliability (lmof); Low landmarks, high optic-flow reliability (lmOF); High landmarks, low optic-flow reliability (LMof); High landmarks, high optic-flow reliability (LMOF).

Participants completed 30 trials for each condition (total 120 trials). Each condition featured the five outbound distances, repeated six times (three returns at 3.5 m/s and three at 4.5 m/s) in random order. The 120 trials were grouped into four blocks of 30 trials. Blocks 1 and 4 used one level of landmark reliability, while Blocks 2 and 3 used the other. The order of high- and low-reliability blocks was counterbalanced across participants. Within each landmark reliability level, half the trials had high optic-flow reliability, and half had low optic-flow reliability, randomized within blocks.

### 2.5 Neuroimaging Data Acquisition

For the neuroimaging data, structural and functional images were acquired using a 7 T MR scanner (Simens, Erlangen, Germany), with a 32-channel head coil (Nova Medical, Wilmington, MA). The functional scan was divided into two runs, each consisting of 60 'homing' trials. Thirty-five contiguous slices of 1 mm thickness, oriented orthogonal to the long axis of the hippocampus, were acquired using a T2*-weighted gradient echo-planar imaging sequence (TR/TE = 2000/22.0 ms; flip angle = 85°, voxel size = 1 mm isotropic, FoV = 216 mm). Prior to the functional scans, high-resolution whole-brain anatomical scans (T1-weighted) were acquired by 176 contiguous sagittal slices of 1 mm thickness (TR/TE = 1700/2.01 ms; flip angle = 5°, voxel size = 1 mm isotropic, FoV = 256 mm). Ten additional images were also acquired of 100 contiguous slices of 1.6 mm thickness: whole-brain echo-planar imaging sequence (TR/TE = 5000/22.0 ms; flip angle = 85°; voxel size: 1.6 mm isotropic, FoV = 205 mm), to facilitate co-registration of the T2 segmented areas to the EPI. A T2 image, on which the areas of interest were segmented, was acquired by 55 contiguous slices of 1 mm thickness (TR/TE = 8000/76 ms; flip angle = 60°, voxel size: $0.4 \times 0.4 \times 1.0$ mm, FoV = 224 mm).

### 2.6 Neuroimaging Data Processing

The fMRI Data processing was done via SPM (Statistical Parametric Mapping) 12. The functional images were motion-corrected and re-sliced, but not smoothed. The entorhinal cortex and the CA1 and CA3 hippocampal-subfields of the right hemisphere were manually segmented, with coronal slices of the T2-weighted structural scan, in ITK-SNAP (Insight Segmentation and Registration Toolkit, v.3.4; www.itksnap.org; [30]), following a manual segmentation protocol [31] (Fig. 1D). Then, on sagittal slices, the voxels of the entorhinal cortex were divided into anterior and posterior halves, to generate posterior- and anterior- EC masks. The four anatomical masks (CA1, CA3, anterior-EC, and posterior-EC) were then co-registered to the mean functional scan of the first run [11].

Neuroimaging and lesion studies in humans indicate that the right-medial temporal lobe is key in spatial navigation [11, 13, 32–34]. Right-hemisphere dominance is also evident in studies on EC spatial-coding during navigations [35–37]. Our analysis therefore focused on the right hemisphere.

For functional-connectivity analysis, each outbound and return trial was entered as a separate regressor in the GLM-design matrix. This GLM yielded a beta estimate of % BOLD signal-change for each return trial. This resulted in 30 beta return-path estimates per condition (i.e., lmof, lmOF, LMof, and LMOF, Fig. 1C) for total of 120 randomized trials. Functional connectivity was then assessed by correlating the beta estimates between pairs of regions of interest: aEC-CA1, aEC-CA3, pEC-CA1, and pEC-CA3 across the 30 return trials of each condition. To perform statistical analysis on the correlation magnitudes, arc-hyperbolic tangent transform was applied on the correlation coefficients [38].

## 2.7 Data Analysis

The behavioral dependent measurements were the mean distance errors and the standard-deviation of distance-errors. The functional connectivity dependent measurements were the Fisher-transformed correlation coefficients of beta estimates between brain regions. All measurements were analyzed by a 2 x 2 repeated-measures ANOVA using SPSS v.23 (IBM, Inc.), with two reliability levels of landmarks and two reliability levels of optic-flow. As functional connectivity from each EC section was measured with two hippocampal-subfields, Holm-Bonferroni corrections were applied for multiple statistical tests, and the Alpha level was adjusted to 0.025.

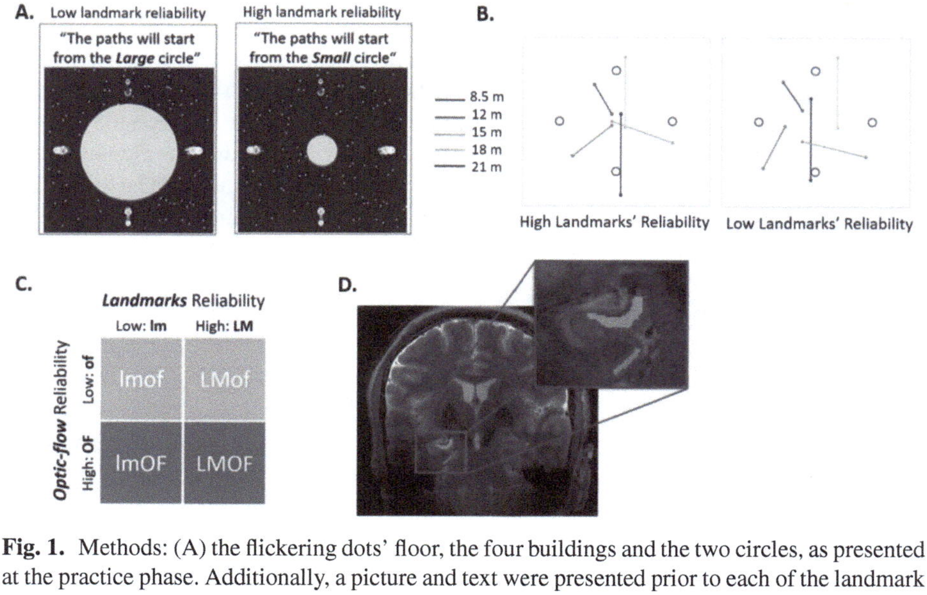


**Fig. 1.** Methods: (A) the flickering dots' floor, the four buildings and the two circles, as presented at the practice phase. Additionally, a picture and text were presented prior to each of the landmark reliability blocks, indicating the starting area of the outbound paths. In the high landmark reliability blocks (right), participants can highly rely on the landmarks' position in order to perform the homing task. (B) the five lengths outbound paths participants traversed at the high and low landmark reliability blocks. (C) reliability levels of landmarks and optic-flow generated four conditions: lmof, lmOF, LMof, and LMOF. Lowercase letters represent low reliability; uppercase letters represent high reliability. (D) an exemplar of manual segmentation on a T2 slice of the CA1 hippocampal-subfield (red), CA3 hippocampal-subfield (yellow), and entorhinal cortex (green) in the right hemisphere, using ITK software (ITK software flips the left-right sides of the image). (Color figure online)

## 3 Results

### 3.1 Behavioral Findings

Navigation performance improved when spatial cues were more reliable. Participants made smaller distance errors when landmark information was reliable and also when optic-flow information was reliable, indicating that both cue types contributed to accurate navigation. The mean distance-errors measurement revealed main effects were found for landmark reliability ($F_{(1,21)} = 30.12$, $p < 0.001$, $\eta^2 = 0.589$) and for optic-flow reliability ($F_{(1,21)} = 16.84$, $p = 0.001$, $\eta^2 = 0.445$); no landmark x optic-flow interaction was seen ($F_{(1,21)} = 3.055$, $p < 0.095$, $\eta^2 = 0.127$) (Fig. 2A, top). Similarly, for distance-error standard-deviations, main effects were found for landmark reliability ($F_{(1,21)} = 45.96$, $p < 0.005$, $\eta^2 = 0.686$) and for optic-flow reliability ($F_{(1,21)} = 9.01$, $p = 0.007$, $\eta^2 = 0.300$); yet no landmark x optic-flow interaction was found ($F_{(1,21)} = 0.74$, $p = 0.399$, $\eta^2 = 0.034$) (Fig. 2A, bottom).

### 3.2 Functional Connectivity Findings

We next asked whether changing the reliability of spatial cues altered communication within the entorhinal-hippocampal network. Functional connectivity reflects the degree to which activity in two brain regions fluctuates together over time. We found that increasing landmark reliability strengthened functional connectivity between the anterior entorhinal cortex (aEC) and hippocampal CA3. In other words, these regions became more tightly coordinated when landmark information could be trusted. The aEC-CA1 functional-connectivity was not significantly modulated by landmark reliability ($F_{(1,21)} = 0.64$, $p = 0.43$, $\eta^2 = 0.03$), optic-flow reliability ($F_{(1,21)} = 1.58$, $p = 0.222$, $\eta^2 = 0.07$) or landmark x optic-flow interaction ($F_{(1,21)} = 0.142$, $p = 0.710$, $\eta^2 = 0.007$) (Fig. 2B, top). However, for the aEC-CA3 functional-connectivity, a main effect was found for landmark reliability ($F_{(1,21)} = 5.992$, $p = 0.023$, $\eta^2 = 0.222$). Specifically, higher landmark reliability increased aEC-CA3 functional-connectivity. No effect was seen for optic-flow reliability ($F_{(1,21)} = 0.035$, $p = 0.854$, $\eta^2 = 0.002$) and no landmark x optic-flow interaction ($F_{(1,21)} = 0.46$, $p = 0.833$, $\eta^2 = 0.002$) (Fig. 2B, bottom).

Next, we tested for modulations in functional connectivity between the *pEC* and the CA1 and CA3 hippocampal subfields. When examining pEC-CA1 functional-connectivity, no effects were found for landmark reliability ($F_{(1,21)} = 0.002$, $p = 0.967$, $\eta^2 = 0.000$), optic-flow reliability ($F_{(1,21)} = 5.15$, $p = 0.034$, $\eta^2 = 0.197$) and no landmark x optic-flow interaction was found ($F_{(1,21)} = 2.219$, $p = 0.151$, $\eta^2 = 0.096$) (Fig. 2C, top). When examining pEC-CA3 functional-connectivity, no effects were seen for landmark reliability ($F_{(1,21)} = 2.352$, $p = 0.140$, $\eta^2 = 0.101$) or for optic-flow reliability ($F_{(1,21)} = 0.163$, $p = 0.691$, $\eta^2 = 0.008$); however, a significant landmark x optic-flow interaction was found ($F_{(1,21)} = 6.339$, $p = 0.020$, $\eta^2 = 0.232$) (Fig. 2C, bottom). Pairwise comparisons revealed that in the high optic-flow-reliability condition, increasing landmark reliability weakened pEC-CA3 connectivity ($p = 0.015$).

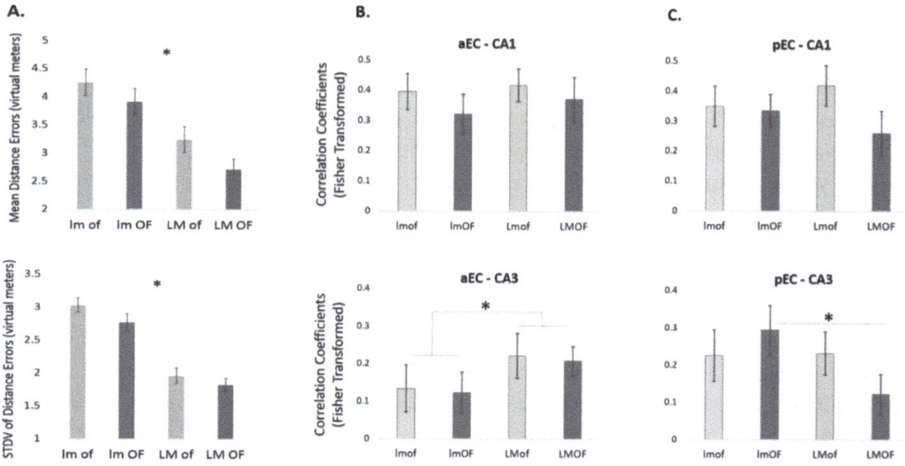


**Fig. 2.** Reliability levels of navigational cues modulate navigational behavior and entorhinal-CA3 connectivity, during a homing task. Data is presented as means ± SEM: (A) Distance-errors (top) and standard deviation of distance errors (bottom). (B) Functional-connectivity of the *anterior* EC with the CA1 (top) and CA3 (bottom) hippocampal subfields. (C) Functional-connectivity of the *posterior* EC with the CA1 (top) and CA3 (bottom) hippocampal subfields

## 4 Discussion

The present study investigated if reliability of navigational cues modulates functional connectivity within the entorhinal-hippocampal network. At the behavioral level, in line with previous findings [29], participants navigated more accurately and more consistently when the available spatial cues were reliable. Thus, when landmarks or self-motion information could be trusted, participants were better able to estimate their location in the environment, consistent with Bayesian accounts of cue integration [7–9]. At the neural level, we observed that when landmarks became more reliable, activity in the aEC and CA3 became more strongly coordinated. This finding suggests that communication between these regions may increase when we rely more heavily on landmark information during navigation. Importantly, the observed behavioral improvements and increases in aEC–CA3 functional connectivity occurred under the same manipulation of landmark reliability. This convergence suggests that stronger coordination between the entorhinal cortex and hippocampus may contribute to the improved navigation performance observed when landmark information is more reliable.

These findings should be interpreted in the context of ongoing debates regarding functional specialization within the human entorhinal cortex. While our results are consistent with proposals that anterior and posterior entorhinal regions differentially contribute to landmark- and self-motion-related processing [11, 19, 20], this dissociation is not universally supported. Human neuroimaging studies have reported mixed and task-dependent findings, and the correspondence between rodent medial-lateral organization and the human anterior-posterior axis remains an open question [15, 17]. Therefore, the present findings contribute to a growing body of work suggesting that entorhinal representations may be modulated by task demands, such as cue reliability.

Within this framework, the observed increase in aEC-CA3 connectivity with higher landmark reliability may reflect enhanced weighting of landmark-based information during navigation. Conversely, the modulation of pEC-CA3 connectivity by interactions between landmark and optic-flow reliability may indicate dynamic reweighting of self-motion information depending on its relative reliability. Thus, when self-motion reliability is high, increasing landmark reliability reduces pEC-CA3 connectivity. Such interpretations are consistent with models of reliability-weighted integration, in which neural systems dynamically adjust the influence of different information sources [26, 28].

The involvement of the CA3 subfield is also notable. While early work identified place cells in the hippocampus [21], more recent accounts emphasize the role of CA3 in pattern completion and the integration of spatial information under uncertainty [23, 24]. Our findings are consistent with the idea that CA3 contributes to combining inputs from entorhinal regions under varying uncertainty conditions. However, given the spatial resolution limits of fMRI and ongoing challenges in precisely isolating hippocampal subfields, these interpretations should be made with caution [25].

A few limitations should be acknowledged. First, self-motion cues in the present study were limited to visual optic-flow and did not include vestibular or proprioceptive inputs, which may limit generalizability to real-world navigation. Second, while our interpretation is guided by proposed functional distinctions within the entorhinal cortex, these distinctions remain an active topic of debate in the literature. Lastly, the sample of twenty-two participants could potentially limit the statistical power and therefore, the interpretation of the findings.

In conclusion, the present findings suggest that entorhinal-hippocampal functional connectivity is modulated by the relative reliability of navigational cues, supporting the idea that this network contributes to adaptive weighing of spatial information. By situating these results within ongoing examinations about entorhinal organization, this study provides new evidence that cue reliability may shape medial temporal lobe interactions during human navigation.

**Acknowledgments.** A thank to Prof. Thomas Wolbers for assisting in developing the research question, Svende Kuebler for supporting the data collection, and Johannes Achtzehn for task programming. This work was funded by a Collaborative US-German Grant of the German Ministry of Education and Research (BMBF) and the National Science Foundation (USA).

**Disclosure of Interests.** None.

## References

1. Gallistel, C.R.: The Organization of Learning. The MIT Press (1990)
2. Etienne, A.S., Jeffery, K.J.: Path integration in mammals. Hippocampus. **14**, 180–192 (2004)
3. Collett, M.: How desert ants use a visual landmark for guidance along a habitual route. Proc. Natl. Acad. Sci. **107**, 11638–11643 (2010)
4. Jeffery, K.J.: Integration of the sensory inputs to place cells: what, where, why, and how? Hippocampus. **17**, 775–785 (2007)

5. Loomis, J.M., Klatzky, R.L., Golledge, R.G., Cicinelli, J.G., Pellegrino, J.W., Fry, P.A.: Non-visual navigation by blind and sighted: assessment of path integration ability. J. Exp. Psychol. Gen. **122**, 73 (1993)
6. Kearns, M.J., Warren, W.H., Duchon, A.P., Tarr, M.J.: Path integration from optic flow and body senses in a homing task. Perception. **31**, 349–374 (2002)
7. Cheng, K., Shettleworth, S.J., Huttenlocher, J., Rieser, J.J.: Bayesian integration of spatial information. Psychol. Bull. **133**, 625 (2007)
8. Nardini, M., Jones, P., Bedford, R., Braddick, O.: Development of cue integration in human navigation. Curr. Biol. **18**, 689–693 (2008)
9. Zhao, M., Warren, W.H.: How you get there from here: interaction of visual landmarks and path integration in human navigation. Psychol. Sci. **26**, 915–924 (2015)
10. Chen, X., McNamara, T.P., Kelly, J.W., Wolbers, T.: Cue combination in human spatial navigation. Cogn. Psychol. **95**, 105–144 (2017)
11. Chen, X., Vieweg, P., Wolbers, T.: Computing distance information from landmarks and self-motion cues-differential contributions of anterior-lateral vs. posterior-medial entorhinal cortex in humans. NeuroImage. **202**, 116074 (2019)
12. Campbell, M.G., Ocko, S.A., Mallory, C.S., Low, I.I., Ganguli, S., Giocomo, L.M.: Principles governing the integration of landmark and self-motion cues in entorhinal cortical codes for navigation. Nat. Neurosci. **21**, 1096–1106 (2018)
13. Doeller, C.F., King, J.A., Burgess, N.: Parallel striatal and hippocampal systems for landmarks and boundaries in spatial memory. Proc. Natl. Acad. Sci. **105**, 5915–5920 (2008)
14. Wolbers, T., Hegarty, M., Büchel, C., Loomis, J.M.: Spatial updating: how the brain keeps track of changing object locations during observer motion. Nat. Neurosci. **11**, 1223–1230 (2008)
15. Epstein, R.A., Patai, E.Z., Julian, J.B., Spiers, H.J.: The cognitive map in humans: spatial navigation and beyond. Nat. Neurosci. **20**, 1504–1513 (2017)
16. Spiers, H.J., Barry, C.: Neural systems supporting navigation. Curr. Opin. Behav. Sci. **1**, 47–55 (2015)
17. Julian, J.B., Keinath, A.T., Marchette, S.A., Epstein, R.A.: The neurocognitive basis of spatial reorientation. Curr. Biol. **28**, R1059–R1073 (2018)
18. Moser, E.I., Kropff, E., Moser, M.-B.: Place cells, grid cells, and the brain's spatial representation system. Annu. Rev. Neurosci. **31**, 69–89 (2008)
19. Maass, A., Berron, D., Libby, L.A., Ranganath, C., Düzel, E.: Functional subregions of the human entorhinal cortex. eLife. **4**, e06426 (2015)
20. Navarro Schröder, T., Haak, K.V., Zaragoza Jimenez, N.I., Beckmann, C.F., Doeller, C.F.: Functional topography of the human entorhinal cortex. eLife. **4**, e06738 (2015)
21. O'Keefe, J., Dostrovsky, J.: The hippocampus as a spatial map: preliminary evidence from unit activity in the freely-moving rat. Brain Res. (1971)
22. Muller, R.U., Kubie, J.L.: The effects of changes in the environment on the spatial firing of hippocampal complex-spike cells. J. Neurosci. **7**, 1951–1968 (1987)
23. Knierim, J.J., Neunuebel, J.P.: Tracking the flow of hippocampal computation: pattern separation, pattern completion, and attractor dynamics. Neurobiol. Learn. Mem. **129**, 38–49 (2016)
24. Moser, M.-B., Rowland, D.C., Moser, E.I.: Place cells, grid cells, and memory. Cold Spring Harb. Perspect. Biol. **7**, a021808 (2015)
25. Reagh, Z.M., Yassa, M.A.: Object and spatial mnemonic interference differentially engage lateral and medial entorhinal cortex in humans. Proc. Natl. Acad. Sci. **111**, E4264–E4273 (2014)
26. Beauchamp, M.S., Pasalar, S., Ro, T.: Neural substrates of reliability-weighted visual-tactile multisensory integration. Front. Syst. Neurosci. **25** (2010)

27. Nath, A.R., Beauchamp, M.S.: Dynamic changes in superior temporal sulcus connectivity during perception of noisy audiovisual speech. J. Neurosci. **31**, 1704–1714 (2011)
28. Vilares, I., Howard, J.D., Fernandes, H.L., Gottfried, J.A., Kording, K.P.: Differential representations of prior and likelihood uncertainty in the human brain. Curr. Biol. **22**, 1641–1648 (2012)
29. Merhav, M.: How spatial-cue reliability affects navigational performance in young and older adults. Aging Neuropsychol. Cognit. **1-17** (2024)
30. Yushkevich, P.A., et al.: User-guided 3D active contour segmentation of anatomical structures: significantly improved efficiency and reliability. NeuroImage. **31**, 1116–1128 (2006)
31. Berron, D., et al.: A Protocol for Manual Segmentation of Medial Temporal Lobe Subregions in 7 T MRI, vol. 15, pp. 466–482. Clinical, NeuroImage (2017)
32. Abrahams, S., Pickering, A., Polkey, C.E., Morris, R.G.: Spatial memory deficits in patients with unilateral damage to the right hippocampal formation. Neuropsychologia. **35**, 11–24 (1997)
33. Philbeck, J.W., Behrmann, M., Levy, L., Potolicchio, S.J., Caputy, A.J.: Path integration deficits during linear locomotion after human medial temporal lobectomy. J. Cogn. Neurosci. **16**, 510–520 (2004)
34. Wolbers, T., Wiener, J.M., Mallot, H.A., Büchel, C.: Differential recruitment of the hippocampus, medial prefrontal cortex, and the human motion complex during path integration in humans. J. Neurosci. **27**, 9408–9416 (2007)
35. Doeller, C.F., Barry, C., Burgess, N.: Evidence for grid cells in a human memory network. Nature. **463**, 657–661 (2010)
36. Howard, L.R., et al.: The hippocampus and entorhinal cortex encode the path and Euclidean distances to goals during navigation. Curr. Biol. **24**, 1331–1340 (2014)
37. Kunz, L., et al.: Reduced grid-cell–like representations in adults at genetic risk for Alzheimer's disease. Science. **350**, 430–433 (2015)
38. Rissman, J., Gazzaley, A., D'Esposito, M.: Measuring functional connectivity during distinct stages of a cognitive task. NeuroImage. **23**, 752–763 (2004)

# How Floor Rotation Fragments 3D Cognitive Maps

Amirtha Varshini Raja[1], Tianyi Xiao[2], Martin Raubal[2], Angela Schwering[1], and Jakub Krukar[1(✉)]

[1] Institute for Geoinformatics, University of Münster, Münster, Germany
{arajason,schwering,krukar}@uni-muenster.de
[2] Institute of Cartography and Geoinformation, ETH Zürich, Zürich, Switzerland
{xiaoti,mraubal}@ethz.ch

**Abstract.** Multilevel buildings impose distinct challenges for mentally integrating vertically stacked spaces, especially when reference frames between floors are misaligned. This study examines how floor rotation affects spatial memory, focusing on horizontal (within-floor) and vertical (across-floor) relations. Thirty-two participants explored two of four three-level virtual buildings: one in aligned and one in 90°-rotated configuration, and reconstructed them using a layer-by-layer 3D sketch mapping platform. The resulting sketch maps were analyzed to quantify landmark accuracy and inter-floor alignment using binomial generalized linear mixed models. Consistent with the established horizontal advantage in multilevel spatial memory, same-floor recall was substantially more accurate (≈86%) than cross-floor recall (≈55%). More importantly, floor rotation selectively impaired vertical memory by ≈80% while within-floor accuracy remained more stable, yielding higher overall accuracy in aligned (82%) than rotated (62%) buildings. These findings indicate that in such buildings people tend to form floor-wise representations rather than unified 3D cognitive maps, and that understanding the building's structural coherence is critical for cross-floor integration of individual locations. This work also introduces a reproducible VR-based workflow for evaluating 3D sketch maps in multilevel environments.

**Keywords:** Spatial memory · floor rotation · cognitive maps · 3D sketch maps · reference frames

## 1 Introduction

Multilevel buildings present a fundamental challenge for spatial cognition: people must integrate separately learnt floor-level representations into a coherent volumetric mental model. Such integration is rarely achieved fully, and the conditions under which it fails remain poorly understood. The present study examines one specific disruptor of this process—the rotation of subsequent floors—and how it impairs spatial memory across floors, while leaving within-floor memory intact.


E. Farran et al. (Eds.): Spatial Cognition 2026, LNAI 16785, pp. 157–172, 2027.
https://doi.org/10.1007/978-3-032-36716-7_11

Spatial memory in complex buildings is consistently anisotropic, meaning that horizontal relations are encoded and recalled more accurately than vertical ones. Thibault et al. showed that floor-by-floor exploration results in significantly better spatial memory than column-by-column exploration, and Bock et al. demonstrated that between-level pointing is less accurate than within-level pointing [3,14]. This shows that integrating separately explored floors into a common representation is error-prone and cognitively demanding. Dollé et al. found that participants defaulted to floor-based encoding regardless of their path during the learning phase, suggesting that this is not an artefact of exploration strategy [6]. Consequently, there are metric distortions in recalling mental representations of vertically-complex buildings: using a pointing task to invisible targets, Brandt et al. reconstructed participants' mental model of a familiar hospital building and found its remembered dimensions to be vertically overestimated by 215% and horizontally compressed by 51% relative to the true structure [4].

However, floor-wise segmentation is not a fixed property of the cognitive system. Lu and Ye found that participants navigating a shopping mall with five open atriums showed equally accurate pointing to same-floor and different-floor targets, and their wayfinding paths gravitated toward globally central spaces across the whole building rather than within individual floors. This provides evidence that volumetric survey knowledge can develop when visual access is available [11]. Gath-Morad et al. further showed that vertical sightlines and the strategic visibility of destinations substantially moderate between-floor navigation success, demonstrating that the horizontal advantage is not architecturally inevitable and can potentially be mitigated by designing cross-floor visibility [7]. Bock extended these insights to physical access: participants in a virtual 3D maze that contained floor transitions at every intersection showed similar recall accuracy for horizontally and vertically arranged objects, suggesting that easy movement between levels can also support volumetric encoding [2]. Evidence from neuroimaging points in the same direction: Kim et al. found that hippocampal encoding of 3D locations is similarly accurate for vertical and horizontal information, suggesting that behavioural anisotropy reflects architectural and locomotor constraints rather than a fundamental limit in how our brain encodes spatial information across dimensions [9]. Taken together, these findings show that the horizontal advantage is not inevitable, but depends on what the architecture affords.

There is early evidence demonstrating that geometric misalignment between floors can be a key understudied design variable compounding this issue. Hölscher et al. showed that navigators routinely assume that floor layouts are identical across levels; when they are not, systematic orientation errors follow [8]. Mastrodonato et al. identified one key mechanism underlying that: 90° turns at staircases often go unnoticed or are not remembered, which results in misalignment in floor's spatial reference frames and large cross-floor pointing errors [12]. In design, rotating floor layouts is a common way of introducing diversification and interestingness to buildings that have an otherwise monotonous (e.g. cubic-like) external structure, as in the GEO1 building of the Institute for Geoinformatics in Münster. "Twisting" buildings are also an explicit skyscraper typology defined by the Council on Tall Buildings and Urban Habitat, as those whose floors or façades gradually rotate as they rise, with the Turning Torso in Malmö being a famous example.

When floors are rotated, a key challenge lies in understanding whether building users are confused because of their misunderstanding of specific place-to-place locations (e.g., knowing that a seminar hall is below an office), or because of their misunderstanding of the overall shape of the building (e.g., realising that floors are rotated). Traditional assessment methods cannot isolate this. Pointing tasks do not carry over participants' understanding of the overall building structure, focusing on place-to-place relations. Sketch maps emphasise the understanding of the floor structure, but force spatial memory onto a flat surface, making it difficult to represent between-floor alignment within a single sketch [13].

The emergence of 3D immersive sketching tools offers a potential solution. VResin [15] addresses this gap directly: the layered system of the tool makes it possible to externalise both horizontal and vertical relations within a single sketch map, making between-floor alignment assumptions explicit and interpretable. Building on these developments we conduct a navigation study in virtual complex buildings, followed by a 3D sketch mapping task to test how floor rotation specifically disrupts the recall of (a) horizontal place-to-place relations, (b) vertical place-to-place relations, and (c) floor shape orientation.

### 1.1 Research Question and Hypotheses

This paper investigates the following Research Question:

> *How does floor rotation influence the way people remember and reconstruct multilevel buildings, and the spatial relations within them, in three dimensions?*

Four controlled three-floor virtual buildings were created—two with floors aligned and two with floors rotated 90° at each level. Participants externalized their memory using VResin after navigation. Four hypotheses are tested:

- **H1:** Within-floor (horizontal) relations are recalled more accurately than cross-floor (vertical) relations.
- **H2:** Rotated-floor conditions impair vertical recall more than aligned conditions.
- **H3:** Horizontal recall is unaffected by floor rotation, indicating partially independent memory structures.
- **H4:** Overall accuracy is higher in aligned than rotated buildings.

## 2 Method

The experiment was conceived to isolate and examine how floor alignment (aligned vs. rotated) and spatial orientation (horizontal vs. vertical) influence the integration of spatial knowledge across dimensions.

### 2.1 Environmental Design

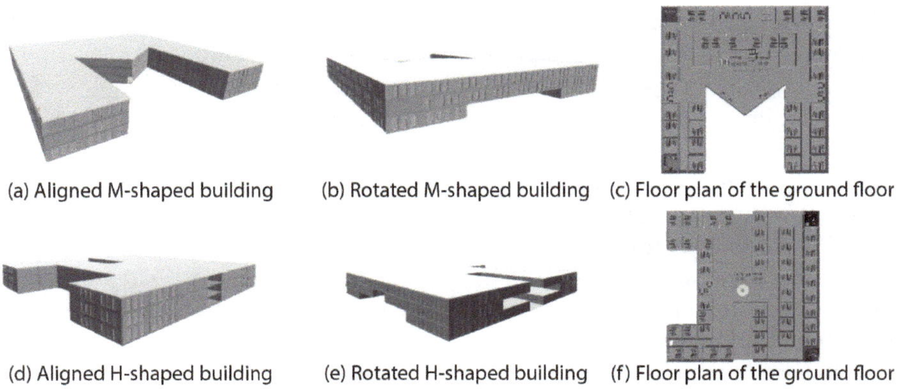


**Fig. 1.** Unity-developed M- and H-shaped buildings.

Four three-floor buildings were constructed: an "M-shaped" and an "H-shaped" building, each in an "aligned" version (floors stacked on top of each other), and a "rotated" version (each subsequent floor rotated counter-clockwise by 90° relative to the lower one). Floors were rotated around the center point of the building which was a round staircase. This staircase was also the only way for changing the floors in the navigation phase. Each building contained six thematically distinct landmark rooms (two per floor) decorated with unique visual features and colors for the task that motivates the participants to explore the building (see the buildings in Figs. 1 and the distinctive rooms in Figs. 4 and 5).

Across the four building configurations, the placement of distinct rooms was planned to manipulate horizontal and vertical spatial relations in a controlled and theoretically diagnostic way (Fig. 2 and 3). Each floor plan also contained multiple visually identical, non-distinctive rooms that formed the building's structure (depicted as empty squares in Figs. 2 and 3); only the six distinctive landmark rooms were relevant to the task and scored.

Horizontal relations were defined by pairs of distinct rooms located within the same floor (e.g., L1–L2 and L5–L6). The memory of these relations will be diagnostic of the within-floor spatial memory. Vertical relations were defined by

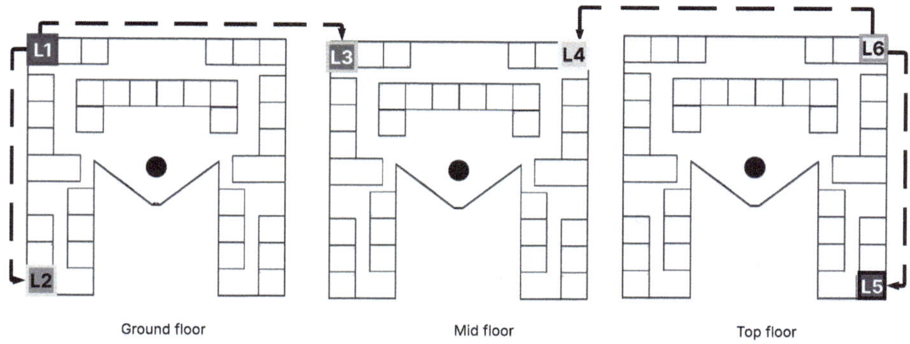


**Fig. 2.** Aligned M-shaped layout (top view). The horizontal relations tested are between rooms on the same floor: L1–L2 (ground floor) and L5–L6 (top floor). The vertical relations tested are between rooms stacked across floors: L1–L3 and L5–L4. Rooms L1 and L6 are anchored, meaning that participants can always see their correct location on the sketch map that they are drawing.

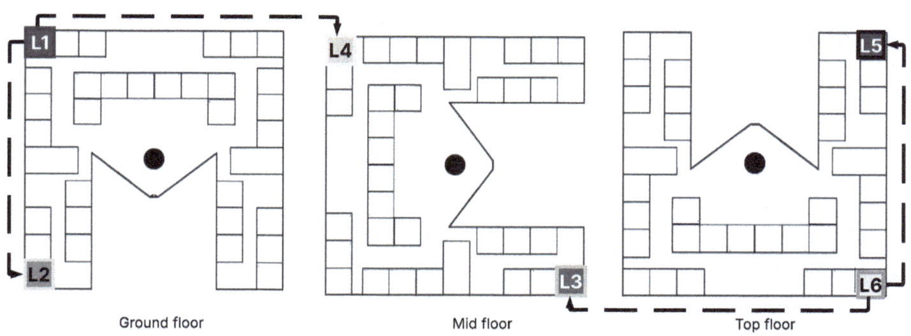


**Fig. 3.** Rotated M-shaped layout (top view). The horizontal relations tested are between rooms on the same floor: L1–L2 (ground floor) and L5–L6 (top floor). The vertical relations tested are between rooms stacked across floors: L1–L4 and L6–L3. Rooms L1 and L6 are anchored, meaning that participants can always see their correct location on the sketch map that they are drawing. The middle floor is rotated 90° and the top floor is rotated 180° relative to the ground floor.

pairs of distinct rooms stacked across floors (e.g., L1–L4 and L6–L3 in the H-layouts). The memory of these relations will be diagnostic of the across-floor memory.

Two rooms, L1 and L6, were designated as fixed anchor rooms and held constant in position across all four configurations. This anchoring ensured that any observed differences in spatial judgement could be attributed to the manipulation of the remaining rooms rather than to global disorientation. The rotation manipulations applied to the non-anchor floors (90° on the middle floor and 180° on the top floor) were designed to test whether participants construct a unified, vertically integrated mental representation of the building or encode

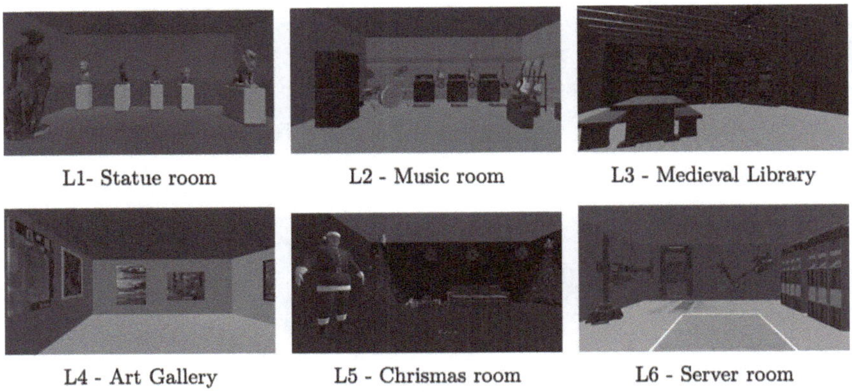


**Fig. 4.** Six visually distinctive rooms used as landmarks in the M-shaped Building.

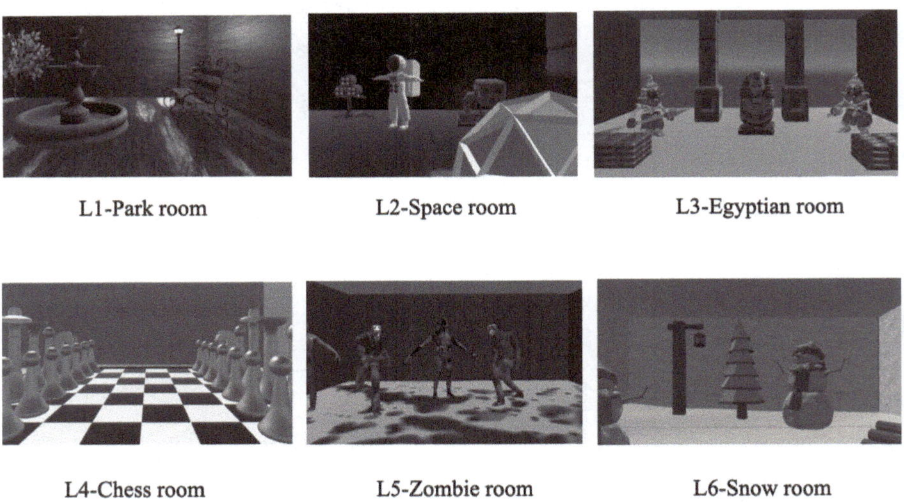


**Fig. 5.** Six visually distinctive rooms used as landmarks in the H-shaped Building.

each floor as an independent spatial frame that is not aligned with the others. So, this design permits the dissociation of qualitatively distinct error types. A participant may correctly reproduce the overall building shape while misplacing distinct rooms within a floor, or may preserve the correct alignment of distinct rooms while misrepresenting the rotational orientation of individual floors (Fig. 6).

Memory was tested using a VR-based 3D sketch mapping. The VR interface used in our experiment is derived from the VResin tool [15]. VResin enables participants to produce freehand three-dimensional strokes directly within a virtual environment using a handheld controller. This interface supports both 3D mid-air sketching of vertical information and 2D surface sketching of horizontal

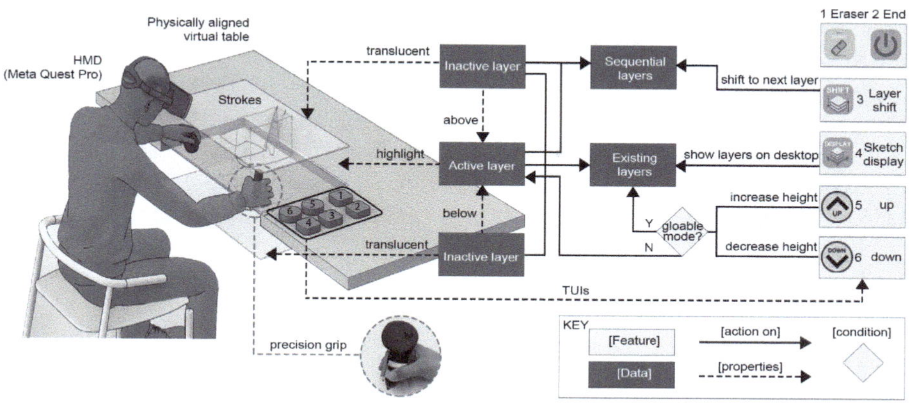


**Fig. 6.** Interface structure of the predefined-layer VResin tool. Users draw on a physical tabletop while viewing their sketch in 3D space, enabling spatial memory to be externalized across multiple floors.

information, allowing users to sketch on a layer aligned with the table surface, adjust the height of layers, and switch between layers. This is methodologically significant for the present study because it allows both horizontal and vertical spatial relations to be externalised within a single sketch. In conventional 2D sketch mapping, participants typically draw each floor on a separate sheet of paper, which makes it difficult to preserve vertical alignment across floors and to interpret it during the analysis [10]. Yet, unlike in freehand 3D sketching, where cross-floor alignment is undermined by hand instability in mid-air, VResin provides a structured interface in which floors are drawn sequentially within a shared spatial frame of reference and the controller acts as a pen using a surface of a physical desk. To simplify the experimental setup, we adopted predefined layers to indicate the positions of the central staircase and two anchor rooms from the start of the drawing.

## 2.2 Participants

Thirty–two volunteers (18–33 years old; $M = 25.22$, $SD = 3.89$, median = 25) took part in the study. The sample comprised 23 males (71.9%), 8 females (25.0%), and one participant who preferred not to specify (3.1%). All reported normal or corrected to normal vision and no history of vestibular disorders or severe motion sickness. Participants were recruited through university mailing lists and notice boards and received a compensation of €12 for participation. The study was approved by the institutional Ethics Committee, and all participants provided informed consent before participation.

## 2.3 Procedure

The study followed a within-subject design. Each participant explored one aligned and one rotated building. In order to avoid learning effects, for each participant one of those conditions was experienced in the M-shape building, and the other one in the H-shaped building. We check for the impact of M/H-shaped building on the results, but do not treat it as a fixed-effect independent variable, as it was not the main focus of the study and the buildings were specifically designed to be similar in complexity. Each experimental session lasted approximately 70 min and consisted of six consecutive phases (Fig. 7): (1) introduction and consent, (2) pre-experiment questionnaire, (3) familiarisation, (4) Building A: navigation and drawing, (5) Building B: navigation and drawing, and (6) post-experiment questionnaire.

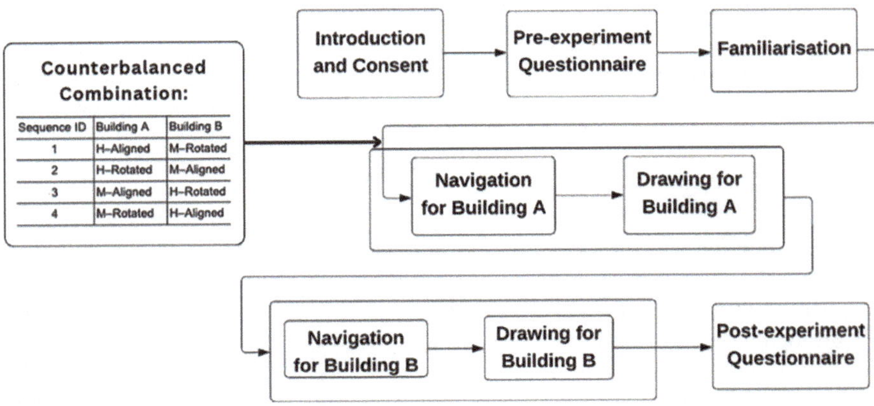


**Fig. 7.** Overview of the six-phase experimental flow implemented in the study

Participants examined two virtual buildings—one *M-shaped* and one *H-shaped*—across two conditions: *aligned* and *rotated*, leading to two trials for each participant. Participants explored the buildings on a PC, using mouse and keyboard.

Participants were instructed to memorize the layout and position of all six distinct rooms (two per floor) and the overall structure of the building. This included a specific focus on the entry point from the staircase, corridor orientations, and the starting position at the entrance door next to the staircase. Participants were informed that they would subsequently be required to recreate the building layouts from memory within a 3D drawing environment. Exploration of each building was limited to 15 min, with a reminder issued every 5 min to encourage thorough exploration.

Immediately after completing each navigation trial, participants proceeded to the drawing task in VR. The drawing space contained three distinct floor layers corresponding to the three floors of the building. Each layer included a staircase and a visible entrance/exit door to preserve the spatial reference frame at the ground floor.

### 2.4 Data Collection and Processing

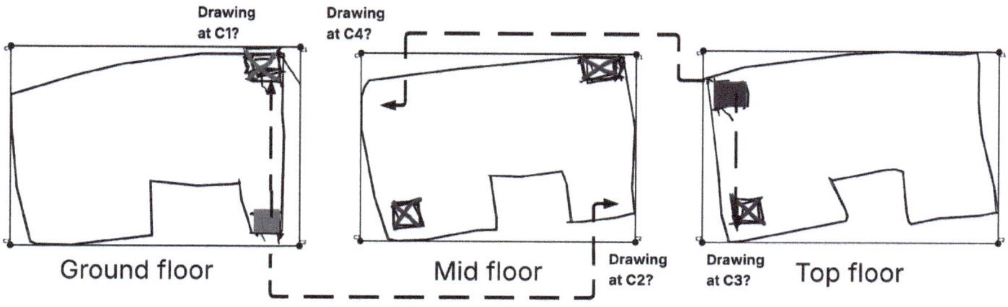


**Fig. 8.** Overview of 3D sketch processing. Polygons marked with a red cross are drawn by participants; green and brown patches are the fixed anchor rooms. The pipeline assigns the polygon to a specific corner of the layout. (Color figure online)

All drawing data were collected from the VR application and exported as three-dimensional meshes in `.obj` format, grouped by participant ID and condition (*aligned* vs. *rotated*). Files were visually inspected for completeness; pre-drawn fixed anchor rooms were reinserted during preprocessing for alignment and were not scored.

An automated pipeline cleaned raw geometry, extracted one floor plan per level via height-based clustering along the vertical axis, and rasterised each level to a fixed-dimension PNG. Each polygon's centroid was matched to the nearest building corner, activating corner flags (c1–c4) that mapped to horizontal and vertical accuracy variables (Fig. 8).

Floor-orientation accuracy measured the angular offset of each non-anchor floor from ground truth, yielding a binary score summed across two floors (0–2), illustrated in Fig. 9. All scores were manually verified in 3D; ambiguous cases were resolved using data from the post-experiment questionnaire.

## 3 Results

Data from 32 participants yielded 128 aggregated observations: calculated by 2 Relations (horizontal vs vertical) $\times$ 2 Conditions (aligned vs rotated) $\times$ 32 Participants. Each row in the aggregated dataset represents the summed count of correct responses ($k_{\text{correct}}$) out of $n = 2$ trials for two distinct rooms—for a given participant, relation type, and condition. Figure 10 shows the correct and incorrect 3d drawings of an M-rotated building.

Figure 11 shows the distribution of correct responses: aligned configurations produced a clear concentration of fully-correct ($k = 2$) responses, whereas rotated configurations showed a wider spread of partial and incorrect trials.

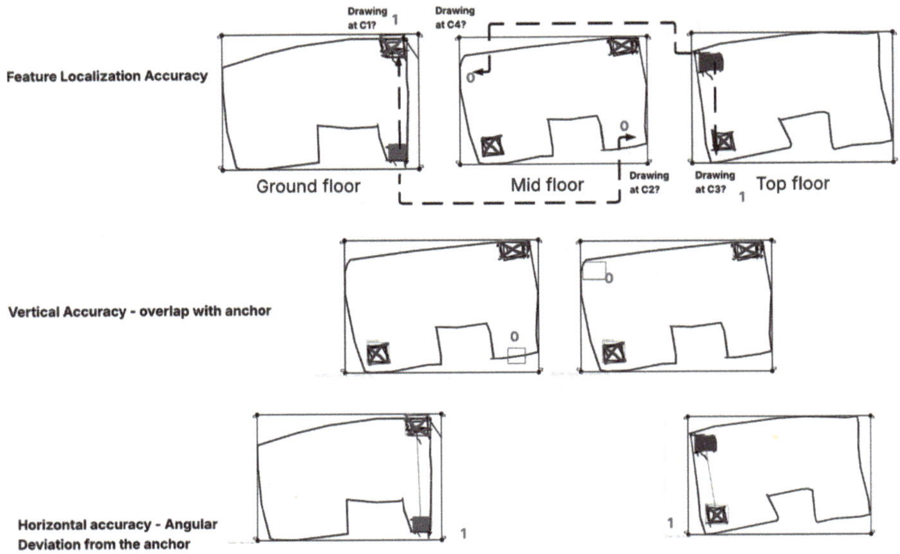


| Relation | Landmark1 | Landmark2 |
|---|---|---|
| Horizontal | 1 AND 1 = 1 | 1 AND 1 = 1 |
| Vertical | 0 AND 0 = 0 | 0 AND 0= 0 |

**Fig. 9.** An example of the automated scoring of the 3D sketch accuracy. (Top) Detection of rooms at corners with 0 depicting no room at the expected location and 1 denoting a room drawn at the expected location. (Middle) Vertical accuracy is scored by verifying whether the locations of drawn rooms from the middle floor overlap with the locations of anchor rooms on the first and third floor - no vertical overlap is detected for either of the anchor rooms marked with violet polygons, resulting in two scores of 0. (Bottom) Horizontal accuracy is assessed by comparing the relative position of rooms on the same floor. The position is scored as correct if the angular deviation is within a 20-degree threshold of the expected location. Here, both rooms were drawn in correct location within-floor relative to the respective anchor room.

### 3.1 Model and Fit

A binomial generalized linear mixed model (GLMM) with participant random intercepts was fitted in R:

$$\text{cbind(k\_correct, n\_trials - k\_correct)} \sim \text{relation} * \text{condition} + (1|\text{participant}),$$

where *relation* denotes the spatial relation tested (horizontal vs. vertical) and *condition* the floor configuration (aligned vs. rotated).

The probability of correct recall of horizontal relations under aligned conditions was high (OR = 6.67, $p < .001$). In isolation, there was no significant effect of relation ($p = .075$) or condition ($p = .629$). The *relation* × *condition*

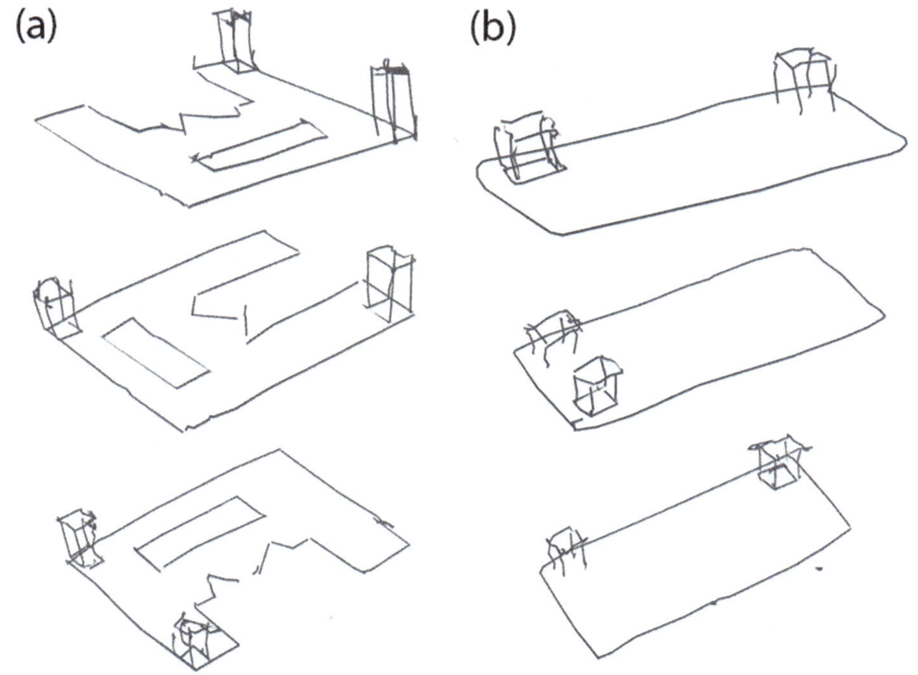


**Fig. 10.** Sketch maps illustrating (a) the correct representation of all three floors and the accurate placement of distinctive rooms, and (b) an incorrect representation of the building with mislocated distinctive rooms.

interaction was significant (OR = 0.21, 95% CI [0.06, 0.77], $p = .018$): whereas horizontal recall accuracy remained stable across aligned and rotated conditions, vertical recall accuracy dropped sharply under rotation, indicating that floor rotation specifically disrupts across-floor spatial integration.

### 3.2 Pairwise Contrasts

Estimated marginal means show high and stable horizontal accuracy across conditions ($\Delta P = -0.029$) against a sharp vertical decline under rotation ($\Delta P = -0.414$). Figure 12 visualizes the interaction (Table 1).

Our approach also lets us split participants by how accurately they encoded the floor rotation, separately from their memory of horizontal/vertical relations between rooms. In order to do this, participants were categorised into two groups based on their floor-orientation accuracy score: those who correctly reproduced the rotation of all non-anchor floors in their sketch (*perfect rotation encoding*, score = 2) and those who did not (*partial rotation encoding*, score <2). Participants with perfect rotation encoding achieved near-ceiling accuracy for vertical room-to-room relations, whereas those with partial encoding showed a

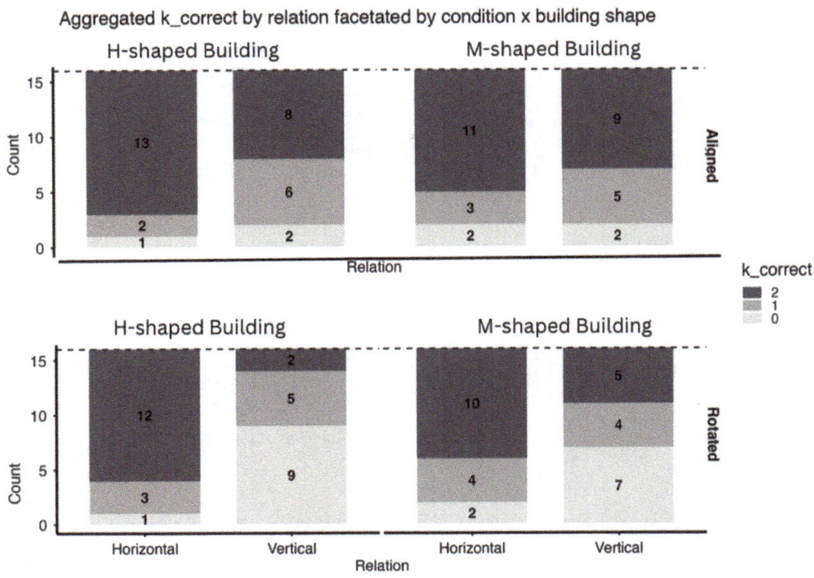


**Fig. 11.** Aggregated $k_{\text{correct}}$ counts by Relation, Condition, and Building Shape. Bars are partitioned into accuracy levels (0, 1, 2). The upper panel depicts results for the Aligned building condition, and the lower panel for the Rotated building condition.

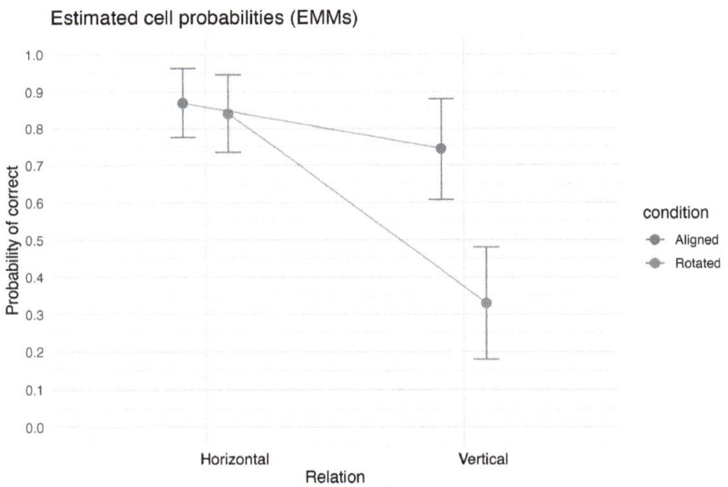


**Fig. 12.** Estimated marginal probabilities for the relation $\times$ condition interaction.

sharp decline (OR $= 0.0163$, SE $= 0.0171$, $z = -3.92$, $p < .001$). Horizontal accuracy was comparatively stable across those groups.

**Table 1.** Pairwise contrasts from the primary GLMM. Each row compares the odds of correct recall between two levels (the first relative to the second). **OR** is the odds ratio: values $> 1$ mean higher odds of correct recall for the first level, values $< 1$ lower odds—e.g. Horizontal/Vertical = 4.94 means horizontal relations were recalled at 4.94× the odds of vertical ones, whereas Vertical: Aligned/Rotated = 0.169 means rotation cut the odds of correct vertical recall to about one-sixth. **SE** is the standard error of the odds ratio, **z** the test statistic, and **p** its significance level.

| Contrast | OR | SE | z | p |
|---|---|---|---|---|
| Horizontal / Vertical (overall) | 4.94 | 1.68 | 4.72 | < .001 |
| Aligned / Rotated (overall) | 2.73 | 0.90 | 3.06 | .002 |
| Vertical: Aligned / Rotated | 0.169 | 0.074 | −4.04 | <.001 |
| Horizontal: Aligned / Rotated | 0.79 | 0.384 | −0.48 | .629 |

## 4 Discussion

Horizontal accuracy was near ceiling across both conditions ($P_{\text{H,Aligned}} = 0.870$; $P_{\text{H,Rotated}} = 0.841$), while vertical relations produced more partial and incorrect responses. The GLMM contrast confirms this: odds of correct recall were nearly five times higher for horizontal than vertical relations (OR = 4.94, $p < .0001$), supporting **H1**. This is consistent with the idea of floor-wise segmentation of multilevel spatial memory discussed in the literature [6,8]. While other studies suggest that the floor-based organisation of 3D spatial memory might be due to constraints in movement and visibility [3,11,14], our results tie the vertical errors to the specific problem: that of understanding and memorising the rotated configuration of the floors. These explanations are not mutually exclusive: richer cross-floor visibility or easier movement between levels could well attenuate the rotation effect we observed, and disentangling these factors is an avenue for future work.

The significant *relation* × *condition* interaction confirms that rotation is a relation-specific disruptor: vertical accuracy dropped from 0.745 to 0.331 under rotation (OR = 0.169, $p < .001$), while horizontal performance remained near ceiling. This pattern supports **H2**, that rotation impairs vertical recall more than alignment does. Participants who failed to encode both floor rotations showed only 1.6% of the vertical recall odds of those with perfect encoding (OR = 0.0163, $p < .001$). This demonstrates that room-to-room vertical memory depends directly on accurate structural encoding of floor orientation [5,12]. Another way to phrase this outcome is that although participants might indeed be able to construct volumetric 3D mental representations of complex buildings [11], the understanding of the horizontal location of a given room, relative to other rooms on the same floor, takes precedence of the recall of vertical relations.

Horizontal accuracy did not differ between conditions (OR = 0.79, $p = .629$), in line with **H3**: within-floor memory is largely independent of floor rotation. Although the null hypothesis cannot be verified with the frequentist test, data shows clear near-ceiling performance in both conditions. This indicates that for buildings of similar complexity to those tested here, floor rotation did not disorient participants so much, that they would get confused about the within-floor relations. This result contrasts findings presented by [8], where each floor was different from the others, and this lack of correspondence resulted in within-floor errors. Our study clarifies this pattern for buildings with identical floor layouts: although they make the construction of a volumetric 3D mental representation challenging, within-floor memory does not seem to be affected by the poor understanding of the general shape of the building.

Finally, in line with **H4**, aligned buildings yielded higher overall accuracy than rotated ones (OR = 2.73, $p = .002$); this difference was driven primarily by the vertical performance drop rather than a condition-wide shift.

It is worth noting that between-participant variability in vertical accuracy was substantial, as captured by the GLMM random intercepts (ICC = 0.40). Participants greatly vary in their ability to memorise vertical relations. Many participants were visibly uncertain about the direction and magnitude of floor rotations; some paused at staircases, physically turned their head or body, or expressed verbal confusion before ascending. Others appeared to abandon the intention of actively tracking rotation after the first floor and defaulted to treating each level as an independent space.

## 5 Limitations and Future Work

Three constraints bound the current findings. First, the constrained building design: three floors, a single spiral staircase, and closed ceilings, which aided experimental control but limited generalizability to natural movement-supporting and atrium-style environments [3,7,11]. Relatedly, ascending a spiral staircase involves continuous rotational motion, which may itself bias participants' sense of how they emerge on each floor relative to their entry point; because the same staircase was used in both conditions it cannot account for the observed aligned–rotated difference, but future studies could compare connector types (e.g., straight versus spiral staircases) to isolate this effect from the floor-rotation manipulation. Second, the study was performed on a PC, reducing vestibular and proprioceptive cues, meaning participants likely relied on visual cues alone to detect floor rotation [1]. Third, despite counterbalancing, some participants appeared to detect the structural regularity (landmarks always at corridor ends) during the second trial, introducing mild strategy transfer.

Future work should introduce systematic manipulation of vertical connectors and cross-floor visibility to clarify whether the misunderstanding of vertical relations in rotated conditions can be prevented with targeted interior design approaches.

## 6 Conclusion

This study examined how floor alignment shapes 3D spatial memory in multilevel environments. Results were consistent across all analyses: within-floor horizontal memory was robust and near-ceiling regardless of condition, while cross-floor vertical integration depended critically on the alignment condition. Aligned buildings supported accurate inter-floor orientation; rotated floors disrupted this, producing fragmented floor-wise representations and sharp vertical accuracy decline unless participants successfully encoded the inter-floor transformations.

These findings show that people do not automatically construct unified volumetric cognitive maps. By dissociating the memory for individual room-to-room relations from the memory of overall building shape using VR-based 3D sketch mapping, this work provides empirical evidence to the structural conditions under which volumetric spatial memory is likely to occur.

**Acknowledgements.** This work has been supported by the Swiss National Science Foundation grant Sinergia 202284.

## References

1. Allen, G.L.: Spatial abilities, cognitive maps, and wayfinding. Wayfind. Behav. Cogn. Mapp. Other Spat. Processes **4680**, 46–80 (1999)
2. Bock, O.: Cognitive representations of multilevel buildings: two- or three-dimensional? Exp. Brain Res. **243**(9), 202 (2025). https://doi.org/10.1007/s00221-025-07136-2
3. Bock, O., Fricke, M., Koch, I.: Human wayfinding in the horizontal versus vertical plane. J. Environ. Psychol. **70** (2020). https://doi.org/10.1016/j.jenvp.2020.101446
4. Brandt, T., Huber, M., Schramm, H., Kugler, G., Dieterich, M., Glasauer, S.: "Taller and Shorter": human 3-D spatial memory distorts familiar multilevel buildings. PLoS ONE **10**(10), e0141257 (2015). https://doi.org/10.1371/journal.pone.0141257
5. Dakin, C.J., Kumar, P., Forbes, P.A., Peters, A., Day, B.L.: Variance based weighting of multisensory head rotation signals for verticality perception. PLoS ONE **15**(1), e0227040 (2020). https://doi.org/10.1371/journal.pone.0227040
6. Dollé, L., Droulez, J., Bennequin, D., Berthoz, A., Thibault, G.: How the learning path and the very structure of a multifloored environment influence human spatial memory. Adv. Cogn. Psychol. **11**(4), 156–162 (2015). https://doi.org/10.5709/acp-0180-5
7. Gath-Morad, M., Grübel, J., Steemers, K., Sailer, K., Ben-Alon, L., Hölscher, C., Aguilar, L.: The role of strategic visibility in shaping wayfinding behavior in multilevel buildings. Sci. Rep. **14**(1), 3735 (2024). https://doi.org/10.1038/s41598-024-53420-6
8. Hölscher, C., Meilinger, T., Vrachliotis, G., Brösamle, M., Knauff, M.: Up the down staircase: wayfinding strategies in multi-level buildings. J. Environ. Psychol. **26**(4), 284–299 (2006). https://doi.org/10.1016/j.jenvp.2006.09.002
9. Kim, M., Maguire, E.A.: Hippocampus, retrosplenial and parahippocampal cortices encode multicompartment 3D space in a hierarchical manner. Cereb. Cortex **28**(5), 1898–1909 (2018). https://doi.org/10.1093/cercor/bhy054
10. Krukar, J., Aly, A., Baecker, L., Heming, L.M., Zhao, J., Schwering, A.: 3D environments require 3D visualisations: the limitations of 2D sketch maps in capturing spatial knowledge. Int. J. Geograph. Inf. Sci., 1–33 (2026). https://doi.org/10.1080/13658816.2026.2684650

11. Lu, Y., Ye, Y.: Can people memorize multilevel building as volumetric map? A study of multilevel atrium building. Environ. Plann. B Urban Anal. City Sci. **46**(2), 225–242 (2019). https://doi.org/10.1177/2399808317705659
12. Mastrodonato, G., Camarda, D., Borri, D., De Lucia, C.: Navigating in multi-level buildings: the effect of rotation. City Territory Architect. **3** (2016). https://doi.org/10.1186/s40410-016-0038-9
13. Simonet, M., et al.: Probing mental representations of space through sketch mapping: a scoping review. Cogn. Res. Principles Implications **10**(1), 59 (2025). https://doi.org/10.1186/s41235-025-00667-w
14. Thibault, G., Pasqualotto, A., Vidal, M., Droulez, J., Berthoz, A.: How does horizontal and vertical navigation influence spatial memory of multifloored environments? Attention Percept. Psychophys. **75** (2012). https://doi.org/10.3758/s13414-012-0405-x
15. Xiao, T., et al.: VResin: externalizing spatial memory into 3D sketch maps. Int. J. Hum.-Comput. Stud., 103322 (2024). https://doi.org/10.1016/j.ijhcs.2024.103322

# Greater Male Variability in Mental Rotation Skills Emerges Early in Childhood

Jillian Lauer(✉)

University of Cambridge, Cambridge CB2 8PQ, UK
jl2345@cam.ac.uk

**Abstract.** This meta-analytic review examined sex differences in mental rotation skills across development through a distributional lens, analysing sex differences in both mean performance and variability to characterise the extent to which boys are overrepresented amongst top performers on mental rotation tasks from early childhood to late adolescence. Across two meta-analyses of 88 articles ($N = 22{,}850$; ages 3–17), there was a robust male advantage in mean mental rotation performance ($d = 0.45$) that increased with age, alongside greater male variability in mental rotation performance (VR = 1.08) that was small and developmentally stable. Distributional analyses indicated that these combined sex differences produced substantial male overrepresentation at the upper tail of the ability distribution, particularly at more extreme percentile thresholds and in older samples. By adolescence, boys were markedly overrepresented among the highest performers in mental rotation ability. These findings support the greater male variability hypothesis, providing novel evidence of early emerging sex differences in the distribution of one key spatial skill, with implications for understanding developmental pathways that contribute to gender disparities in STEM attainment.

**Keywords:** spatial cognition · mental rotation · sex differences · meta-analysis · developmental

## 1 Introduction

Sex differences in cognitive ability have long garnered significant interest in psychological science, both because of their theoretical relevance and because of their perceived implications for educational and occupational inequalities. Prior work on this topic has often focused on mean differences between men's and women's performance across various cognitive domains, but there has also been considerable interest in sex differences in variability in cognitive performance for well over a century (Ellis, 1894). Today, it is widely argued that men and boys exhibit greater variability in cognitive performance than women and girls, a contention known as the "greater male variability hypothesis". This hypothesis proposes that sex differences in variability yield male overrepresentation at both the high and low ends of ability distributions, even in the absence of mean sex differences (Feingold, 1992; Hedges & Nowell, 1995).

The greater male variability hypothesis has also featured in broader academic and public discussions about gender representation in science, technology, engineering, and


E. Farran et al. (Eds.): Spatial Cognition 2026, LNAI 16785, pp. 173–183, 2027.
https://doi.org/10.1007/978-3-032-36716-7_12

maths (STEM) fields. Some have argued that even small differences in variance in cognitive performance between men/boys and women/girls could have large consequences for women's representation in elite scientific fields that demand high cognitive abilities (Feingold, 1992; Hedges & Nowell, 1995; O'Dea et al., 2018). The core statistical point underlying this claim is straightforward: when two groups share similar means but differ in variance, the more variable group will be disproportionately represented at both tails of the distribution. If men are more variable in their spatial reasoning abilities than women, and prestigious STEM occupations disproportionately select for individuals with exceptional spatial abilities, then one may expect that men would be overrepresented in such STEM occupations relative to women. However, the validity of this argument depends on whether variability differences are present in spatial cognition.

Sex differences in spatial cognition have been central to debates on gender disparities in STEM attainment, given that spatial cognition robustly varies by sex (Voyer et al., 1995) and is closely related to STEM achievement across development (Geer et al., 2018; Hodgkiss et al., 2018; Lauer & Lourenco, 2016; Wai et al., 2009). Mental rotation skills, in particular, have consistently produced male advantages in mean performance across development (Lauer et al., 2019; Voyer et al., 1995), and are linked to sex differences in STEM outcomes (Casey et al., 1995; Ganley et al., 2014). Nevertheless, most of the research in this area has focused on how mean sex differences in mental rotation might contribute to the underrepresentation of women in highly selective STEM pathways, rather than the distributional properties of these sex differences or their developmental emergence.

Despite longstanding interest in the greater male variability hypothesis, relatively little is known about the extent to which greater male variability characterises spatial performance, and, if so, when this sex difference in variability emerges during development. Minimal research has examined whether sex differences in variability in spatial reasoning are already present in early development, and to our knowledge, no previous meta-analysis has quantified sex differences in variability in children's spatial performance. Identifying any early emerging sex differences in variability in mental rotation performance may be informative for our understanding of the origins of gender disparities in STEM, as developmental trajectories of sex differences in variability constrain the plausibility of different explanations for these disparities.

The present research provides the first meta-analytic review of sex differences in both the mean and variability of mental rotation performance across childhood and adolescence. First, we conduct a meta-analysis to characterise the developmental emergence and trajectory of the male advantage in mean mental rotation performance. Second, we conduct a meta-analysis to examine the presence, magnitude, and developmental stability of any sex differences in variability in mental rotation performance between 3 and 17 years of age. Finally, we combine the effect size estimates from both meta-analyses to model the expected representation of boys and girls at the upper tail of the mental rotation ability distribution. In doing so, we provide the first quantitative account of how mean and variability differences jointly shape the distribution of mental rotation performance across development, informing ongoing debates surrounding the greater male variability hypothesis and its implications for gender disparities in STEM.

## 2 Methods

This research provides the first developmental meta-analysis of sex differences in both the mean and variability of mental rotation performance across childhood and adolescence. The meta-analytic dataset was created in two steps. First, we obtained statistics from a previously published dataset of mean sex differences in children's mental rotation performance (Lauer, Yhang, & Lourenco, 2019), extracting only those from studies that met our inclusion criteria (described below). This yielded 159 effect sizes. Second, we systematically searched the developmental literature published since 2015, identifying an additional 31 effect sizes that met our inclusion criteria. The resulting dataset therefore combines studies from the Lauer et al. review with newly identified studies, enabling an up-to-date and comprehensive examination of developmental sex differences in both mean performance and variability.

Using this dataset of 190 effect sizes, we conducted two meta-analyses to characterise the presence and development of both mean-level and variability-based sex differences across childhood and adolescence. First, we estimated sex differences in *mean* mental rotation performance using standardised mean differences ($d$), providing an updated synthesis on the developmental trajectory of sex differences in average mental rotation performance. Second, we derived variance ratios (VRs) from each study in the meta-analytic dataset, allowing us to estimate sex differences in *variance* in mental rotation performance across development. Finally, we used the meta-analytic estimates of sex differences in both mean and variability to model the expected overrepresentation of boys and girls across the upper tail of the mental rotation ability distribution.

### 2.1 Identifying Articles for Inclusion

From the dataset published in Lauer and colleagues (2019), we extracted data for all studies that reported both the mean and standard deviation or standard error for boys and girls, as these descriptive statistics were necessary to compute variance ratios. This led to 159 effect sizes (excluding 46 effect sizes from Lauer et al. due to lack of reporting of necessary statistics).

We then sought to identify material published since 2015 that met these inclusion criteria: must include a mental rotation measure, administered to samples with a mean age of 3 to 17 years (with an age range of less than 5 years); must have studied a healthy typically developing population without a focus on children with any exceptional academic, physical or intellectual differences (e.g. giftedness); and must report the necessary statistics for effect-size computation. We considered 70 articles published since 2015 for inclusion, identifying 12 articles and 31 effect sizes for inclusion. The most common reason that articles could not be included in the meta-analyses was a lack of sufficient descriptive statistics for effect size computation.

### 2.2 Data Extraction and Coding

For each study in the meta-analytic sample, we extracted the sample sizes for girls and boys and the means and standard deviations for girls' and boys' mental rotation performance. We used these statistics to compute Cohen's $d$s and variance ratios (VRs).

A $d$ greater than 0 corresponds to a male advantage in mental rotation performance, and a $d$ less than 0 corresponds to a female advantage; a VR greater than 1 corresponds to greater male variability in mental rotation performance, and a VR less than 1 corresponds to greater female variability. The *metafor* package in R (Viechtbauer, 2010) was used for all effect size calculations.

**Coding.** We coded the following sample- and measure-level characteristics: age, country of residence, stimulus dimensionality (2-D vs. 3-D), stimulus type (abstract shapes vs. recognisable shapes, such as animals or letters), test setting (individual testing vs. group testing), and timing conditions (with a time limit vs. without a time limit).

### 2.3 Analytic Approach

All meta-regression analyses were conducted in R using the *robumeta* package (Tanner-Smith et al., 2016).

**Standardised Mean Differences.** First, we conducted a meta-analysis of standardised mean differences to quantify the sex difference in mean mental rotation performance across all studies, via a hierarchical meta-regression analysis using the robust variance estimation (RVE) method (Hedges et al., 2010a, 2010b). We next examined the effects of sample- and measure-level variables of interest on effect size magnitudes by conducting a series of hierarchical meta-regression analyses.

**Variance Ratios.** Second, we conducted a meta-analysis of VRs to quantify the sex difference in variance in mental rotation performance across all studies via a hierarchical meta-regression analysis with RVE. Then, we examined the effects of sample- and measure-level variables of interest on VRs through a series of hierarchical meta-regression analyses.

## 3 Results

Data from 88 articles were included in the meta-analyses. These articles produced 190 standardised mean differences ($d$s) and variance ratios (VRs). These effect sizes were derived from 144 unique samples comprising 22,850 children aged 3 to 17 years. Samples were collected in 20 countries (90% Global North) across a timespan of more than 75 years (70% published in the 21$^{st}$ century).

### 3.1 Meta-Analysis of Standardised Mean Differences

Across all effect sizes in the meta-analytic sample ($k$ = 190, $m$ = 88), the mean effect size ($d$) equaled 0.45, 95% CI[0.37, 0.52], $p < .001$ (see Fig. 1). This indicates that there is a medium-sized male advantage in mental rotation performance across childhood and adolescence. There was notable heterogeneity among effect sizes ($\tau^2 = 0.05$, $\omega^2 = 0.03$), suggesting that moderator analyses are appropriate.

**Age-Related Change in the Male Advantage in Mean Performance.** The magnitude of the male advantage in mental rotation performance increased with age ($B$ = 0.04, $P < .001$). The male advantage first emerges and becomes small in size ($d$ =

0.20) around age 5 and increases by 0.04 standard deviation units each year, reaching a medium effect size by age 13.

**Sample Characteristics and the Male Advantage in Mean Performance.** There were no effects of sample country or year of birth on mean sex differences when accounting for the effect of age (*p*s > .18).

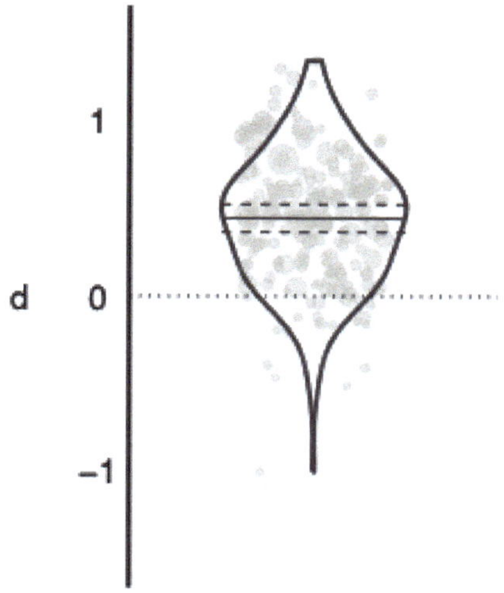


**Fig. 1.** Violin plot displaying the distribution of effect sizes in the meta-analysis of standardised mean differences (*d*). Reported *d*s are on the y-axis; *d*s above 0 reflect a male advantage and *d*s below 0 reflect a female advantage in performance. Markers correspond to individual effect sizes, and the size of markers corresponds to the standard error of the effect size. The dark blue solid line denotes the meta-analytic *d* of 0.45, and the dark blue dashed lines correspond to its 95% confidence interval

**Task Features and the Male Advantage in Mean Performance.** Tasks with 3-D stimuli resulted in larger effect sizes ($d = 0.54$, $p < .001$, $m = 58$, $k = 100$) than tasks with 2-d stimuli ($d = 0.34$, $p < .001$, $m = 41$, $k = 89$); $b = .19$, $p = .001$. The effect of stimulus dimensionality remained significant even when accounting for the effect of age on effect sizes ($b = 0.11$, $p = .027$).

There were no significant main effects of timing conditions, test setting, or stimulus type when controlling for the effect of age on reported *d*s (*p*s > .20).

### 3.2 Meta-Analysis of Variance Ratios

Across all effect sizes in the meta-analytic sample ($k = 190$, $m = 88$), the variance ratio (VR) equaled 1.08, 95% CI[1.04, 1.13], $p < .001$ (see Fig. 2). This indicates that there is a small sex difference in variance on mental rotation tasks (Howes & Chapman, 2024). Some heterogeneity among effect sizes was detected ($\tau^2 = 0.01$, $\omega^2 = 0.02$), suggesting that moderator analyses are appropriate.

**Sample Characteristics and Greater Male Variability in Performance.** There was no significant effect of age on vrs ($b = 0.005$, $p = .368$). That is, the presence and

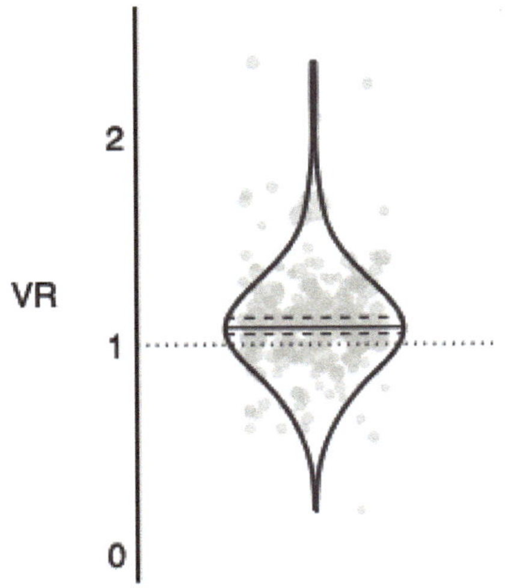


**Fig. 2.** Violin plot displaying the distribution of effect sizes in the meta-analysis of variance ratios (VR). Reported VRs are on the y-axis. VRs above 1 reflect greater male variability and VRs below 1 reflect greater female variability in performance. Markers correspond to individual effect sizes, and the size of markers corresponds to their standard error. The dark blue solid line denotes the meta-analytic VR, and the dark blue dashed lines correspond to its 95% confidence interval

magnitude of greater variability in mental rotation performance are consistent across samples aged 3 to 17 years.

There were no effects of sample country or year of birth on variance ratios (*p*s > .40).

**Task Features and Greater Male Variability in Performance.** Tasks with 3-d stimuli resulted in larger vrs (vr = 1.15, $p < .001$, $m = 58$, $k = 100$) than tasks with 2-d stimuli (vr = 1.01, $p = .775$, $m = 41$, $k = 89$); $b = .12$, $p < .001$. Tasks that were timed also resulted in larger vrs (vr = 1.12, $p < .001$, $m = 48$, $k = 112$) than tasks that were untimed (vr = 1.02, $p = .524$, $m = 43$, $k = 76$); $b = .09$, $p = .024$. However, when both stimulus dimensionality and timing conditions were included as predictors in the same model, only stimulus dimensionality had a significant effect on reported VRs ($b = .11$, $p = .007$).

There were no significant effects of test setting or stimulus type on reported VRs (*p*s > .05).

### 3.3 Distributional Implications of Sex Differences in Mental Rotation Ability

We next sought to quantify how sex differences in mental rotation performance translate into male overrepresentation at the upper end of the ability distribution across development. To do this, we combined our meta-analytic estimates of *d*s and VRs across ages. Specifically, we used the meta-regressions reported above to obtain age-varying estimates of the standardised mean difference between boys' and girls' mental rotation abilities and the log variance ratio of them. These estimates were then used to parameterise sex-specific normal distributions at each age, assuming girls as the reference distribution and allowing the mean and variance of boys' scores to vary with age. From these distributions, we derived the expected proportion of boys and girls exceeding a percentile threshold relative to the pooled population distribution. We then computed male-to-female ratios in the upper tail of the distribution for four percentile thresholds: top 50%, 25%, 10%, and 2% of scores, respectively, for all ages 3 to 17 years. Thus, the resulting ratios indicated the degree to which boys were overrepresented at each percentile threshold.

This analysis indicated that, at all ages in the meta-analytic sample, we would expect boys to be overrepresented relative to girls in the top 50%, top 25%, top 10%, and top 2% of all scorers (see Fig. 3). By 10 years of age, we would expect more than twice as many boys as girls in the top 10% of scorers and more than thrice as many boys as girls in the top 2% of scorers. By 17 years of age, we would expect 3.6 times as many boys as girls in the top 10% of scorers and 6.6 times as many boys as girls in the top 2% of scores.

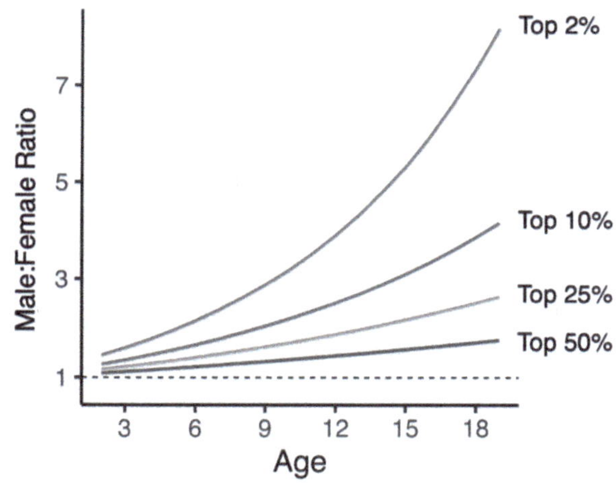


**Fig. 3.** Male-female ratios in the upper tail of mental rotation performance as a function of age (years) and distributional threshold (top 2%, 10%, 25%, and 50% of the distribution)

## 4 Discussion

This meta-analytic review provides the first quantitative synthesis of sex differences in both the mean and variability of mental rotation performance across development. Consistent with prior meta-analyses (Lauer et al., 2019; Linn & Petersen, 1985; Voyer et al., 1995), we observed a reliable male advantage in mean mental rotation performance ($d$ = 0.45), which increased considerably between the ages of 3 and 17 years. In novel findings, we observed greater male variability in mental rotation performance (VR = 1.08) that was modest in magnitude but early emerging and stable across childhood and adolescence. Together, these findings suggest that sex differences in mental rotation performance are characterised by both an age-dependent male advantage in mean performance and an age-independent greater male variability in performance. When these sex differences were modelled jointly, boys were consistently overrepresented at the upper tail of the ability distribution from early childhood onwards, and this overrepresentation of boys at very high levels of ability becomes progressively larger with age through late adolescence.

The meta-analytic findings provide novel support for the greater male variability hypothesis, which has been widely held for over a century (Ellis, 1894; Feingold, 1992; Hedges & Nowell, 1995; Maccoby & Jacklin, 1974) but not previously quantified in the spatial development literature. This research is, to our knowledge, the first to estimate the magnitude of such sex differences in variability in a key spatial ability: mental rotation. The sex difference in variance in mental rotation performance observed in our meta-analysis was modest in size; however, when combined with an increasing male advantage in mean performance across development, it produced substantial male overrepresentation among the highest-performing individuals. That is, relatively small sex differences in means and variances translated into much larger sex differences in representation at the extremes of the performance distribution, with boys being multifold more likely than girls to demonstrate very high levels of mental rotation ability by late adolescence (see Fig. 3). This distributional modelling provides the principal contribution of the present research, directly quantifying the preponderance of boys at the highest levels of mental rotation skill.

These findings are also interesting to consider in relation to the broader literature on sex differences, and the lack thereof, in spatial cognition. Mental rotation consistently produces some of the largest sex differences observed across spatial abilities, and perhaps across cognition more broadly, yet many other spatial tasks produce much smaller or no sex differences in mean performance (Linn & Petersen, 1985; Voyer et al., 1995). This specificity suggests that explanations for the emergence of sex differences in spatial ability should focus on the particular cognitive demands of mental rotation rather than spatial cognition more generally. Importantly, to our knowledge, no previous meta-analysis has examined sex differences in variability for other spatial skills. It therefore remains unclear whether greater male variability is similarly specific to mental rotation or reflects a broader characteristic of spatial cognition. Determining whether comparable sex differences in variability are observed across different spatial tasks represents an important direction for future research.

Our results further suggest that the observed sex differences in mental rotation are themselves sensitive to task demands. Tasks that required the mental rotation of three-dimensional stimuli produced larger sex differences in both mean performance and variability than those with two-dimensional stimuli, whereas other task characteristics showed comparatively little influence on the magnitude of sex differences. The marked specificity of observed sex differences, both across different forms of spatial ability and across different mental rotation paradigms, suggests that explanations of sex differences should focus on the cognitive processes uniquely engaged in mental rotation rather than consider spatial cognition to be a unitary construct. Future research should therefore move beyond asking whether sex differences exist in spatial cognition and instead identify the task characteristics that reliably increase or reduce both mean and variability differences. Such work has the potential to provide important constraints on competing explanations for the origins of sex differences in spatial ability.

The meta-analytic findings indicate that the mean male advantage in mental rotation abilities exhibits considerable age-related change while the observed greater male variability in mental rotation performance emerges early in life and is stable across development. What might account for this pattern of effects? Historically, greater male variability in cognition has most often been attributed to biological influences, including sex-linked neurodevelopmental processes and hormonal factors operating during prenatal and early postnatal development (Halpern et al., 2007). The early emergence and developmental stability of greater male variability in mental rotation performance are broadly consistent with this possibility. However, early-emerging differences should not be interpreted as evidence that they are biologically determined (Lauer, 2025). By three years of age, children have already accumulated extensive experience within their physical and social environments, and biological and environmental influences are likely to be highly intertwined. Accordingly, the present findings are informative about when sex differences in variability emerge but do not distinguish between the biological and environmental mechanisms that produce them. Future research should therefore seek to identify the developmental processes that generate early mean and variability differences between girls and boys and characterise the mechanisms of developmental stability and change within them.

The results of this meta-analytic review may have implications for understanding gender disparities in STEM outcomes, although these implications should be interpreted cautiously as the present research did not examine such outcomes directly. Mental rotation ability is a robust predictor of STEM achievement (Casey et al., 1995; Ganley et al., 2014; Wai et al., 2009), making it reasonable to consider the potential implications of the present findings for debates on gender inequalities in STEM. One longstanding argument has been that greater male variability in cognitive performance may contribute to the overrepresentation of men in highly selective STEM fields by increasing the proportion of males at the upper tail of relevant ability distributions (Feingold, 1992; Hedges & Nowell, 1995), although the importance of this mechanism remains debated (e.g. Spelke, 2005). The meta-analytic results presented here refine this debate. Although we observed evidence of greater male variability in mental rotation performance, the distributional analyses indicate that the substantial male overrepresentation at the highest levels of ability arises primarily through the combination of increasing mean differences and consistently modest variability differences, with the increasing male advantage in mean performance contributing more strongly to upper-tail disparities than the slight greater male variability. These findings therefore suggest that discussions of cognitive contributions to gender disparities in highly selective STEM pathways should consider both differences in average performance and differences in variability, rather than treating greater male variability as a primary explanation.

Several limitations to these meta-analyses should be acknowledged. First, effect sizes could only be computed for studies reporting both group means and variances for each sex, resulting in the exclusion of otherwise eligible studies that did not report sufficient descriptive statistics. This reporting practice seems unlikely to systematically bias estimates of sex differences in variability but may be more likely to bias estimates of mean sex differences, potentially over-inflating effects. Given the robust evidence of sex differences in mental rotation performance across development, we encourage authors to report both types of sex differences to increase the robustness of future meta-analytic endeavours.

Another limitation of this research lies in the geographic representation of samples: the overwhelming majority of studies included in the meta-analyses were conducted in Global North nations, as would be expected given the lack of cultural diversity in the spatial development literature (Lauer, 2025). Although we considered the effects of national context on reported sex differences in our meta-analyses, the dearth of samples from Global South contexts greatly reduced our power to detect significant effects. This is a notable limitation as our findings cannot be generalised to global-majority contexts. Thus, future research should examine whether similar sex differences (both in means and in variance) are observed in more geographically and culturally diverse populations. Such research would have the potential not only to diversify our evidence base but also advance our theorising on the origins of sex differences in mental rotation skills.

Taken together, the present findings indicate that greater male variability in mental rotation emerges early in childhood, remains stable across development, and combines with an increasing male advantage in mean performance to produce substantial sex differences at the upper tail of the ability distribution. More broadly, these findings demonstrate the importance of considering the full distribution of cognitive performance, rather than mean differences alone, when evaluating sex differences in early spatial skills and their potential implications for educational and occupational outcomes later in life.

**Acknowledgments.** The author thanks members of the Cambridge University Development and Learning Lab for support. This research was funded in part by NIH F32HD100149.

**Disclosure of Interests.** The author has no competing interests.

## References

1. Casey, M.B., Nuttall, R., Pezaris, E., Benbow, C.P.: The influence of spatial ability on gender differences in mathematics college entrance test scores across diverse samples. Dev. Psychol. **31**(4), 697–705 (1995). https://doi.org/10.1037/0012-1649.31.4.697
2. Ellis, H.: Man and Woman. Walter Scott, London (1894)
3. Feingold, A.: Sex differences in variability in intellectual abilities: a new look at an old controversy. Rev. Educ. Res. **62**(1), 61–84 (1992)
4. Ganley, C.M., Vasilyeva, M., Dulaney, A.: Spatial ability mediates the gender difference in middle school students' science performance. Child Dev. **85**(4), 1419–1432 (2014)
5. Geer, E.A., Quinn, J.M., Ganley, C.M.: Relations between spatial skills and math performance in elementary school children: a longitudinal investigation. Dev. Psychol. **55**(3), 637–652 (2018)
6. Halpern, D.F., Benbow, C.P., Geary, D.C., Gur, R.C., Hyde, J.S., Gernsbacher, M.A.: The science of sex differences in science and mathematics. Psychol. Sci. Public Interest. **8**(1), 1–51 (2007)
7. Hedges, L.V., Nowell, A.: Sex differences in mental test scores, variability, and numbers of high-scoring individuals. Science. **269**(5220), 41–45 (1995)
8. Hedges, L.V., Tipton, E., Johnson, M.C.: Robust variance estimation in meta-regression with dependent effect size estimates. Res. Synth. Methods. **1**(1), 39–65 (2010)

9. Hodgkiss, A., Gilligan, K.A., Tolmie, A.K., Thomas, M.S., Farran, E.K.: Spatial cognition and science achievement: the contribution of intrinsic and extrinsic spatial skills from 7 to 11 years. Br. J. Educ. Psychol. **88**, 675–697 (2018)
10. Howes, O.D., Chapman, G.E.: Understanding variability: the role of meta-analysis of variance. Psychol. Med. **54**(12), 3233–3236 (2024)
11. Lauer, J.: Revisiting intrinsic sex differences in STEM aptitude: insights from infant development research twenty years after Spelke (2005). Infant Behav. Dev. **79**, 102064 (2025)
12. Lauer, J.E., Yhang, E., Lourenco, S.F.: The development of gender differences in spatial reasoning: a meta-analytic review. Psychol. Bull. **145**(6), 537–565 (2019)
13. Lauer, J.E., Lourenco, S.F.: Spatial processing in infancy predicts both spatial and mathematical aptitude in childhood. Psychol. Sci. **27**(10), 1291–1298 (2016)
14. Linn, M.C., Petersen, A.C.: Emergence and characterization of sex differences in spatial ability: a meta-analysis. Child Dev. **56**(6), 1479–1498 (1985)
15. Maccoby, E.E., Jacklin, C.N.: The Psychology of Sex Differences. Stanford University Press, Stanford, CA (1974)
16. O'Dea, R.E., Lagisz, M., Jennions, M.D., Nakagawa, S.: Gender differences in individual variation in academic grades fail to fit expected patterns for STEM. Nat. Commun. **9**, 3777 (2018)
17. Spelke, E.S.: Sex differences in intrinsic aptitude for mathematics and science?: a critical review. Am. Psychol. **60**(9), 950–958 (2005)
18. Tanner-Smith, E.E., Tipton, E., Polanin, J.R.: Handling complex meta-analytic data structures using robust variance estimates: a tutorial in R. J. Dev. Life-Course Criminol. **2**(1), 85–112 (2016)
19. Viechtbauer, W.: Conducting meta-analyses in R with the metafor package. J. Stat. Softw. **36**, 1–48 (2010)
20. Voyer, D., Voyer, S., Bryden, M.P.: Magnitude of sex differences in spatial abilities: a meta-analysis and consideration of critical variables. Psychol. Bull. **117**(2), 250–270 (1995)
21. Wai, J., Lubinski, D., Benbow, C.P.: Spatial ability for STEM domains: aligning over fifty years of cumulative psychological knowledge solidifies its importance. J. Educ. Psychol. **101**(4), 817–835 (2009)

# STEM Attitudes and Aspirations Across Early and Mid-Adolescence: Associations with Spatial Ability and Visuospatial Working Memory

Styliani Malkogeorgou[1], Gavin Duffy[1(✉)], Marianna Pagkratidou[2], and Petra Jansen[3]

[1] School of Electrical and Electronic Engineering, Technological University Dublin, Grangegorman D07 ADY7, Ireland
gavin.duffy@tudublin.ie

[2] School of Psychology, Dublin City University, Dublin 9, Ireland

[3] Faculty of Human Sciences, University of Regensburg, Universitätsstr. 31, 93053 Regensburg, Germany

**Abstract.** Given ongoing concerns about shortages of STEM graduates, it is important to understand why young people pursue STEM education and careers. This study examined associations between spatial ability, visuospatial working memory and STEM attitudes and aspirations in adolescents, considering grade, gender, socioeconomic status (SES), and differences between the Greek and Irish subsamples. Participants were 763 grade 6 and grade 10 students from public schools in Greece and Ireland. Measures assessed spatial ability, visuospatial working memory, STEM attitudes, advanced STEM lesson interest, and STEM career aspirations. Higher levels of spatial ability and working memory were associated with more positive STEM attitudes and aspirations. Grade 6 students reported more positive STEM attitudes and stronger aspirations than grade 10 students. Boys reported more positive engineering/technology attitudes than girls, whereas girls performed better than boys on some spatial measures. Students in the Irish subsample and students from higher SES groups showed more positive STEM attitudes and aspirations and stronger cognitive performance than students in the Greek subsample and lower SES groups. Working memory statistically partially mediated the association between spatial ability and STEM attitudes. Overall, the findings underline the combined importance of cognitive, grade-level, socioeconomic, and sample-context factors in STEM engagement among adolescents.

**Keywords:** STEM attitudes · Spatial ability · Working memory · STEM careers · Gender

## 1 Introduction

Students' engagement with science, technology, engineering, and mathematics (STEM) is shaped by cognitive, motivational, and contextual factors [1, 2]. Among the cognitive variables most consistently associated with STEM learning and performance are spatial


E. Farran et al. (Eds.): Spatial Cognition 2026, LNAI 16785, pp. 184–195, 2027.
https://doi.org/10.1007/978-3-032-36716-7_13

abilities, particularly spatial visualization and mental rotation, which support reasoning, problem solving, and the interpretation and transformation of visual information across STEM domains [3–5]. Although spatial abilities are well established in relation to STEM achievement, less is known about how they relate to students' attitudes toward STEM and aspirations for future STEM participation.

In this study, STEM attitudes refer to students' current evaluations of and interest in STEM subjects, whereas STEM aspirations refer to future-oriented intentions to continue engaging with STEM, including interest in advanced STEM study and STEM-related careers [6, 7]. This distinction is important because students may hold positive views of STEM subjects without necessarily intending to pursue STEM pathways. The present study focuses on Grade 6 students aged 11–12 years-old and Grade 10 students aged 15–16 years-old because these educational stages are relevant to the formation of academic preferences, self-perceptions, and future study intentions [1, 2, 8, 9]. Despite the importance of these grade groups, relatively little research has examined how spatial abilities relate specifically to STEM attitudes and aspirations within the same study across grade groups and national contexts.

The present study assessed spatial ability using two complementary measures: the Paper Folding Test, which captures spatial visualization, and the PMA Spatial Relations subtest, which indexes mental rotation/spatial relations. Examining both measures makes it possible to capture distinct but related aspects of spatial ability that may contribute to students' STEM attitudes and aspirations. In addition, the study considered visuospatial working memory (VSWM) as a complementary cognitive factor. Visuospatial working memory supports the temporary storage and manipulation of spatial information and has been linked both to spatial performance and to achievement in STEM-related domains [10, 11]. It may also be relevant to students' attitudes toward STEM, given evidence that working memory capacity is associated with more positive attitudes toward mathematics and science [12, 13]. VSWM was not included simply as a second cognitive predictor, but as a theoretically relevant candidate mediator. Spatial tasks require students to temporarily hold, update, and manipulate visuospatial representations, so students with stronger spatial ability may also be better able to manage the working-memory demands involved in STEM-related reasoning. In this way, VSWM may help account for part of the statistical association between spatial ability and STEM attitudes. This potential indirect association remains underexplored.

The study also considers gender and socioeconomic status (SES) as important individual-difference variables. Gender has long featured in research on both spatial ability and STEM participation, but recent work increasingly emphasizes that observed differences are often domain-specific and shaped by contextual, educational, and sociocultural influences rather than reflecting fixed or universal patterns [5, 14, 27]. SES is similarly relevant, as it has been associated with variation in neurocognitive development, academic performance, and future educational expectations [2, 15, 16]. A further contribution of the study is its inclusion of students from two national contexts, while recognizing that the Greek and Irish subsamples are unequal in size. By comparing Greek and Irish subsamples, the study explores whether patterns are similar across two national contexts, while treating these comparisons cautiously because of the smaller Irish subsample.

The study addressed four research questions: (1) whether STEM attitudes, STEM aspirations, spatial ability, and visuospatial working memory differ by grade, gender, SES, and national subsample; (2) whether spatial ability and visuospatial working memory are associated with STEM attitudes and aspirations; (3) whether spatial ability and visuospatial working memory predict overall STEM attitudes; and (4) whether visuospatial working memory statistically mediates the association between spatial ability and overall STEM attitudes. The core contribution of the study is therefore to examine how spatial ability and visuospatial working memory are associated with STEM attitudes and aspirations, and to test whether visuospatial working memory statistically mediates the association between spatial ability and overall STEM attitudes, while treating grade, gender, SES, and national subsample as contextual factors.

## 2 Method

### 2.1 Participants

Participants were 763 students from public schools in Greece and Ireland: 297 in Grade 6 and 466 in Grade 10. Mean age was 11.48 years (SD = 0.50) in Grade 6 and 15.61 years (SD = 0.49) in Grade 10. Overall, 339 students identified as male, 407 as female, and 17 preferred not to report gender. The Greek subsample comprised 691 students: 270 Grade 6 students (M age = 11.44, SD = 0.50) and 421 Grade 10 students (M age = 15.61, SD = 0.49); 324 identified as male, 353 as female, and 14 preferred not to report gender. The Irish subsample comprised 72 students: 27 Grade 6 students (M age = 11.93, SD = 0.67) and 45 Grade 10 students; 15 identified as male, 54 as female, and 3 preferred not to report gender. Schools were recruited through nonprobability school-based sampling based on willingness to participate and access. No participants were excluded from the analytic sample.

### 2.2 Measures

All measures were administered in computerized format via Qualtrics and included spatial ability, visuospatial working memory, STEM attitudes and aspirations, and sociodemographic characteristics.

**Paper Folding Test (PFT).** Spatial visualization was assessed using the Paper Folding Test [17]. The test comprises 20 items in which participants view drawings of a sheet of paper being folded and punched with a hole, then select from five options the pattern that would appear when the paper is fully unfolded. Scores were calculated as the total number of correct responses across both parts, with higher scores indicating stronger spatial visualization. The PFT was included because spatial visualization is relevant to STEM tasks requiring interpretation and transformation of visual representations.

**Primary Mental Abilities-Spatial Relations (PMA-SR).** Mental rotation/spatial relations ability was assessed using the Spatial Relations subtest of the Primary Mental Abilities battery [18]. The test comprises 20 items assessing the ability to recognize and interpret two-dimensional figures despite changes in spatial orientation. For each item, participants inspected six response options and identified those matching the target figure after mental rotation or spatial transformation. Scores were corrected for guessing using the standard PMA-SR scoring procedure, in which the number of incorrect responses is subtracted from the number of correct responses, with higher scores indicating stronger spatial relations ability. Administration time was approximately 5–10 min.

**Visuospatial Working Memory.** Visuospatial working memory was assessed using a computerized Forward Corsi Block Test, based on the original Corsi block-tapping task [19] and implemented following established parameters [20]. Participants reproduced sequences of spatial locations in the same order presented, with span length and accuracy used as performance indicators.

**STEM Attitudes and Aspirations.** STEM attitudes and aspirations were measured using the Student Attitudes toward STEM (S-STEM) questionnaire [6]. The measure yielded scores for overall STEM attitudes, attitudes toward mathematics, science, and engineering/technology, and aspiration-related indicators including interest in advanced STEM lessons and STEM-related careers. Attitude items captured students' current views of STEM subjects, whereas lessons and careers items captured future-oriented intentions to continue engaging with STEM through further study and possible occupations. The $21^{st}$-century skills subscale was omitted because it did not align directly with the study's focus on subject-specific STEM attitudes and aspirations.

**Sociodemographic and Socioeconomic Variables.** A self-report questionnaire collected information on age, grade, gender, nationality, and socioeconomic indicators. SES items were adapted from the TIMSS 2019 student questionnaire [21] and assessed home and educational resources. Responses were summed to create an SES index, with scores of 1–4 classified as low SES, 5–7 as medium SES, and 8 or higher as high SES.

## 2.3 Procedure

The study used a cross-sectional school-based design in Greece and Ireland. Schools were recruited through direct contact with principals and teachers, and eligible students in the relevant grades were invited to participate. Ethical approval was obtained from the relevant institutional research ethics committee (approval number REIC22146), and permission to conduct the study in Greek schools was granted by the Greek Ministry of Education.

Data collection took place in schools using PCs, laptops, or tablets. Students accessed the study through a secure Qualtrics link. Measures were administered in a fixed order to ensure procedural consistency across schools and countries and minimize variation in administration: (a) sociodemographic and SES questionnaire, (b) Paper Folding Test, (c) PMA-SR, (d) S-STEM questionnaire, and (e) Corsi Block Test. In Greece, data collection was supervised by the researcher and classroom teacher. In Ireland, teachers administered the study using a standardized guide with step-by-step instructions, example items, and practice trials to support procedural consistency across sites.

## 2.4 Data Analysis

Analyses were conducted in IBM SPSS Statistics 23 with $\alpha = .05$ (two-tailed). Descriptive statistics and assumption checks preceded inferential analyses. Associations among spatial ability, visuospatial working memory, STEM attitudes and aspirations, and SES were examined using Spearman's rho or Pearson correlations. Simple and multiple regressions assessed spatial ability and working memory as predictors of STEM attitudes. Group differences by gender, grade, country, and SES were tested using chi-square, t, Mann-Whitney U, ANOVA, and Kruskal-Wallis tests. A statistical mediation analysis examined visuospatial working memory as a mediator between spatial ability and STEM attitudes via PROCESS Model 4 [22] with 5,000 bootstrap samples and bias-corrected 95% CIs.

## 3 Results

Descriptive statistics and tests of normality were conducted before the main analyses. Because most continuous variables deviated from normality, nonparametric tests were used for group comparisons where appropriate, whereas parametric analyses were conducted for overall STEM attitudes and regression models.

### 3.1 Group Differences in STEM Attitudes, Aspirations, Spatial Ability, and Visuospatial Working Memory

Group differences were most consistent for grade group, SES, and national subsample. Grade 6 students reported higher overall STEM attitudes ($M = 3.15$, $SD = 0.49$) than Grade 10 students ($M = 3.07$, $SD = 0.44$), $t(758) = 2.19$, $p = .029$, $d = 0.16$. Grade 6 students also reported greater interest in advanced STEM lessons and stronger STEM career aspirations, whereas Grade 10 students scored higher on Paper Folding, PMA-SR, overall spatial ability, and visuospatial working memory. These findings indicate differences between grade groups in this cross-sectional sample and should not be interpreted as evidence of developmental change.

Gender differences were limited and domain specific. Male students reported higher engineering/technology attitudes ($M = 3.41$, $SD = 0.74$) than female students ($M = 3.09$, $SD = 0.71$), $H(2) = 36.98$, $p < .001$, $f = .21$. In contrast, female students scored higher on Paper Folding ($M = 7.77$, $SD = 3.52$) than male students ($M = 7.01$, $SD = 3.38$), $H(2) = 8.50$, $p = .014$, $f = .08$. No broader gender differences were observed for overall STEM attitudes, STEM aspirations, PMA-SR, overall spatial ability, or visuospatial working memory.

SES differences were observed across motivational and cognitive outcomes. Overall STEM attitudes differed by SES group, $F(2, 654) = 27.14$, $p < .001$, $\eta^2 = .08$, with the highest scores reported by students in the high-SES group ($M = 3.30$, $SD = 0.47$), followed by the medium-SES group ($M = 3.06$, $SD = 0.43$) and low-SES group ($M = 2.94$, $SD = 0.44$). SES was also associated with STEM aspirations, spatial ability, and visuospatial working memory, with higher-SES students generally reporting higher STEM attitudes and aspirations and showing higher cognitive scores than students in lower SES groups.

Differences were also observed between national subsamples. Students in the Irish subsample reported higher overall STEM attitudes ($M = 3.38$, $SD = 0.45$) than students in the Greek subsample ($M = 3.08$, $SD = 0.45$), $t(758) = -5.40$, $p < .001$, $d = 0.68$. Students in the Irish subsample also reported higher STEM aspirations and scored higher on several cognitive measures. However, these national subsample comparisons should be treated as exploratory because the Irish subsample was small and may have differed from the Greek subsample in SES distribution, gender distribution, school context, and recruitment conditions.

### 3.2 Associations Among STEM Attitudes, Aspirations, Spatial Ability, Visuospatial Working Memory, and SES

Table 1 presents the correlations among STEM attitudes, STEM aspirations, spatial ability, visuospatial working memory, and SES. Overall STEM attitudes were positively associated with STEM career aspirations, interest in advanced STEM lessons, spatial ability, visuospatial working memory, and SES. The strongest associations outside the STEM attitude subscales were observed between overall STEM attitudes and STEM career aspirations, and between overall STEM attitudes and visuospatial working memory. Spatial ability and visuospatial working memory were also positively correlated. These findings indicate that more positive STEM attitudes were associated with stronger STEM aspirations, higher cognitive performance, and higher SES.

**Table 1.** Correlations among STEM attitudes, cognitive abilities, and SES

| Variable | 1 | 2 | 3 | 4 | 5 | 6 | 7 | 8 |
|---|---|---|---|---|---|---|---|---|
| 1. STEM | – | | | | | | | |
| 2. Maths | .588*** | | | | | | | |
| 3. Science | .766*** | .443*** | | | | | | |
| 4. Eng-Tec | .701*** | .253*** | .336*** | | | | | |
| 5. STEM Careers | .579*** | .332*** | .548*** | .386*** | | | | |
| 6. STEM Lessons | .467*** | .420*** | .555*** | .214*** | .545*** | | | |
| 7. Spatial | .361*** | .168*** | .217*** | .162*** | .258*** | .147*** | | |
| 8. WM | .461*** | .240*** | .287*** | .276*** | .260*** | .183*** | .590*** | |
| 9. SES | .312*** | .280*** | .276*** | .122** | .220*** | .299*** | .258*** | .187*** |

*Note. Correlations are Spearman's rho coefficients. SES = socioeconomic status. **$p < .01$. ***$p < .001$.*

### 3.3 Regression Analysis

Regression analysis examined spatial ability and visuospatial working memory as predictors of overall STEM attitudes. In separate simple regression models, spatial ability was significantly associated with overall STEM attitudes, $R^2 = .13$, $F(1, 758) = 113.25$, $p < .001$, and visuospatial working memory was also significantly associated with overall STEM attitudes, $R^2 = .21$, $F(1, 758) = 204.86$, $p < .001$.

When both predictors were entered simultaneously, the overall model was significant, $R^2 = .23$, $F(2, 757) = 109.74$, $p < .001$. Both spatial ability, $B = 0.011$, $SE = 0.003$, $\beta = .136$, $p < .001$, and visuospatial working memory, $B = 0.105$, $SE = 0.011$, $\beta = .381$, $p < .001$, were significant predictors of overall STEM attitudes (Table 2). Visuospatial working memory showed the stronger unique association with overall STEM attitudes.

**Table 2.** Regression analysis of spatial abilities and visuospatial working memory as predictors of attitudes toward STEM

| | | | 95% CI | | | |
|---|---|---|---|---|---|---|
| Variable | B | SE | LL | UL | β | p |
| Constant | 2.484 | .057 | 2.372 | 2.595 | | <.001 |
| Spatial Abilities | .011 | .003 | .005 | .017 | .136 | <.001 |
| VWM | .105 | .011 | .084 | .127 | .381 | <.001 |

*Note.* The model was significant, $R^2 = .225$, $F(2, 757) = 109.74$, $p < .001$. Durbin-Watson = 1.70. Collinearity statistics were acceptable, tolerance = .652, VIF = 1.53. N = 760. CI = confidence interval; LL = lower limit; UL = upper limit.

### 3.4 Mediation Analysis

The statistical mediation analysis tested whether visuospatial working memory was part of the indirect association between spatial ability and overall STEM attitudes and the results are provided in Table 3 and Fig. 1. Spatial ability was positively associated with visuospatial working memory, $B = 0.166$, $SE = 0.008$, $\beta = .590$, $p < .001$. In the final model, visuospatial working memory was positively associated with overall STEM attitudes, $B = 0.105$, $SE = 0.011$, $\beta = .381$, $p < .001$, and the direct association between spatial ability and overall STEM attitudes remained significant, $B = 0.011$, $SE = 0.003$, $\beta = .136$, $p = .001$. The indirect effect was statistically significant, 95% bootstrap CI [0.013, 0.022], indicating a statistical indirect association through visuospatial working memory. Because the data are cross-sectional, this model should be interpreted as a statistical mediation model rather than evidence of a causal process.

**Table 3.** Mediation model results for spatial ability, visuospatial working memory, and STEM attitudes

| | | M (WM) | | | | | Y (STEM attitudes) | | | |
|---|---|---|---|---|---|---|---|---|---|---|
| | | B | SE | p | β | | B | SE | p | β |
| X (Spatial) | a | .166 | .008 | .001 | .590 | c′ | .011 | .003 | .001 | .136 |
| M (WM) | | – | – | – | – | b | .105 | .011 | .001 | .381 |
| | | R2 = .348 F(1, 758) = 404.515, p < .001 | | | | | R2 = .225 F(2, 757) =109.725, p < .001 | | | |

Note. Bootstrap resampling indicated a significant indirect effect, with a 95% confidence interval ranging from .013 at the lower level to .022 at the upper level

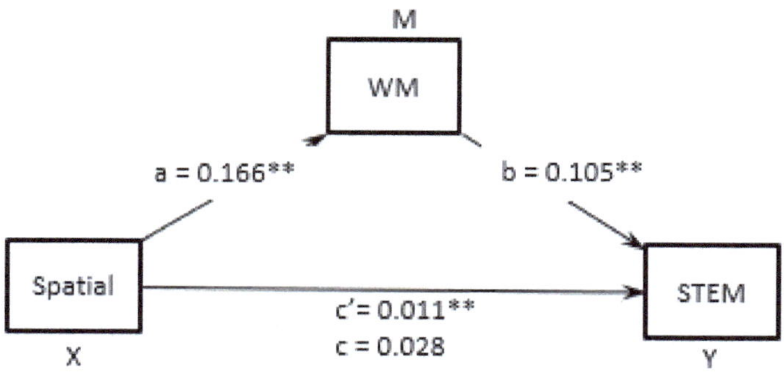


**Fig. 1.** Mediation Model Results. Path c is the total effect of Spatial, path ab is the indirect effect and path c' is the direct effect

## 3.5 Summary of Main Group Differences

To provide a concise synthesis of the group-comparison findings, Table 4 summarizes the main patterns observed by grade group, gender, SES, and national subsample.

**Table 4.** Summary of main group differences

| Comparison | Main pattern |
|---|---|
| Grade group | Grade 6 students reported higher STEM attitudes and aspirations, whereas Grade 10 students scored higher on spatial ability and working memory. |
| Gender | Boys reported higher engineering/technology attitudes, whereas girls scored higher on Paper Folding. Other gender differences were not significant. |
| SES | Higher-SES students reported higher STEM attitudes and aspirations and showed higher spatial ability and working memory scores. |
| National subsample | Students in the Irish subsample reported higher STEM attitudes and aspirations and scored higher on several cognitive measures than students in the Greek subsample. These comparisons are exploratory because of the small size of the Irish subsample. |

## 4 Limitations

A major limitation is the imbalance between the Greek and Irish subsamples, with the Irish subsample comprising about 10% of the total sample and being drawn from a small number of schools. As a result, comparisons between the Greek and Irish subsamples should be interpreted cautiously and treated as exploratory, particularly because SES, gender distribution, and school-level composition may have influenced the observed differences. Because the study was cross-sectional, differences between Grade 6 and Grade 10 should be interpreted as grade-group differences rather than evidence of developmental change, as they may reflect cohort effects. The mediation model should likewise be interpreted as a statistical indirect association rather than a causal process, and alternative reciprocal explanations remain possible. Because several exploratory group comparisons were conducted without formal correction for multiple testing, these findings should be interpreted with emphasis on effect sizes and consistency of patterns rather than isolated p-values. STEM attitudes, STEM aspirations, and SES were measured using self-report questionnaires, so responses may have been affected by response bias. The study also did not include objective STEM achievement, later subject choices, or long-term educational outcomes, so conclusions about STEM participation remain indirect. The adapted SES index was used as a contextual indicator rather than a fully validated psychometric scale in this sample, so SES-related findings should be interpreted cautiously.

## 5 Discussion

The present study examined the associations between spatial ability, visuospatial working memory, and STEM attitudes and aspirations among Grade 6 and Grade 10 students. Its main contribution is the integration of spatial ability and visuospatial working memory in relation to STEM attitudes, including a statistical mediation model in which visuospatial working memory was tested as an indirect associate between spatial ability and overall STEM attitudes. Grade, gender, SES, and national subsample were considered as contextual factors to clarify how these associations varied across student groups.

Both spatial ability and WM were positively associated with STEM attitudes, interest in advanced STEM lessons, and STEM career aspirations. In the regression analyses, both predicted overall STEM attitudes, with working memory showing the stronger unique contribution. This suggests that STEM engagement is linked not only to background or motivational factors, but also to cognitive capacities supporting visuospatial processing and manipulation. These findings are consistent with prior research linking spatial ability to STEM outcomes and working memory to mathematics- and science-related performance, while extending this literature to broader attitudinal outcomes [11, 12]. One interpretation is that students with stronger spatial and working memory skills may experience STEM tasks as more manageable, supporting more positive attitudes and aspirations.

Significant differences in STEM attitudes and aspirations were observed between grade groups, with Grade 6 students reporting more positive attitudes than Grade 10 students in this study. Grade 6 students reported more positive attitudes toward mathematics, science, and overall STEM, as well as greater interest in advanced STEM lessons and stronger STEM career aspirations. This is consistent with previous research reporting lower STEM interest among older adolescent groups; however, because the present study is cross-sectional, it cannot determine whether individual students' attitudes decline over time [2]. The absence of a grade difference in engineering/technology attitudes suggests that attitudes to STEM should be measured for each of its constituent subjects as differences can arise between each of the STEM subjects.

Differences were also observed between the Greek and Irish subsamples, with students in the Irish subsample reporting more positive STEM attitudes and aspirations, particularly in Grade 10, and performing better on spatial ability measures. These differences may reflect contextual factors, such as school context, STEM exposure, recruitment conditions, or broader educational experiences. More broadly, cross-national STEM patterns may be shaped by sociocultural and structural factors rather than national context alone [23, 24]. However, the comparisons in the present study should be treated as exploratory because the Irish subsample was small and may have differed from the Greek subsample in SES distribution, gender distribution, school composition, or number of participating schools. Therefore, the observed differences should not be attributed to national context alone.

Gender differences were limited and domain-specific and did not support a generalized male advantage in spatial or STEM-related outcomes. Boys reported more positive attitudes toward engineering/technology, particularly in Grade 10, whereas girls outperformed boys on spatial visualization ability. No gender differences were found for overall STEM attitudes, mathematics attitudes, science attitudes, STEM lesson interest, STEM career aspirations, PMA-SR performance, or visuospatial working memory. This pattern suggests a decoupling between cognitive performance and STEM-related motivation: girls' stronger Paper Folding performance did not correspond to stronger engineering/technology attitudes, while boys' more positive engineering/technology attitudes were not accompanied by stronger spatial performance. The findings therefore suggest that STEM motivation is not simply a reflection of cognitive ability. Instead, engineering/technology attitudes may be shaped by sociocultural factors such as gendered STEM identity, stereotypes, exposure to engineering/technology activities, and perceived fit with STEM pathways [5, 14, 27].

SES was another consistent source of difference. Higher-SES students reported more positive STEM attitudes, stronger aspirations, higher spatial ability, and better working memory. This pattern is consistent with previous literature linking SES to cognitive development, educational performance, and access to STEM-related opportunities [15, 16, 25]. In the present study, SES appears to function not simply as a background characteristic, but as a contextual condition associated with the cognitive and motivational resources supporting STEM engagement.

The statistical mediation analysis showed a significant indirect association, suggesting that spatial ability was associated with STEM attitudes both directly and indirectly through its association with working memory. Although the cross-sectional design does not allow causal conclusions, this finding is consistent with the possibility that working memory is one cognitive factor involved in the association between spatial ability and

STEM engagement [10, 11, 26]. The remaining direct association also suggests that additional factors, such as confidence, perceived competence, or prior learning experiences, may be relevant to this relationship.

**Acknowledgments.** This study was funded by the European Union's Horizon 2020 research and innovation programme under the Marie Skłodowska-Curie grant agreement No 956124, 'SellSTEM'.

**Disclosure of Interests.** The authors have no competing interests to declare that are relevant to the content of this article.

## References

1. Godwin, A., Potvin, G., Hazari, Z., Lock, R.: Identity, critical agency, and engineering: an affective model for predicting engineering as a career choice. J. Eng. Educ. **105**(2), 312–340 (2016). https://doi.org/10.1002/jee.20118
2. McDaniel, A.: The role of cultural contexts in explaining cross-National Gender Gaps in STEM expectations. Eur. Sociol. Rev. **32**(1), 122–133 (2016). https://doi.org/10.1093/esr/jcv078
3. Newcombe, N.S., Shipley, T.F.: Thinking about spatial thinking: new typology, new assessments. In: Gero, J.S. (ed.) Studying Visual and Spatial Reasoning for Design Creativity, pp. 179–192. Springer Netherlands, Dordrecht (2015). https://doi.org/10.1007/978-94-017-9297-4_10
4. D. H. Uttal and C. A. Cohen, Spatial Thinking and STEM Education. When, Why, and How?. In: Psychology of Learning and Motivation - Advances in Research and Theory, vol. 57. 2012. http://www.scopus.com/inward/record.url?eid=2-s2.0-84860615431&partnerID=40&md5=9e7bafd47ed3bb637fcef4311e09dfd7
5. Khine, M.S. (ed.): Visual-Spatial Ability in STEM Education. Springer International Publishing, Cham (2017). https://doi.org/10.1007/978-3-319-44385-0
6. M. Faber, A. Unfried, E. N. Wiebe, J. Corn, L. W. Townsend, and T. L. Collins, "Student attitudes toward STEM: The development of upper elementary school and middle/high school student surveys. In: 2013 ASEE Annual Conference & Exposition, pp. 23–1094 (2013). Accessed: Jun. 16, 2026. https://peer.asee.org/student-attitudes-toward-stem-the-development-of-upper-elementary-school-and-middle-high-school-student-surveys.pdf
7. Unfried, A., Faber, M., Stanhope, D.S., Wiebe, E.: The development and validation of a measure of student attitudes toward science, technology, engineering, and math (S-STEM). J. Psychoeduc. Assess. **33**(7), 622–639 (2015). https://doi.org/10.1177/0734282915571160
8. Archer, L., DeWitt, J., Osborne, J., Dillon, J., Willis, B., Wong, B.: 'Doing' science versus 'being' a scientist: examining 10/11-year-old schoolchildren's constructions of science through the lens of identity. Sci. Educ. **94**(4), 617–639 (2010). https://doi.org/10.1002/sce.20399
9. Pagkratidou, M., Michaelides, M.P., Pitsia, V., Karakolidis, A.: Factors associated with STEM career expectations of Greek 15-year-old students. J. STEM Educ. Res. **8**(1), 59–87 (2025). https://doi.org/10.1007/s41979-024-00124-1
10. Cornoldi, C., Vecchi, T.: Visuo-Spatial Working Memory and Individual Differences. Psychology Press (2004) Accessed 16 Jun 2026. https://api.taylorfrancis.com/content/books/mono/download?identifierName=doi&identifierValue=10.4324/9780203641583&type=googlepdf

11. Miyake, A., Friedman, N.P., Rettinger, D.A., Shah, P., Hegarty, M.: How are visuospatial working memory, executive functioning, and spatial abilities related? A latent-variable analysis. J. Exp. Psychol. Gen. **130**(4), 621–640 (2001). https://doi.org/10.1037/0096-3445.130.4.621
12. Jung, E.S., Reid, N.: Working memory and attitudes. Res. Sci. Technol. Educ. **27**(2), 205–223 (2009). https://doi.org/10.1080/02635140902853665
13. Nazir, A., Rana, R.A., Khan, K.A.: Effect of working memory on students' attitude towards mathematics at secondary level. PJE. **35**(3) (2018)
14. Sellami, A.L., Al-Rakeb, N.A., Tok, E.: Secondary school students' interest in STEM careers in Qatar. Educ. Sci. **13**(4), 369 (2023). https://doi.org/10.3390/educsci13040369
15. Johnson, T., Burgoyne, A.P., Mix, K.S., Young, C.J., Levine, S.C.: Spatial and mathematics skills: similarities and differences related to age, SES, and gender. Cognition. **218**, 104918 (2022). https://doi.org/10.1016/j.cognition.2021.104918
16. Noble, K.G., McCandliss, B.D., Farah, M.J.: Socioeconomic gradients predict individual differences in neurocognitive abilities. Dev. Sci. **10**(4), 464–480 (2007). https://doi.org/10.1111/j.1467-7687.2007.00600.x
17. Ekstrom, R.B., French, J.W., Harman, H.H., Dermen, D.: Manual for kit of factor-referenced cognitive tests. Princet. NJ Educ. Test. Serv. (1976)
18. L. L. Thurstone, "Primary mental abilities," in The Measurement of Intelligence, Springer, 1973, pp. 131–136.
19. Corsi, P.M.: Human Memory and the Medial Temporal Region of the Brain. McGill University (1972)
20. Kessels, R.P.C., van Zandvoort, M.J.E., Postma, A., Kappelle, L.J., de Haan, E.H.F.: The Corsi block-tapping task: standardization and normative data. Appl. Neuropsychol. **7**(4), 252–258 (2000). https://doi.org/10.1207/S15324826AN0704_8
21. Broer, M., Bai, Y., Fonseca, F.: Methodology: constructing a socioeconomic index for TIMSS trend analyses. In: Broer, M., Bai, Y., Fonseca, F. (eds.) Socioeconomic Inequality and Educational Outcomes: Evidence from Twenty Years of TIMSS, pp. 19–34. Springer International Publishing, Cham (2019). https://doi.org/10.1007/978-3-030-11991-1_3
22. Hayes, A.F.: Introduction to Mediation, Moderation, and Conditional Process Analysis, Second Edition: a Regression-Based Approach. Guilford Publications, New York, United States (2017) Accessed 21 Nov 2023. http://ebookcentral.proquest.com/lib/tudublin/detail.action?docID=5109647
23. B. Anghel, N. Rodríguez-Planas, and A. Sanz-de-Galdeano, "Culture, gender, and math: a Revisitation," IZA discussion papers, working paper 12371 2019. Accessed 16 Jun 2026. https://www.econstor.eu/handle/10419/202717
24. Stoet, G., Geary, D.C.: Can stereotype threat explain the gender gap in mathematics performance and achievement? Rev. Gen. Psychol. **16**(1), 93–102 (2012). https://doi.org/10.1037/a0026617
25. J. J. Jirout and N. S. Newcombe, "Building blocks for developing spatial skills: evidence from a large, representative U.S. sample," Psychol. Sci. 0956–7976, vol. 26, no. 3, pp. 302–310, Mar. 2015, doi:https://doi.org/10.1177/0956797614563338.
26. Kaufman, S.B.: Sex differences in mental rotation and spatial visualization ability: can they be accounted for by differences in working memory capacity? Intelligence. **35**(3), 211–223 (2007)
27. Kucuk, S., Sisman, B.: Students' attitudes towards robotics and STEM: differences based on gender and robotics experience. Int. J. Child-Comput. Interact. **23**, 100167 (2020). https://doi.org/10.1016/j.ijcci.2020.100167

# Author Index





E. Farran et al. (Eds.): Spatial Cognition 2026, LNAI 16785, p. 197, 2027.
https://doi.org/10.1007/978-3-032-36716-7

FSC
www.fsc.org
MIX
Papier | Fördert gute Waldnutzung
FSC® C083411

Kolibri 360 GmbH
Ferdinand-Jühlke-Straße 7
99095 Erfurt, Deutschland
produktsicherheit@kolibri360.de